19:1 / March 2022

LABOR
Studies in Working-Class History

Special Issue: Class and Consent

T0341470

NOTES AND DOCUMENTS

CLASS AND CONSENT

Christopher Phelps

Perhaps the tremors began with the criminal charges filed against Dominique Strauss-Kahn in 2011 and Bill Cosby in 2015, or the lawsuit of Gretchen Carlson against Fox News CEO Roger Ailes in 2016. The real earthquake, though, was the election of President Donald Trump just weeks after footage leaked of him boasting that he liked to "grab 'em by the pussy." Global women's protests on the day after his inauguration in January 2017 featured a pink sea of clever hand-knitted "pussyhats." That set the context when, eight months later in October 2017, *New York Times* and *New Yorker* reporters broke allegations of sexual assault by the movie mogul Harvey Weinstein. Actress Alyssa Milano used a #MeToo hashtag on Twitter, echoing the "Me Too" phrase introduced eleven years before by Tarana Burke. The tremendous consequent outpouring exposed numerous men as alleged serial sexual harassers, dethroning them from positions of power. The very long list would include, among others, NBC *Today* host Matt Lauer, CBS CEO Leslie Moonves, Senator Al Franken, New York attorney general Eric Schneiderman, MSNBC contributor Mark Halperin, *New Republic* figures Leon Wieseltier and Hamilton Fish, Metropolitan Opera director James Levine, Amazon Studios president Roy Price, actor Kevin Spacey, and comedian Louis C.K.

Lost in the corporate media's predictable concentration on famous names was, all too often, the everyday sexual harassment and violence at ordinary workplaces. To be sure, some journalists investigated the sexual abuse of hotel workers, fast-food workers, farmworkers, autoworkers, and other wage-earning women—as well as abuse within labor unions—but their exposés, however excellent, rarely broke

I would like to thank Leon Fink, this journal's editor, and Patrick Dixon, its John Henry, for many hours of consultation and collaboration in the shaping of this special issue, as well as all my fellow contributors for their brilliant work. Mara Keire deserves a special shout-out for her spirited attempts to refine my thinking. Margot Canaday, Vanessa May, Robyn Muncy, David Sartorius, Katrin Schultheiss, and Leslie Rowland were chairs and commentators at the symposium that tested drafts of these essays. Thanks to the many students over the years who gave me an education in labor history and the history of sexuality. Dedicated to Rosa Hollier Phelps, smasher of the patriarchy.

Labor: Studies in Working-Class History, Volume 19, Issue 1
DOI 10.1215/15476715-9475646   © 2022 by Labor and Working-Class History Association

through the endless salacious stories of celebrity misconduct.[1] This special issue of *Labor* seeks to contribute to a more rounded view from below, with a focus on sexual harassment in the history of labor and the working class from the nineteenth century to the present. It arises out of an online symposium sponsored by the journal, "Class and Consent: Labor, Work, Gender, and the Problems of Sexual Harassment and Violence," which took place September 24–25, 2020, and involved every contributor here. What motivates the issue is the belief that the field of labor history can and must do more to speak to sexual harassment, even if this journal deserves credit for paying attention to the question from its very first issue in 2004.[2]

What constitutes sexual harassment has, of course, varied across time and place. The term itself was devised less than fifty years ago, in 1975.[3] A generative definition is provided by Mary Bularzik: "any unwanted pressure for sexual activity," including "verbal innuendos and suggestive comments, leering, gestures, unwanted physical contact (touching, pinching, etc.), rape and attempted rape."[4] Whether construed as sexual harassment or not, such behavior—and resistance to it—has pervaded the history of work and labor for centuries. A notice by maidservants in the *New York Weekly Journal* on January 28, 1734, stated that women driven to service in hard times "think it reasonable we should not be beat by our Mistresses Husband, they being too strong, and perhaps may do tender women Mischief."[5] Friedrich Engels, in his 1844 investigation of the social conditions of the English working class, held that "the factory owner wields complete power over the persons and charms of the girls working for him," and that "nine times out of ten, nay, in ninety-nine cases out of a hundred, the threat of dismissal is sufficient to break down the inclination of girls who at the best of times, have no strong inclination to chastity."[6] Harriet Jacobs, in *Incidents in the Life of a Slave Girl* (1861), told how upon entering her fifteenth year—"a sad epoch in the life of a slave girl," as she put it—"my master began to whisper foul words in my ear. . . . He tried his utmost to corrupt the pure principles my grandmother had instilled."[7] As these examples show, workplace sexual harassment has occurred throughout American history across a variety of labor conditions, free and unfree, in field, home, factory, and office, from the colonial era to neoliberal global capitalism.

The following articles provide a narrative arc from the Civil War to the present. They identify a common theme of women's resistance to sexual harassment in the

---

1. For exemplary work, see Mueller, "For Hotel Workers, Weinstein Allegations Put a Spotlight on Harassment"; Chira and Einhorn, "How Tough Is It to Change a Culture of Harassment? Ask Women at Ford"; Malone, "Will Women in Low-Wage Jobs Get Their #McToo Moment?"; Yeung, "Unreckoned"; Sainato, "'It Was Like Hell'"; Smith, "Powerful Reporter Got Away with Sexual Misconduct"; and Covert, "McDonald's Has a Real Sexual Harassment Problem."

2. Meyer, "Workplace Predators."

3. The best history of its origins may be found in Baker, *Women's Movement against Sexual Harassment*.

4. Bularzik, "Sexual Harassment at the Workplace," 25.

5. Quoted in Foner, *History of the Labor Movement*, 26.

6. Engels, *Condition of the Working Class*, 167–68.

7. [Jacobs], *Incidents in the Life of a Slave Girl*, 44.

workplace, featuring a diversity of tactics, evolving frames of reference, differing categories of workers, and myriad proposals for its regulation and overcoming. Crystal N. Feimster mines a rich documentary vein to unearth the extraordinary story of how African American laundresses for the US Army in Louisiana during the Civil War used tribunals to contest their harassment. Black women's resistance to sexual abuse in the Civil War and Reconstruction era is traced more broadly by Kaisha Esty, who carries out an intellectual history of what she creatively calls their assertions of "sexual sovereignty." Mara Keire examines internal investigations by Macy's department store in the Progressive Era and finds management so preoccupied with women's morality as to excuse verbal and sexual harassment by male supervisors. Annelise Orleck profiles two strikes a century apart, by corset workers in Kalamazoo, Michigan, in 1912, and McDonald's workers in 2018–19, to examine the efficacy of the strike tactic against sexual harassment. Emily E. LB. Twarog recounts how 9to5, an organization of office workers, initiated a sexual harassment hotline in the 1980s, using telecommunications to support and counsel women. A global horizon is established by Eileen Boris, who reconstructs in detail how, in a complex process stretching across decades, the International Labour Organization passed its Violence and Harassment Convention (No. 190) in 2019. Anne Balay draws on her oral histories of queer blue-collar workers and her own work as a union organizer to provide a personal essay on the class dimensions of consent and its implications for labor organizing. In a concluding essay, Christopher Phelps provides a synthetic overview of the value of class as an analytic category for understanding sexual harassment, drawing together evidence of labor movement activity against it from the Gilded Age to the present. Finally, in a documentary bonus, a short story by Margaret Sanger from 1912 published here for the first time provides a fictional dramatization of a nurse's repudiation of a doctor's attempted sexual assault.

  Read holistically, this special issue traces how working-class women, in resisting work-related sexual abuse between the nineteenth and twenty-first centuries, helped reframe behavior once viewed as "virtue" forsaken as, instead, sexual harassment. A powerful rotation in perspective, this shifted blame from the harassed to the harassers. Nevertheless, these essays merely scratch the surface of what labor history might contribute to our understanding of sex, class, and consent. Future research could expand our comprehension in many areas. The women's resistance that is at the core of the contributions here, for example, should be complemented by more investigations of working-class male behavior and supervisory predation. The relationship between sex work and sexual harassment, often existing on a continuum, deserves fuller treatment. The way lesbian, gay, transgendered, and queer workers experienced harassment historically has barely begun to be told. Transnational and comparative approaches to this topic remain surprisingly rare.[8] Structural analyses of workplaces as institutional contexts for sexual regulation could augment a history of capitalism too often delimited as political economy. Finally, work as a locus of consensual sex—the

---

8. One exception is Zippel, *Politics of Sexual Harassment.*

joys of workplace sex and sexual banter—deserves a greater secondary literature, one brought into dialogue with the history of sexual harassment and violence, because the workplace has always been a site of mutual desire, lust, and pleasure as well as danger and violation.[9] If these essays arrive at the end of a very long historical process, then, they represent but a beginning. ◢

References

Baker, Carrie N. *The Women's Movement against Sexual Harassment*. Cambridge: Cambridge University Press, 2008.

Berebitsky, Julie. *Sex and the Office: A History of Gender, Power, and Desire*. New Haven, CT: Yale University Press, 2012.

Bularzik, Mary. "Sexual Harassment at the Workplace: Historical Notes." *Radical America* 12, no. 4 (1978): 25–43.

Chira, Susan, and Catrin Einhorn. "How Tough Is It to Change a Culture of Harassment? Ask Women at Ford." *New York Times*, December 19, 2017. www.nytimes.com/interactive /2017/12/19/us/ford-chicago-sexual-harassment.html.

Covert, Bryce. "McDonald's Has a Real Sexual Harassment Problem." *The Nation*, July 28, 2020. www.thenation.com/article/society/mcdonalds-sexual-harassment-feature.

Engels, [Friedrich]. *The Condition of the Working Class in England*. New York: Macmillan, 1958.

Foner, Philip S. *History of the Labor Movement in the United States*, vol. 1: *From Colonial Times to the Founding of the American Federation of Labor*. New York: International Publishers, 1947.

[Jacobs, Harriet]. *Incidents in the Life of a Slave Girl*. Boston: L. Maria Child, 1861.

Malone, Clare. "Will Women in Low-Wage Jobs Get Their #MeToo Moment?" *FiveThirtyEight*, December 14, 2017. https://fivethirtyeight.com/features/the-metoo-moment-hasnt -reached-women-in-low-wage-jobs-will-it.

Meyer, Steve. "Workplace Predators: Sexuality and Harassment on the U.S. Automotive Shop Floor, 1930–1960." *Labor: Studies in Working-Class History of the Americas* 1, no. 1 (2004): 77–93.

Mueller, Benjamin. "For Hotel Workers, Weinstein Allegations Put a Spotlight on Harassment." *New York Times*, December 17, 2017. www.nytimes.com/2017/12/17/us/harvey -weinstein-hotel-sexual-harassment.html.

Saintano, Michael. "'It Was Like Hell': California Hotel Workers Break Their Silence on Abuse." *The Guardian*, October 16, 2018. www.theguardian.com/world/2018/oct/16 /hotel-workers-sexual-assault-harassment-terranea-resort.

Smith, Ben. "A Powerful Reporter Got Away with Sexual Misconduct for Decades. His Paper, and His Union, Looked the Other Way." *New York Times*, December 6, 2020. www.nytimes.com/2020/12/06/business/media/pittsburgh-post-gazette-news-guild.html.

Williams, Christine L., Patti A. Giuffre, and Kirsten Dellinger. "Sexuality in the Workplace: Organizational Control, Sexual Harassment, and the Pursuit of Pleasure." *American Review of Sociology* 25 (1999): 73–93.

9. For examples of such a fused approach, see Berebitsky, *Sex and the Office*; and Williams, Giuffre, and Dellinger, "Sexuality in the Workplace."

Yeung, Bernice. "The Unreckoned: Seventeen Women Tell Why #MeToo Still Hasn't Come for Them." *The Cut*, September 5, 2018. www.thecut.com/2018/09/unreckoned-left -behind-by-metoo.html.

Zippel, Kathrin S. *The Politics of Sexual Harassment: A Comparative Study of the United States, the European Union, and Germany.* Cambridge: Cambridge University Press, 2006.

What to Do with Pennies Left as Tips

Karen J. Weyant

Yes, it still happens. You find them tossed
on the table, tangled in crumpled napkins or resting

rather innocently in spots of dribbled gravy.
Sometimes they are stacked neatly by a coffee cup,

or arranged in a cryptic smile near an overturned plate.
Once you even found one wedged in the napkin holder,

Lincoln's head turned, his chin against stainless steel.
You will want to sweep them into the garbage can

along with bread crumbs, bits of stuffing, chicken bones,
and lettuce stained white with swirls of ranch dressing.

Don't. Instead, shove them deep into your pocket.
On your walk home, toss them into drainage ditches lined

with cattails or into potholes overfilling with rainwater.
Every tossed penny is a wish, you learned this as a child.

So this is what you want: the ingrown toenail to heal,
a pay raise, or a way to turn back time, so you could

spit in a rude customer's food or, at the very least,
substitute regular coffee for their requested decaf with cream. ◢

Labor: Studies in Working-Class History, Volume 19, Issue 1
DOI 10.1215/15476715-9475660   © 2022 by Karen J. Weyant

The author of two poetry chapbooks, KAREN J. WEYANT has published poems and essays in the *Briar Cliff Review, Chautauqua, Crab Creek Review, Crab Orchard Review, Coal Hill Review, Fourth River, Lake Effect, Spillway, Stoneboat, Rattle,* and *River Styx*. She is associate professor of English at Jamestown Community College in Jamestown, New York.

Toward a New Social Compact

James C. Benton

The quest to improve conditions for working people during and after the COVID-19 pandemic was the focus of a four-day online convention, "Constructing a New Social Compact: A Public Forum on Empowering the Post-pandemic Working Class," held April 28–May 1.

Nearly 1,200 participants attended the convening, which featured three plenary sessions, twenty-five panels, and 150 presenters from five continents. Attendees heard and discussed issues aimed at reconstructing a social compact in ways that are fairer and more inclusive. Among the topics discussed were the future of workers and democracy, immigration, climate change, the care economy, and approaches to bargaining for the common good.

An arts event included an online screening of *Union Time: Fighting for Workers' Rights*, a documentary on the successful organizing of a Smithfield Foods pork-processing plant, and a question-and-answer session with *Union Time* director Matthew Barr and Gene Bruskin, former director of the Justice@Smithfield organizing campaign.

Presenters included Sharan Burrow, the general secretary of the International Trade Union Confederation; Sara Nelson, president of the Association of Flight Attendants; Randi Weingarten, president of the American Federation of Teachers; Mary Kay Henry, SEIU president; LAWCHA president Will Jones; J. J. Rosenbaum, executive director, Global Labor Justice; Ai-Jen Poo, executive director, National Domestic Workers Alliance; William Spriggs, chief economist, AFL-CIO; Sarita Gupta and Rebecca Coakley of the Ford Foundation; and Rep. Jamaal Bowman (D-NY).

Conceptualized by the Kalmanovitz Initiative for Labor and the Working Poor at Georgetown University and developed by an organizing committee of roughly forty representatives from academia, labor, faith, and nonprofit organizations, the New Social Compact project envisions building a stronger, more durable social compact for workers in the aftermath of the COVID-19 pandemic. It is designed to bring together representatives of various groups to discuss shortcomings of the safety net that exists in most nations and conceive of how that safety net can be improved, in

Labor: Studies in Working-Class History, Volume 19, Issue 1
DOI 10.1215/15476715-9475674   © 2022 by Labor and Working-Class History Association

ways that help the working class and avoid barriers to people based on gender, race, or class. From these discussions, the NSC organizers plan to build coalitions of leaders and activists with the purpose of creating change in communities—local, regional, national, and global.

Major crises, such as wars, depressions, and the ongoing COVID-19 pandemic "create windows where major changes that once seemed unthinkable are possible," said Lane Windham, associate director of the Kalmanovitz Initiative. The NSC project, Windham said, is an effort to bring together people to think about, and propose, ways to change or even replace the current social compact.

In the United States, much of that compact dates to the New Deal and World War II and is largely based around employment. Unfortunately, that safety net also excluded large swaths of people—mainly women and Black and Brown workers who worked in economic sectors not addressed by the compact. That compact has weakened, especially in the past half century, as employers sidestepped their responsibilities, aided by laws, including labor laws, that were too weak to protect workers or force the private sector to abide by its duties.

"The pandemic has forced a national reckoning that's been years in the making," said Henry, the SEIU director, adding that multiple crises triggered by the pandemic—including loss of jobs, healthcare, and housing—are affecting communities, but especially Black communities and communities of color.

Henry added that workers, employers, and government all have duties to help create a new social compact. Employers of all sizes, especially the wealthiest and most powerful, and government must value the work performed by workers, particularly service and care workers, in part through the elimination of poverty wages. Workers also need a voice at work, including greater freedom to unionize and bargain collectively.

"All of us, no matter what our race or where we come from, want the same things: health, safety, security, a fair chance at a decent life, a better future for our families, and that creating a new social compact has to be grounded in a shared analysis that those basic things are only possible [now] for a very few in America," she said.

Rev. Alvin Herring, executive director of Faith in Action, added that he saw "a new kind of social theology" in the massive protests nationwide following the murder of George Floyd by a Minneapolis police officer. He described this new change as a theology predicated on justice, equity, respect for the planet, and an understanding of the moral underpinnings of human societies. "If we are to build a new social compact, we'll have to have a moral discussion in this country," he said.

The New Social Compact project plans more meetings and gatherings over the coming years that it anticipates will lead to greater networking, coalition-building, and further actions to shape social policy. Additional information on the New Social Compact, as well as recordings of all the sessions, are available at lwp.georgetown .edu. ◪

JAMES C. BENTON is the director of the Race and Economic Empowerment Project at Georgetown University. His forthcoming book, *Fraying Fabric: How Trade Policy and Industrial Decline Transformed America*, explains how missteps by business, labor, and government leaders on trade policy after World War II contributed to the backlash that benefited Donald Trump in the 2016 presidential election.

Rape and Mutiny at Fort Jackson:
Black Laundresses Testify in Civil War Louisiana

Crystal N. Feimster

The racial and sexual violence that defined slavery did not disappear with Lincoln's Emancipation Proclamation. In the context of war, however, formerly enslaved men and women did not hesitate to defend themselves. Just as runaways had forced the administration to begin to make policy about slavery in 1861, Black men and women who served and labored in the Union, whether soldiers on the battlefield or laundresses in the contraband camps, put the question of free Black labor and equal protection under the law squarely on the national agenda. Countless Black women, many of them laundresses who labored in the Union army, were sexually harassed and assaulted by Union soldiers and officers. In the context of the Civil War and their military service, Black women, for the first time, were granted access to military tribunals that allowed them to bring charges of sexual assault against their assailants. The military's strict code of conduct, which empowered commanding officers to court-martial soldiers accused of criminal activity, along with the 1863 Lieber Code, which defined rape as a war crime, created a legal opening for Black women. Acknowledging rape as a crime against Black women, Union military courts ignored state laws and for the first time allowed Black women to testify against white men.

In Civil War Louisiana, Black laundresses took the lead in claiming rights and protections as free labor, by challenging white men's violent sexual power. As early as June 1862, Mary Ellen DeRiley, a twenty-three-year-old "washerwoman" for the Twenty-Sixth Massachusetts Regiment, stationed at Fort Saint Philip, brought rape charges against Corporal William W. Chinock of Company F, Twenty-Sixth Massachusetts Regiment. Chinock was court-martialed and charged with "conduct to the prejudice of good order and discipline." According to the "specifications" of the charge, Chinock had "enticed" DeRiley into a boat, where he engaged in "unlawful sexual intercourse with her." Testifying in graphic detail, DeRiley recounted the assault: "He told me to lay down and let him ride me and I told him that I would not. . . . He beat me with his fist, pulled my clothes over my head and rode me—for an hour." Even though the court found Chinock "not guilty" of the specifications

Labor: Studies in Working-Class History, Volume 19, Issue 1
DOI 10.1215/15476715-9475688 © 2022 by Labor and Working-Class History Association

("unlawful sexual intercourse"), it found him "guilty" of the charge ("conduct to the prejudice of good order and discipline") and sentenced him to be stripped of his ranks in the presence of his regiment and to "forfeit to the United States ten dollars per month of his monthly pay for four months."[1]

Undergirding Chinock's rape of DeRiley and the court's "not guilty" verdict was the common and long-held belief that Black women lacked virtue and sometimes invited, and always welcomed, white men's illicit sexual advances. A dangerous fiction of the antebellum "sexual economy of slavery," the trope of the lascivious Black woman was the product of the systematic expropriation of enslaved women's productive labor, reproductive capacity, and sexuality.[2] Required to engage in physical and domestic labor, enslaved women, unlike Black men and white women, were also forced to perform sexual and reproductive labor. The legal doctrine of *partus sequitur ventrem* that established that children of enslaved women were born into slavery and the refusal of law to recognize rape as a crime against Black women engendered Black women's sexual vulnerability, enabled a sexual double standard that enforced chastity on white women, and promoted aggressive sexual promiscuity for white men.

This essay examines sexual violence against Black laundresses by white Union officers in Civil War Louisiana. The first part concerns the Union occupation of New Orleans in the spring of 1862 and General Benjamin Butler's orders and policies regarding the treatment of Black laundresses who labored in the Union army. The second and third parts focus on the violent interracial interactions between white officers and Black soldiers and laundresses of the Fourth Regiment of the Native Guard (also known as the Corps d'Afrique) stationed at Fort Jackson. Over the course of six weeks, in December 1863 and January 1864, these Black soldiers and laundresses engaged in open mutiny to protest the racial and sexual violence inflicted by white officers. Illuminating the connections between the mutiny of Black soldiers at Fort Jackson and sexual violence against Black laundresses by white Union officers, this essay maps the shifting racial and sexual terrain on which Black women in Civil War Louisiana battled for their rights as free labor.

Butler's General Order No. 38

On May 15, 1862, two weeks after the fall of New Orleans, the Thirteenth Connecticut Regiment dressed in their "best attire" and with "great pomp" marched down Canal Street to the US Custom House.[3] The designated headquarters of the Department of the Gulf, the federal building took up a whole city block and stood four stories high without a roof. The newly constructed but unfinished Custom House had

---

1. Trial of Corporal William W. Chinock, Twenty-Sixth Massachusetts Regiment, RG 153, Records of the Judge Advocate General's Office (US Army), National Archives and Records Administration (NARA), Washington, DC. Hereafter, cases from these records are cited as RG 153, NARA.

2. Davis, "'Don't Let Nobody Bother Yo' Principle'"; Glymph, *Out of the House*; Hunter, *To Joy My Freedom*; and Brown, *Good Wives, Nasty Wenches*.

3. Sprague, *History of the 13th Infantry Regiment of Connecticut Volunteers*, 51.

recently served as headquarters for rebel forces, who according to Captain Homer B. Sprague of the Thirteenth Connecticut Regiment had left the building "filthy beyond expression."[4]

Within days of moving into the Custom House, the regiment was confronted with the arrival of Black people desperate for work, shelter, food, and protection. Following the "contraband" policy initiated by Butler during his command of Fort Monroe (and made official with the passage of the Confiscation Acts of 1861 and 1862), the Thirteenth Connecticut Regiment put the first arrivals to work "cleaning the floors, ceilings, stairways, walls, drains, casement."[5] The Quartermaster's Department hired Black people as blacksmiths, carpenters, shoemakers, wagoners, cooks, and laundresses. Sprague recalled that once the Thirteenth Regiment "had established itself in the Customs House," most of the companies "employed, as laundresses, colored women, who had run away or been driven off to the Yankees."[6]

The US Army had a long tradition of employing women as laundresses in military camps and hospitals.[7] Adopted from the British, the practice was made official in 1802, when Congress passed an act that prescribed four laundresses to a company and dictated a daily ration and quarters for each laundress.[8] From the War of 1812 until 1883, when the practice was officially ended, Black women were among the thousands of women who labored as military laundresses. The 1821 *General Regulations for the Army* dictated that "laundresses employed to wash soldiers' clothes will be paid by the piece" at a rate set by the Council of Administration.[9] In other words, the regimental officers at a given post determined how much a laundress was paid. Regulations further provided laundresses with a common tent, straw for bedding, cords of wood for fuel, an iron kettle, two tin pans, and a hatchet.[10] In 1841, revised regulations stipulated that the Council of Administration could decide whether to pay laundresses "by the month, or by the piece." More importantly, regulations made clear that "debts due the laundress by soldiers, for washing" were to be settled at the "pay-table" and taken from soldiers' monthly wage.[11] Because the price of washing was set at each post by the Council of Administration, it is difficult to know exactly how much laundresses were paid. It seems, however, that by 1861 washerwomen were

4. Sprague, *History of the 13th Infantry Regiment of Connecticut Volunteers*, 52–53.

5. Sprague, *History of the 13th Infantry Regiment of Connecticut Volunteers*, 53.

6. Sprague, *History of the 13th Infantry Regiment of Connecticut Volunteers*.

7. Gaines, "Westward Expansion: Laundresses," 537–39; Mescher, "Tubs and Suds"; Sibbald, "Camp Followers All"; Stallard, *Glittering Misery*; Stewart, "Army Laundresses"; Kellie K. B. Wilson, "'Troublesome Hellions' and 'Belligerent Viragos'"; Wood, "Army Laundresses and Civilization on the Western Frontier"; Glymph, "Noncombant Military Labor in the Civil War" and "I'm a Radical Black Girl"; King, "In Search of Women of African Descent Who Served in the Civil War Union Navy," 302; Barber and Ritter, "Dangerous Liaisons"; and Schultz, "Race, Gender, and Bureaucracy" and *Women at the Front*.

8. Callan, *Military Laws of the United States*; and US War Department, *The Military Handbook and Soldiers' Manual of Information*.

9. US War Department, *General Regulations for the Army*, 48.

10. US War Department, *General Regulations for the Army*, 94.

11. *General Regulations for the Army of the United States, 1841*, 37.

making on average between $6 and $12 per month, and benefits had expanded to include rations for their children and access to military doctors.[12]

During the Civil War, Black women labored as laundresses in both the Confederate and Union armies. Confederate muster rolls list Anne Green, a "colored (free)" woman, as a laundress at the Confederate General Hospital in Mount Jackson, Virginia; and Julia Bellman, a "free" woman as a laundress at the Confederate Jackson Hospital in Richmond, Virginia.[13] In August 1864, the Confederate State paid Martha Bragg, "a free girl of color," $44 ($11 per month) for "services as Laundress" at Breckinridge Confederate Hospital in Marion, Virginia.[14] But the majority of laundresses who labored in Confederate hospitals and camps were enslaved women pressed into service by the men and women who held them in bondage. Most likely, Andrew Green collected the wages earned by the four enslaved women—Fanny, Riney, Jennie, and Jennette—he sent to work as laundresses at Breckinridge Military Hospital in Marion, Alabama. For enslaved women who were able to secure jobs as laundresses in the Union army, however, the position came with the dual benefits of freedom and wages.[15]

Under normal circumstances washing was grueling work, but in the context of war the relentless regime of soaking, washing, boiling, rinsing, drying, starching, ironing, mending, and altering war-stained and battered uniforms was dangerous work at best—and deadly work at its worst. Black women who traveled with the Union army and labored as laundresses in "contraband camps," military posts, and hospitals were particularly vulnerable to sexual violence.[16] Those who did not have husbands or male relatives to protect them were easy targets. For many enslaved women, however, the combined benefits of freedom and reliable wages made the job a risk worth taking. In fact, many had already suffered racial and sexual violence at the hands of the men and women who held them in bondage.

Without question, the arrival of Union forces in Louisiana in the spring 1862 created opportunities for enslaved women to seize their freedom and to gain waged labor. Captain Sprague of the Thirteenth Regiment did not hesitate to help Black women secure their freedom within Union lines. A native of Massachusetts and a Yale University graduate, Sprague was an abolitionist who had called for immediate emancipation with the outbreak of war. Thus, it is not surprising that he hired as a laundress Carolina, a twenty-two-year-old enslaved woman who had sought refuge in the Custom House to escape a whipping. In fact, the Thirteenth quickly garnered

12. Schultz, "Race, Gender, and Bureaucracy"; Stewart, "Army Laundresses," 424; and US War Department, *Revised United States Army Regulations of 1861*.

13. Unfiled Papers and Slips Belonging in Confederate Compiled Service Records, in Fold3 database, www.fold3.com//title/656/civil-war-service-records-cmsr-confederate-miscellaneous (accessed January 21, 2021).

14. Unfiled Papers and Slips Belonging in Confederate Compiled Service Records.

15. Unfiled Papers and Slips Belonging in Confederate Compiled Service Records.

16. For discussions of Black women in contraband camps, see Glymph, *Women's Fight*; Downs, *Sick from Freedom*; Schwalm, *Hard Fight for We*; Manning, *Troubled Refuge*; and Taylor, *Embattled Freedom*.

a reputation as "an antislavery regiment."[17] Moreover, the commanding officer, Colonel Henry Warner, was notorious for allowing fugitives of slavery to seek refuge within the Custom House and refusing entry to slaveholders in search of runaways.[18]

On May 26, however, General Butler gave a Mrs. Benedict permission to enter the Custom House to search and retrieve Caroline, the enslaved woman whom Sprague had employed as one of his company's laundresses. Catching sight of Caroline, Mrs. Benedict confronted the young woman, insisted on her return, and warned that she would never see her enslaved mother again if she refused. Unintimidated and confident in her status as a military laundress, Caroline declared: "You have treated me badly. You have beaten my mother over her head with a pan. I would rather stay and be free than see my mother again. You know you will be cruel to me. You can't take me from *here*."[19]

While the commanding officers of the Thirteenth Connecticut Regiment were committed to protecting the freedom of self-emancipated enslaved people, Butler was more interested in appeasing loyal slaveholders and preventing officers from harboring and protecting fugitives. On the same day that Butler gave the spurned Mrs. Benedict permission to search for Caroline in the Custom House, he issued Special Order No. 44: "All females, white and black, must be excluded from remaining in any portion of the United States custom-house after the hours of 4 o'clock p.m. or before the hour of 9 a.m."[20] The order's expulsion of "all females, black and white" from the Custom House included Black laundresses. Offended by the order's implications that the presence of Black women promoted sexual promiscuity and disorder, some of the officers, including Captain Sprague, protested Butler's removal of the laundresses. In Butler's office, Sprague advocated, "Many of our soldiers are debilitated by this climate, and it is a most welcome relief to have this work transferred to more skillful hands; besides contributing greatly to increased cleanliness, comfort and health."[21] More to the point, the officers argued that official regulations allowed every company four laundresses, whose rations, quarters, and fuel was to be provided by the army.[22] Butler flatly defended the removal of the laundresses "on the ground of the difficulty of preventing improper intercourse between soldiers and these women." The officers, however, managed to convince Butler to allow "rooms to be rented outside of the Custom-house for the colored laundresses."[23] The issue, however, as far as Butler and the Benedicts were concerned, was not settled.

17. Sprague, *History of the 13th Infantry Regiment of Connecticut Volunteers*, 60.

18. *New London Daily Chronicle*, June 17, 1862; *Minnesota Pioneer*, June 27, 1862; and *New York Times*, July 3, 1862.

19. Sprague, *History of the 13th Infantry Regiment of Connecticut Volunteers*, 341–47.

20. Special Orders, No. 44 New Orleans, May 26, 1862, in *War of the Rebellion* (hereafter cited as *OR*), ser. 1, vol. 15, 444; Sprague, *History of the 13th Infantry Regiment of Connecticut Volunteers*, 60; and *New York Times*, July 3, 1862.

21. Sprague, *History of the 13th Infantry Regiment of Connecticut Volunteers*, 345.

22. US War Department, *Revised United States Army Regulations of 1861*, 24, 12, 160, 162, 246.

23. *New York Times*, July 3, 1862.

Despite Caroline's rejection of them, the Benedicts continued their campaign to return her to their ownership. On May 30, Mr. Benedict confronted Captain Sprague with a letter endorsed by Butler. Caroline, the letter explained, "was the property of a poor man whose wife is sick in bed and needs this negress for a nurse." It is unclear whether this sick wife was the Mrs. Benedict who marched into the Custom House four days earlier. In an appeal to "Capt. Sprague's humanity," the letter urged him to "drive [Caroline] out, so that she may return to her master."[24]

In a written reply, Sprague explained his unwillingness to "drive" Caroline out. The Confiscation Act 1862, he argued, forbade "military officers to deliver fugitive slaves to their masters, on penalty of being cashiered."[25] The law, he insisted, "makes no exception in the case of '*poor*' masters. No; not even if the 'poor man's wife is sick in bed, and needs the negress as a nurse.'" Nor does the law "make any exception on grounds of '*humanity*,'" he reasoned. Moreover, he considered the choice clear if faced with a humanitarian appeal made by Caroline, "a young and helpless girl, innocent of any crime, pleading with me to save her from hopeless and perpetual slavery," and another claim made by Benedict, "'a *poor* man, with a sick wife,' and in need of this girl's unpaid toil, and the money which you might coin out of her body and soul, if you could only keep her degraded and enslaved, or sell her for labor or breeding or lust!"[26]

Benedict took Sprague's letter to Butler, who in turn summoned Sprague to his office. Butler asked Sprague a series of questions in which he all but accused the captain of being involved in an illicit relationship with Caroline. Sprague challenged Butler's assumptions and insisted that Caroline not only was "regularly employed as a laundress" and that her services were "very much needed," but also that she was "an intelligent, smart girl, anxious for her freedom." Moreover, he explained, she had "been cruelly treated by her mistress."[27] Uninterested in the "humanitarian" aspects of the case, Butler cut to the chase. The case raised "military questions" about how to best bring Louisiana back into the Union and how to promote discipline and morality among the troops. After a "long discussion" in which Butler reiterated the reasons he thought it best for Caroline to be returned to her "loyal masters," he directed Sprague to "procure a statement of the facts" from Chaplain Salter about Caroline's character. On June 3, Sprague sent Butler a statement from Chaplain Salter regarding Caroline and a letter in which he addressed head on Butler's "objection" to employing Black women as laundresses. Sprague recounted how in two separate meetings, Butler had charged enslaved women with licentiousness and having a demoralizing influence on the regiment. The problem, if there was one all, wrote Sprague, had been "entirely obviated" by moving the laundresses out of the Custom House and into nearby private quarters. "These women are almost completely isolated from the world," he

24. Sprague, *History of the 13th Infantry Regiment of Connecticut Volunteers*, 341.
25. Sprague, *History of the 13th Infantry Regiment of Connecticut Volunteers*, 342.
26. Sprague, *History of the 13th Infantry Regiment of Connecticut Volunteers*, 342.
27. Sprague, *History of the 13th Infantry Regiment of Connecticut Volunteers*, 342.

explained. "Their seclusion is unbroken by any male person, except momentarily for the transmission of laundry articles or rations."[28] More to the point, Sprague challenged Butler's assumptions regarding Black women's sexuality: "Whatever may have been their habits at home—obliged to submit of course to their masters' lusts, as you told us in that interview—they are necessarily virtuous in their conduct *here*, and are likely to continue so while in this service."[29]

Even though Butler allowed Caroline to continue to wash for the regiment, he was not convinced that the relationships between the "colored laundresses" and the men of the Thirteenth Connecticut Regiment were purely professional. In fact, as soon as he had received Sprague's letter and approved Caroline's appointment, he issued General Order No. 38: "The Laundresses of Companies are not permitted to come into the quarters of the men. They must be kept in their own quarters, and the clothing sent to them and sent for." The order warned, "Any officer who permits a woman, black or white, not his wife, in his quarters, or the quarters of his company, will be dismissed from the service."[30] Butler's order mobilized long-standing ideas that simultaneously defined Black women as lascivious and poor working women as promiscuous. According to Butler's logic, laundresses who dared to enter the "quarters of the men" were engaging in illicit sexual behavior.

Even as the order sexualized Black laundresses, it challenged the racial sexual double standard that permitted white men unfettered access to Black women's bodies. Indeed, Butler's order suggested that Black laundresses were no different from prostitutes and implied that Union officers were not above sexually exploiting them. It was one thing for Butler to issue a public order that perpetuated the myth of unrestrained Black sexuality, but it was something else altogether to suggest that federal officers were sexually exploiting the Black women who labored under their command. The order was printed in every issue of the *New Orleans Daily Delta* for the next two months and was reprinted in northern and southern newspapers.[31] The Confederate press took the opportunity to mock Union soldiers. The *Louisville Daily Journal* reported, "General Butler has issued an order at New Orleans forbidding the admission of laundresses to the quarters of the men. It is probably thought a great hardship that the poor soldiers can't have a chance to court their washer-women."[32] In defense of the Thirteenth Connecticut Regiment, Chaplain Salter published an open letter in the *New York Times* protesting Butler's General Order No. 38: "This order insulted the officers by intimating a state of things such as did not exist. It played into the hands of the rebels. It cast odium upon the retention of negro servants. If designed to counteract charges, it struck harder than it defended."[33] Less concerned with the

28. Sprague, *History of the 13th Infantry Regiment of Connecticut Volunteers*, 342.
29. Sprague, *History of the 13th Infantry Regiment of Connecticut Volunteers*, 345–46.
30. Parton, *General Butler in New Orleans*, 557.
31. *Daily Delta*, July 4, July 31, and August 5, 1862; *Boston Traveler*, July 26, 1862.
32. *Louisville Daily Journal*, July 11, 1862.
33. *New York Times*, July 3, 1862.

"insult" against the laundresses, Salter defended the officers as men who "merited honor."

Ultimately, Butler remained unfazed by the insult that General Order No. 38 offered to Black women. But he regretted the damage done to the reputation of the Thirteenth Connecticut Regiment. On June 14, in an effort to diminish the aspersions his order had cast on the regiment, Butler issued Special Order No. 99, in which he praised the men at length and declared: "Soldiers, your behavior in New Orleans has been admirable. Withstanding the temptations of a great city so as to present such discipline and efficiency is the highest exhibition of soldierly qualities. You have done more than win a great battle; you have conquered Yourselves."[34] Without question, New Orleans was a city rife with "temptations," especially for many young men who were away from home and the moral influences of their families for the first time. Nonetheless the young soldiers, he insisted, had remained true to their "New England training" and "religious influences."

While Butler was willing to let the Thirteenth off the hook, he doubled down on his critique of the Black women. Butler reiterated his belief that all Black women were eager for sex with white men when testifying before the American Freedmen's Inquiry Commission in May 1863. Butler described his so-called difficulty with Black laundresses: "I was obliged to make some stringent regulations in regard to them, because the women are all brought up to think that no honor can come to them equal to that of connection with a white man. And I am sorry to say that white men are not all above taking advantage of this feeling."[35] Butler, like slaveholders who justified the sexual exploitation of enslaved women with charges of licentiousness, ultimately blamed Black women for any and all illicit sexual relations with white men. The powerful ideology that portrayed Black women as sexually depraved made it difficult for most white Union officers to see Black laundresses as a victim of sexual violence. Butler's General Order No. 38, however, not only perpetuated the racist and sexist double standards that made Black laundress easy prey for white officers, but also exposed efforts to prevent Union officers from taking sexual advantage of the Black women who depended on them for employment and the protection of their freedom.

Cruelty and Mutiny at Fort Jackson

On the afternoon of December 15, 1863, Brigadier General William Dwight retreated to his new quarters at Fort Jackson, a Mississippi River garrison almost seventy miles south of New Orleans, and carefully penned a letter to his mother, Elizabeth Dwight, in Newton, Massachusetts. He recounted in painstaking detail the mutiny of the Fourth Regiment Corps d'Afrique at Fort Jackson that had compelled Major-General Nathaniel P. Banks, commander of the Department of the Gulf, to issue orders for

---

34. Special Order, No. 99, June 14, 1862 in Marshall, *Private and Official Correspondence of General Benjamin F. Butler* 1:591–92; *New York Times*, June 23, 1862; *National Anti-slavery Standard*, June 28, 1862.
35. Berlin et al., *Freedom*, ser. 1, vol. 3, 445.

Figure 1. Military laundresses and Union soldiers, Virginia, 1862. Prints and Photographs Division, Library of Congress, Washington, DC.

him to take "temporary command" of the fort.[36] According to initial reports on December 9, the Fourth Regiment had risen up in arms against their white officers. It was rumored that twenty-seven white officers were murdered, the fort was in possession of Black soldiers, and the river was blockaded.[37] "I was ordered down here to assume command, to enforce discipline, to arrest the ring leaders of the riot," he explained, "in short to deal with the difficult case—I was given white troops with which to force matters, if need be, with the edge of the sword."[38]

Organized by General Banks in February 1863 as the Fourth Native Guard and renamed the Fourth Corps d'Afrique in June 1863, the regiment was made up largely of men who had escaped plantations throughout Louisiana and Mississippi for Union lines. Unlike the First, Second, and Third Native Guard Regiments, which had been organized in August 1862 by General Benjamin Butler and mustered in with Black officers, the Fourth Regiment was commanded by white officers. When Banks replaced Butler as head of the Gulf Department in December 1862, he forced

36. William Dwight to Elizabeth Dwight, Fort Jackson, December 15, 1863, Dwight Family Papers, Massachusetts Historical Society, Boston (henceforth cited as MHS).

37. *Tri-weekly Mercury*, December 29, 1863.

38. William Dwight to Elizabeth Dwight, Fort Jackson, December 15, 1863, MHS.

Butler's commissioned Black officers to resign and appointed less than capable white men to command the Corps d'Afrique. Indeed, it was difficult to find good white officers who wanted to command Black soldiers. The best men were able to secure promotions within their own regiment, and as Banks later explained, "men disqualified by want of character and capacity for the discharge of the humblest duties in the regiments to which they belonged, and others, seeking promotion for personal objects, indifferent to the success of the corps, have in some cases been appointed."[39] Banks's promotion of Augustus W. Benedict to lieutenant-colonel of the Fourth Regiment in the spring of 1863 was a case in point.

Benedict, who came from the Finger Lakes region of western New York, joined the war effort as a second lieutenant in the Seventy-Fifth New York Infantry in the fall of 1861. In February 1863, Benedict wrote to Lieutenant Colonel Richard B. Irwin to request the major's position in the Corps d'Afrique. Eager for promotion, Benedict saw the Fourth as an easy opportunity to jump a grade or two. Benedict informed Irwin that Charles W. Drew, the Fourth's newly appointed colonel, with whom he had served in the Seventy-Fifth New York Regiment, had urged him to seek the position. With little if any qualifications, Benedict was appointed major of the newly organized Fourth Regiment and four months later, when the unit's lieutenant-colonel resigned, he was promoted to second-in-command despite his inexperience.

Benedict quickly garnered a reputation as a brutal and cruel officer. He cursed and hit soldiers whose brass buckles or boots did not shine to his satisfaction. When a punch to the face or kick to the back was insufficient, he did not hesitate to use his sword.[40] At his worst, Benedict tortured men who failed to live up to his expectations. On one occasion he had a soldier tied up by his thumbs. Stationed in Baton Rouge in August 1863, the men had gone months without fresh meat or vegetables, and signs of scurvy had begun to appear. When Benedict caught two of his men "stealing corn to roast," he ordered the officer of the guard to "lay them on the ground, straighten their legs and arms out, and stake them—tie them down." Once the men were tied spread-eagle to the ground, Benedict had their faces, feet, and hands covered with molasses. For two days the men suffered in the blistering summer heat as ants, flies, and bees attracted by the sweet syrup swarmed their exposed flesh.[41]

The regiment's transfer from Fort St. Philip to Fort Jackson in December 1863 did little to change Benedict's behavior. The soldiers, however, were growing impatient with his brutality. On at least two occasions the men, to no avail, complained of Benedict's maltreatment.[42] For almost a year they had tolerated Benedict's cruelty and the failure of their commanding officers to act on their behalf. Thus, when it came time for the men of the Fourth to depart for Fort Jackson, many of

39. *OR*, ser. 1, vol. 26, pt. 1, 457–59.

40. *OR*, ser. 1, vol. 26, pt. 1, 473.

41. Note that this was August 7 in Baton Rouge, and this punishment would be repeated at Fort Saint Philip on August 25. See *OR*, ser. 1, vol. 26, pt. 1, 468, 471.

42. *OR*, ser. 1, vol. 26, pt. 1, 473.

them asked "to remain at Fort Saint Philip, so that they would not have to be under Lieutenant Colonel Benedict."[43]

Less than twenty-four hours after their arrival at Fort Jackson, Benedict again resorted to violence to punish two of his men. With a rawhide teamster's whip, he flogged Harry Williams and Munroe Miller for attempting to leave the grounds of the fort without proper permission. The sound of the whip cracking on the men's backs and their pleas for mercy outraged the Black soldiers, who watched in horror. Colonel Drew, as well as two other officers, looked on as Benedict beat the men like enslaved people. Their failure to stop the flogging or to reprimand Benedict for his abuse of power made matters worse. The soldiers knew that flogging was illegal; Congress had outlawed the practice two years earlier.[44] Moreover, the soldiers had "been constantly assured . . . that under no circumstances whatever were they to be subjected to the degrading punishment of flogging," and in a recent address by Adjutant General Lorenzo Thomas they had been promised that any officer who maltreated them would be dismissed.[45] For the Black soldiers the whipping was too reminiscent of their recent enslavement. More importantly, the racialized violence contradicted their ideas of freedom.

The soldiers who had witnessed the brutal beatings grudgingly dispersed on Benedict's orders, but back in their quarters they decided it was time to put an end to the lieutenant-colonel's violent regime. Within an hour they had organized 250 men, and with muskets in hand they rushed onto the parade ground in protest. Making clear their discontent, they demanded, "Give us Colonel Benedict; we did not come here to be whipped by him. Kill Colonel Benedict; shoot him."[46] Firing their guns into the air they declared, "We know what [Adjutant General Thomas] told us!" While many remained on the parade field shooting their guns into the air, others went in search of Benedict. As the mutineers continued to fire their rifles in the air, white officers tried to reason with them. Promising that justice would be meted out, Colonel Drew persuaded the men to put down their weapons and return peacefully to their quarters.

Dwight's mother would be relieved to know that initial reports had been "greatly exaggerated." Dwight assured her that the "trouble" at Fort Jackson was not with "the insubordination of the negro" but had everything to do with "the bad administration of affairs" and with "having inferior and incompetent officers over [the] troops." The primary cause of the mutiny, he concluded "was a foolish and passionate Lt Col who so little understood his character as an officer as to raise his own hand against a soldier; and who had no more sense than to put the lash to the Negro whose idea of freedom is that he is raised by it beyond the pale of that worst degra-

43. *OR*, ser. 1, vol. 26, pt. 1, 471.

44. Witt, *Lincoln's Codes*.

45. *OR*, ser. 1, vol. 26, pt. 1, 456; Foner, *Fiery Trail*, 251; and *Washington Daily Morning Chronicle*, April 20, 1863.

46. *OR*, ser. 1, vol. 26, pt. 1, 460.

dation of servitude."[47] Indeed, here lay the crux of the issue—the violent gap between Black and white people's "idea of freedom" in the aftermath of slavery.

Twelve soldiers were court-martialed on charges of mutiny. After three days of testimony, the court announced its verdict. Two of the most aggressive offenders—including Private Frank Williams, who had tried to bayonet Captain Miller after declaring, "God damn you! I have been looking for you all night"—were sentenced "to be shot to death with musketry."[48] Private Julius Boudro was sentenced to prison for twenty years, while five other soldiers received terms ranging from one to ten years. Private James H. Moore was sentenced to a month confined in the guardhouse. Four of the accused were found innocent of all charges. At the same time, Benedict was charged with "inflicting cruel and unusual punishment, to the prejudice of good order and military discipline."[49] The court found him guilty. The sentence was dishonorable discharge. Banks heartily approved and immediately dismissed Benedict from the army. Banks, however, was more sympathetic toward the Black soldiers. While he endorsed the six prison sentences, he suspended the two death sentences and ordered both men to serve a sentence of hard labor instead.[50] By the end of the month, with Benedict and the mutineers removed, Dwight pronounced the regiment's discipline "excellent."[51] This, however, as Dwight would soon learn, was only part of the unsavory story of the mutiny at Fort Jackson.

Sexual Coercion and Resistance

On January 27, 1864, only a few weeks after the court-martial and two days after petitioning General Banks for reassignment, Dwight wrote again pleading to be reassigned. The delay, he complained, had required the "discharge of the most unpleasant duty."[52] Dwight reported in graphic detail the circumstances that compelled him to arrest four white officers.

On the night of January 25, Dwight explained, "Officer of the Day" Captain Charles A. Goff, and "Officer of the Guard" Lieutenant Henry E. Blakeslee left the Fort "for the ostensible purpose" of inspecting the "contraband quarters." Captain William H. Knapp and Lieutenant William H. Odell were asked to join in the inspection of the quarters, which were "occupied by negro women," who served as regimental laundresses. The officers began their "inspection" by first forcing their way into "the hut" of Keziah Davis, a laundress for Company F, whom Dwight

47. William Dwight to Mother, Fort Jackson December 15, 1863, MHS.

48. *OR*, ser. 1, vol. 26, pt. 1, 476–77.

49. *OR*, ser. 1, vol. 26, pt. 1, 476–79.

50. *OR*, ser. 1, vol. 26, pt. 1, 26, 457, 476–79.

51. For further discussion of the mutiny, see Harrington, "Fort Jackson Mutiny"; Dobak, *Freedom by the Sword*, 96–97, 112–13; Keith P. Wilson, *Campfires of Freedom*, 204–5; Messner, *Freedmen and the Ideology of Free Labor*, 157–63; and Ripley, *Slaves and Freedmen*, 115–16.

52. William Dwight Jr. to Chief of Staff General Charles P. Stone, January 27, 1864, MHS. All quotations that follow are from this same document, unless otherwise noted.

described as "an old negro crone . . . whom more than fifty summers under the inspiration of the lash of the slaveholder, have not spared." The exchange between the officers and "Aunt Keziah," explained Dwight, "was characterized first by looseness" and "soon became indecent and obscene." The men insisted that Davis have sex with at least one of them. Dwight described Davis as a "hideous creature" and admitted that "it would appear strange" to Banks "that from this revolting embrace she was the one to shrink." Dwight found it difficult to believe a Black woman was capable of rejecting a white man's sexual advances. Davis, he admitted, eventually managed to drive the officers out of her quarters with the contents of her chamber pot.

The officers moved on to "the cabin" of "Mrs. Rose Plummer," a laundress in Company A, whom Dwight described as "a young octoroon widow not without pretention to good looks." On entering Plummer's quarters, the men were allegedly "quiet and respectful, for the fair skin and bright eyes of the widow, scandal reports and she asserts, have obtained for her the protection of Captain Knapp." In this case, Dwight better understood the officers' desire and reported that Knapp was left "to the smiles and favors of this bewitching laundress." Plummer had confessed, "He [Knapp] alone obtains from her the rights and acknowledgment of husband." Even as Dwight admitted that Plummer's consent was offered in exchange for Knapp's protection, he could not resist racist stereotypes of Black women as seductresses. Clearly, Plummer had consented to a sexual relationship with Knapp to "obtain" protection against the unwanted sexual advances of other officers. Rendering their relationship in the contractual terms of the rights and privileges of marriage, Plummer sought to position herself within the frame of respectable womanhood.

Leaving Knapp at Plummer's "cabin," Goff, Blakeslee, and Odell moved on to the "dwellings" of Emma Smith, Elizabeth Dallas, and Laura Davis. Davis told Dwight that she was so soundly asleep that she did not realize that one of the officers had entered her quarters until he was lying on top of her. Davis and Smith, both reported that Goff and Blakeslee warned they "would lose their places" and be forced to leave the fort by the first boat "if they longer refused them the favors granted by Mrs. Rose Plummer to Captain Knapp."

By the time the three officers arrived at Elizabeth Taylor's contraband quarters, the laundress was asleep. It was late now, and the officers who stood banging on Taylor's door had already forced entry into the quarters of at least four other laundresses. Goff was particularly aggressive: when she refused to open the door, declaring that the men "were out on no very respectable business," he broke it down. Goff climbed into Taylor's bed and Odell tried to hold her down. Taylor screamed for help and fought the men as best she could. Eventually Goff gave up and called Taylor a "bitch" as he stormed out of her quarters. Hot on his heels, Taylor brazenly responded in like terms that he had "descended from a similar animal." Goff, not missing a beat, turned and struck her across the face with his sword.

Taylor's "appeal for help" drew the attention of Private Edward Idell of Company C, who lived in the boathouse at the landing of the camp. Idell shouted from his doorway "that if he had a sister in those contraband quarters he would send her away from this 'Port' before she should be so abused by the officers." In response, Goff had Idell arrested and confined him to the guardhouse.

Dwight, explained that his account was a "very brief and inadequate description of the conduct of these officers during this pretend inspection," based on statements taken from five of the laundresses and four Black soldiers. The statements, he claimed, were "in some degree corroborated" by Goff, who conceded that the inspection was not "properly conducted" and that he had in fact "pushed" Elizabeth Taylor with his sword. Blakeslee also admitted it was "not a proper inspection" and that Goff did strike Taylor with his sword, but added that because she had called Goff "a son of a bitch," he thought the captain was justified in striking her. Moreover, Blakeslee insisted, "it would have been better to have shot Elizabeth at once." Dwight explained that "this would be woman-killer" declared, "It is hard enough for a person to take *that* from a white man let alone a black woman." Odell, reported Dwight, denied holding Taylor down but admitted "to putting his hands upon her" and thought he might have struck her in "vindication of Captain Goff's birth." Knapp also admitted that the inspection was not properly made but claimed he had no idea what occurred after the party left him with Mrs. Plummer. The four officers, concluded Dwight, "are of course in close arrest."

The officer's assaults on the laundresses on the night of January 25 were just the tip of the iceberg. Dwight underscored that this kind of assault happened regularly. "These women, and the soldiers who live in their vicinity, as well as the soldiers who have from time to time for months past been placed 'on Post' near these 'contraband quarters,' all concur in stating, that scenes similar to the one of Monday evening have been of frequent, almost nightly, occurrences for a long time past," explained Dwight. The laundresses insisted that officers other than those arrested "have been at other times equally guilty." The names of many officers, reported Dwight, "have long been held up to the scandal and contempt of the soldiers of the Regiment."

Dwight hoped that Banks would agree with his assessment that "the disgusting details of the late affair render it unfit for the investigations of a military tribunal." The "publicity" of another court-martial, he reasoned, would bring more negative attention and further injure the reputation of "a most important corps of the service." Moreover, he maintained that the only witnesses to be produced against white officers would be "negro women, of more than questionable character, and the negro soldiers who stand in terror of all who have exercised authority over them—an inherited terror, increased by an average of twenty years of personal bondage, and only to be eradicated by the influences of time and the elevation of freedom." Dwight recommended "the immediate dishonorable dismissal of these officers from the service of the United States."

Banks, however, ordered Dwight to convene a military commission of officers from the Fourth Regiment Corps d'Afrique "to inquire into the facts." Dwight appointed Major William Nye, Captain George E. Wentworth, and First Lieutenant Daniel C. Payne to the commission. Within hours of the inquiry, however, Dwight found himself forced to "dissolve" the commission. In a letter to Bank's chief of staff, he recounted how one of the laundresses had testified that Captain Wentworth of the commission had also tried to force his way into her quarters. Whether this was a case of mistaken identity, or merely a mistake as to time, Dwight explained that it was clear that "a similar occurrence with this actor having been so recent as not easily to be distinguished in the dull mind and dim memory of this heavy looking negress." Dwight believed it was of "no consequence" whether or not the woman's testimony was true. "The immediate effect," he explained, "can only be likened to the bursting of a shell loaded with Greek fire—it not only destroyed the efficiency of the commission but threw a glare of light upon the whole subject—a light which nothing could dim or put out." Moreover, he observed, "It completely dazzled Captain Wentworth who exclaimed with a pathos and simplicity seldom found combined with guilt 'that it would never do to prosecute such an inquiry as this, for that every officer in the Regiment might be implicated!'" Dwight insisted he had no choice but to dissolve the commission and requested permission to appoint Captain E. P. Loring of the First Heavy Artillery, Corps d'Afrique, at Fort St. Philip to the commission.[53] He concluded, "I can find but one officer of sufficient rank in the 4th Regiment Corps d'Afrique fit to sit on the commission."[54] The problem, however, had less to do with finding an officer of sufficient rank within the regiment and more to do with finding a "fit" officer—in other words, an officer who was not implicated in the assaults.

Moreover, Dwight insisted that the officers, under the direction of Colonel Drew, had "banded together for self-preservation." Prior to the convening of the commission, Dwight explained that the four officers "most implicated" in the attacks had spent the time "concocting" a unified story, which compelled him to put a sentinel over each man. Then three other officers—Captain James Miller (whom Private Frank Williams had attacked during the late mutiny), Captain Wentworth (of the commission), and Captain Charles H. Merritt, "of notoriously bad character"—had tried to intimidate some of the laundresses. According to Dwight, when Miller asked Keziah Davis not to mention him in her testimony, she berated him, "Go on! Go on! You know what you have done." As for Merritt, she reassured him, "Go long! You be not so bad as the worst of these—maybe I'll let you off this time." Davis's reprimand of Miller—"You know what you have done"—suggests that it may in fact have been his treatment of the laundresses in the contraband quarters that provoked Williams's attack on him during the mutiny.[55]

Taken together, the whippings of the soldiers and the sexual assaults against the laundresses left little doubt in Dwight's mind that Drew and the white officers under his command were "pro-slavery officers," who had entered the service "only for increased rank and pay." He believed they were just as bad as, if not worse than, southern slaveholders, who whipped and raped enslaved people. Dwight poured out his frustrations in a single sentence:

53. William Dwight to Charles P. Stone, January 31, 1864, MHS.
54. William Dwight to Charles P. Stone, January 31, 1864, MHS.
55. William Dwight to Charles P. Stone, January 31, 1864, MHS.

We are dealing with difficulties in a Regiment which has been driven to mutiny by one of the officers highest in command using in person upon its black soldiers the lash which even the slave-driver directed through other hands,—and in which the officers with great publicity have indulged with the colored women, or forced these women to indulge with them, in all the vices which have most stained slavery in the eyes of the civilized world as a curse and a shame.[56]

Whereas the slaveholder had delegated the whip to the "bad and brutal" overseer and sought discretion in the sexual exploitation of enslaved women, Dwight argued that these white officers had "repeated in worse forms the methods through which the slave-holders ruled." He reasoned that the officers' "beastliness has not the virtue of the amalgamation practiced by the slave-holders, for it tends to destroy, not to create." Moreover, he insisted, "it affords to those who desire to use them the best arguments upon what are called 'the curses of freedom.'"[57] Dwight promised to do his "part" to "purify" the regiment.[58] Responding on Banks's behalf, General Stone wrote, "Do the work thoroughly and fearlessly. Those men have no more right to the negro than the slave holder had."[59]

On February 1, the commission reconvened, with Loring taking Wentworth's place. Over the course of two days, the commission interviewed many witnesses, including six laundresses, three Black soldiers, and the four accused white officers. On February 3, the commission "after mature deliberation on the evidence" completed and submitted its official report. While laden with racist and sexual stereotypes, the report took seriously the laundress's testimonies: for example, "The testimony of Keziah Davis who is of a decent and respectable appearance was unmistakable, and was given in a straightforward and truthful manner."[60] More to the point, when the commission had asked Davis, "Are there officers here in the habit of doing the same thing?" she did not hesitate to name names: "Yes sir, Captain Miller." Miller had been the target of Frank Williams's bayonet during the mutiny.[61]

The commission praised Emma Smith, a laundress who was married to a soldier in the regiment, for giving "her testimony with apparent truthfulness but with some timidity."[62] Smith swore that the officers had threatened to get rid of her if she continued to reject their sexual advances. She also recounted that "Captain Merritt came and sat on my bed, and I told him that it was wrong to do so, because he knew my husband was under arrest. He said he knew it and asked my pardon."[63] Smith's testimony suggests that some of the laundresses tried to use their marital status to

---

56. William Dwight to Charles P. Stone, January 31, 1864, MHS.

57. William Dwight to Charles P. Stone, January 31, 1864, MHS.

58. William Dwight to Charles P. Stone, January 31, 1864, MHS.

59. C. P. Stone to William Dwight, January 31, 1864, RG 393, part 1, vol. 6, entry 1738, NARA.

60. Report of Military Commission, February 3, 1864, RG 153, NN 1332, NARA.

61. Military Commission Convened at Fort Jackson, February 1, 1864, RG 153, NN1332, NARA.

62. Military Commission Convened at Fort Jackson.

63. Military Commission Convened at Fort Jackson.

fend off assaults, and that some of the officers may have avoided sexually harassing laundresses who were married to soldiers in the regiment.

The commission, however, critiqued Laura Davis, as "somewhat heavy looking, and less intelligent in appearance than the other witnesses" and for exhibiting "more indignation and vindictiveness in regard to the Officers against whom she testified."[64] A close examination of Davis's testimony leaves little doubt as to why she was more forthright than the other laundresses in her testimony. Davis took particular aim at Blakeslee, a lieutenant in the company that she served: "Lieutenant Blakeslee said . . . he had as much right to stay with me as Captain Knapp had to stay with his laundress."[65] And it was Davis who had implicated Wentworth (of the commission), when she testified that he had come to her quarters "the night before . . . and tried to do the same thing." Davis made it clear that the officers demanded sex as part of the labor they expected of the laundress who served their regiment. In fact, the commission unwittingly exposed the implications of Davis's statement when it asked, "Whose laundress are you?" instead of asking her which company she served. Of greater significance, however, was Davis's answer: "I was Captain Cranes, Company K, but they have turned me off. I was turned off the day after this happened."[66] Without question, laundresses who resisted the sexual advances of the officers they served risked losing not only their jobs but also their freedom in Louisiana, where emancipation had not yet freed the enslaved people. Given that Davis had lost her positions, it is not surprising that her testimony was filled with "indignation" and bitterness.

While the report concluded that "nothing of importance took place" at Plummer's quarters and that the officers "unnecessarily annoyed" Keziah Davis and behaved with "gross indecency" in her presence, it declared that in the quarters of Emma Smith, Laura Davis, and Elizabeth Taylor the officers "behaved with violence and gross indecency."[67] Furthermore, the report made clear that "scenes similar that of the night of January 25, in which other officers of the Regiment have been equally implicated, have been of not unfrequent occurrence."[68] The committee concluded "that the good of the service requires the summary punishment."[69] Dwight approved the report and attached his recommendation that six officers, including the four he had arrested as well as Miller and Wentworth, be "dishonorably dismissed the service of the United States."[70] Banks ultimately agreed. On February 10, he issued Special Order No. 36, which declared the officers guilty of "conduct highly prejudicial to good order and military discipline, and unbecoming officers and gentlemen, in disturbing the peace of the garrison by forcing an entrance in the quarter occupied by

64. Military Commission Convened at Fort Jackson.
65. Military Commission Convened at Fort Jackson.
66. Military Commission Convened at Fort Jackson.
67. Military Commission Convened at Fort Jackson.
68. Military Commission Convened at Fort Jackson.
69. Military Commission Convened at Fort Jackson.
70. Military Commission Convened at Fort Jackson.

colored laundresses" and "dishonorably dismissed" them, "subject to the approval of the President."[71]

But Dwight was not finished yet. There was still the problem of Colonel Drew, who Dwight now believed was to blame for the "rotten" behavior of the officers under his command. In a separate letter written to General Stone, Dwight announced that he had arrested Drew and confined him to his quarters. He said that he had arrested Drew with "reluctance" but insisted his actions were necessary: "This Regiment will again rise in revolt if the abuse of the soldiers is suffered to continue, and the next revolt will not be bloodless."[72]

Dwight recounted in detail four acts of violence committed by Drew between January 24 and February 3. He described Drew kicking Private Idell (the soldier who had been arrested for speaking out in defense of the laundresses) twice in the back for "not moving quickly enough"; striking First Sergeant Williams (possibly related to the lead mutineer Frank Williams) in the face and kicking him several times for being out of his quarters without permission; striking Sergeant Eugene Charles twice with a pole, when he was sick and unable to drill; and threatening Private Sheldon with his pistol, for not facing properly in saluting and appealing to a higher authority for protection against punishment. The assault against Sheldon, on the very day that the commission had concluded its investigation and submitted its final report, proved the tipping point for Dwight.

Drew's conduct was not discipline, declared Dwight; it was the kind of physical terror that, if endured too long, provoked mutiny. The problem, he suggested, was rooted in the fact that Drew and Benedict, two inexperienced young men with "violent passions and unchastened temper" and proslavery sentiments, had selected "many of the Regiment's worst Officers." There could be no mistake, Dwight explained at length:

> In this Regiment thus commanded was practiced every species of disgusting vice; what should have been the performance of duty was made a means of low and vile licentiousness among the Officers, of outrage which could not fail to be known to these soldiers, towards the women of their race, and the demoralization thus caused was repressed by violent punishment miscalled discipline. These are the traditions possessed by this Regiment.[73]

Dwight again called for the regiment to be broken up and for the officers under arrest—there were now seven of them—to be discharged from the service.[74] Whether driven by his belief that truth will out, or inspired by the Black men and women who mutinied against the white officers at Fort Jackson, Dwight's vision of military justice was at odds with the racial and sexual hierarchies that justified white violence against Black people.

71. *Weekly Times-Democrat*, March 26, 1864.
72. William Dwight to Chief of Staff Charles P. Stone, February 4, 1864, MHS.
73. William Dwight to Chief of Staff Charles P. Stone, February 4, 1864, MHS.
74. William Dwight to Chief of Staff Charles P. Stone, February 4, 1864, MHS.

In the end Banks refused to hold Drew responsible, and President Lincoln revoked the commission's dismissals of the six officers. As for their laundresses, the *Weekly Times-Democrat* reported that it had "been found necessary, for the good order of the men and the good behavior of the officers, to send all colored women out of this camp, except a few who are lawfully married to privates in the regiment, and are retained as laundresses for the regiment."[75] Nonetheless, while the commission's report had failed to bring justice, the women hoped a proper court-martial might succeed. In September 1864, seven months after testifying before the commission, three laundresses, Keziah Davis, Emma Smith, and Elizabeth Dallas, testified at the courts-martial of officers Wentworth, Goff, Blakeslee, and Knapp.[76] Despite the women's testimony, the court found the men not guilty.

The case of rape and munity at Fort Jackson is an extraordinary example of how Black men and women sought to defend themselves against racial and sexual violence and raise questions about the links between slavery and Black women's wartime labor. Bringing into focus how sexual and racial violence informed emerging ideas about freedom, and not least, the capacity of Black women to refuse to be treated as enslaved labor, the Black laundresses at Fort Jackson spoke truths that had long been denied under slavery—truths rooted in ideas about the past, what was possible, what was likely, and what was just. ◪

CRYSTAL N. FEIMSTER is an associate professor at Yale University in the Department of African American Studies and the American Studies Program. Feimster is the author of *Southern Horrors: Women and the Politics of Rape and Lynching* (2009).

References

Barber, Susan E., and Charles F. Ritter. "Dangerous Liaisons: Working Women and Sexual Justice in the American Civil War." *European Journal of American studies* 10, no. 1 (2015). http://journals.openedition.org/ejas/10695; DOI: https://doi.org/10.4000/ejas.10695.

Berlin, Ira, Thavolia Glymph, Julie Saville, Leslie S. Rowland, Steven F. Miller, and Joseph Reidy, eds. *Freedom: A Documentary History of Emancipation: Selected from the Holding of the National Archives of the United States*. Series 1, vols. 1–53. New York: Cambridge University Press, 1982–2008.

Brown, Kathleen M. *Good Wives, Nasty Wenches, and Anxious Patriarchs: Gender, Race, and Power in Colonial Virginia*. Chapel Hill: University of North Carolina Press, 1996.

Callan, John F. *Military Laws of the United States, 1777–1863*. Philadelphia: George Childs, 1863.

Davis, Adrienne D. "'Don't Let Nobody Bother Yo' Principle': The Sexual Economy of American Slavery." In *Sister Circle: Black Women and Work*, edited by Sharon Harley, 15–38. New Brunswick, NJ: Rutgers University Press, 2002.

75. *Weekly Times-Democrat*, March 26, 1864.
76. Trials of G. E. Wentworth, C. A. Goff, W. H. Knapp, H. F. Blakeslee, and W. H. O'Dell, Fourth Corps d'Afrique, RG 153, NN1332 and LL2744, NARA.

Dobak, William A. *Freedom by the Sword: The U.S. Colored Troops 1862–1867*. Washington, DC: US Army Center of Military History, 2011.

Downs, Jim. *Sick from Freedom: African-American Illness and Suffering during the Civil War and Reconstruction*. New York: Oxford University Press, 2012.

Foner, Eric. *The Fiery Trial: Abraham Lincoln and American Slavery*. New York: W. W. Norton & Company, 2010.

Gaines, John J. "Westward Expansion: Laundresses." In *Encyclopedia of Prostitution and Sex Work*, vol. 2, edited by Melissa Hope Ditmore, 537–39. Santa Barbara, CA: Greenwood, 2006.

Glymph, Thavolia. "'I'm a Radical Black Girl': Black Women Unionists and the Politics of Civil War History." *Journal of the Civil War Era* 8, no. 3 (September 2018): 359–87.

Glymph, Thavolia. "Noncombant Military Labor in the Civil War." *OAH Magazine of History* 26, no. 2 (2012): 25–29.

Glymph, Thavolia. *Out of the House of Bondage: The Transformation of the Plantation Household*. Cambridge: Cambridge University Press, 2012.

Glymph, Thavolia. *The Women's Fight: The Civil War's Battles for Home, Freedom and Nation*. Chapel Hill: University of North Carolina Press, 2019.

Harrington, Fred Harvey. "The Fort Jackson Mutiny." *Journal of Negro History* 27, no. 4 (1942): 420–31.

Hunter, Tera. *To Joy My Freedom*. Cambridge, MA: Harvard University Press, 1998.

King, Lisa Y. "In Search of Women of African Descent Who Served in the Civil War Union Navy." *Journal of Negro History* 83, no. 4 (1998): 302.

Manning, Chandra. *Troubled Refuge: Struggling for Freedom in the Civil War*. New York: Knopf, 2016.

Marshall, Jessie Ames. *Private and Official Correspondence of General Benjamin F. Butler: During the Period of the Civil War*. Norwood, MA: The Plimpton Press, 1917.

Mescher, Virginia. "Tubs and Suds: Civil War Laundresses in the Field, Camp and Hospital." *Camp Chase Gazette*, (August–September 2003), online at http://www.raggedsoldier.com/final_laundry_vv.pdf (accessed November 15, 2020).

Messner, William F. *Freedmen and the Ideology of Free Labor*. Baton Rouge: Louisiana State University Press, 1978.

Parton, James. *General Butler in New Orleans: History of the Administration of the of the Department of the Gulf in the Year 1861*. New York: Mason Brothers, 1864.

Ripley, C. Peter. *Slaves and Freedmen in Civil War Louisiana*. Baton Rouge: Louisiana State University Press, 1976.

Schultz, Jane E. "Race, Gender, and Bureaucracy: Civil War Army Nurses and the Pension Bureau." *Journal of Women's History* 6, no. 2 (1994): 45–69.

Schultz, Jane E. *Women at the Front: Hospital Workers in Civil War America*. Chapel Hill: University of North Carolina Press, 2004.

Schwalm, Leslie. *A Hard Fight for We: Women's Transition for Slavery to Freedom in South Carolina*. Urbana: University of Illinois Press, 1998.

Sibbald, John R. "Camp Followers All." *American West* 3, no. 2 (1966): 56–67.

Sprague, Homer. *History of the 13th Infantry Regiment of Connecticut Volunteers, during the Great Rebellion*. Hartford, CT: Case, Lockwook and Co., 1867.

Stallard, Patricia Y. *Glittering Misery: Dependents of the Indian-Fighting Army*. San Rafael, CA: Presidio Press, 1978.

Stewart, Miller J. "Army Laundresses: Ladies of the 'Soap Suds Row.'" *Nebraska History* 60 (1980): 421–36.

Taylor, Amy Murrell. *Embattled Freedom: Journeys through the Civil War's Slave Refugee Camps*. Chapel Hill: University of North Carolina Press, 2018.

US War Department. *General Regulations for the Army of the United States*. Washington, DC: Louis Le Grand, MD, 1841.

US War Department. *General Regulations for the Army or Military Institutes*. Philadelphia: M. Carey & Sons, 1821.

US War Department. *The Military Handbook and Soldiers' Manual of Information*. New York: Beadle and Company, 1861.

US War Department. *Revised United States Army Regulations of 1861, with an Appendix Containing the Changes and Laws Affecting Army Regulations and Articles of War to June 25, 1863*. Washington, DC: Government Printing Office, 1863.

US War Department. *The War of the Rebellion: A Compilation of the Official Records of the Union and the Confederate Armies*. Series 1, vols. 1–53. Washington, DC: Government Printing Office, 1885.

Wilson, Keith P. *Campfires of Freedom: The Camp Life of Black Soldiers during the Civil War*. Kent, OH: Kent State University Press, 2002.

Wilson, Kellie K. Buford. "'Troublesome Hellions' and 'Belligerent Viragos': Enlisted Wives, Laundresses, and the Politics of Gender on Nineteenth-Century Army Posts." *Military History of the West* 41 (2011): 13–30.

Witt, John Fabian. *Lincoln's Codes: The Laws of War in American History*. New York: Free Press, 2012.

Wood, Cynthia A. "Army Laundresses and Civilization on the Western Frontier." *Journal of the West* 41, no. 3 (2002): 26–34.

"I Told Him to Let Me Alone, That He Hurt Me": Black Women and Girls and the Battle over Labor and Sexual Consent in Union-Occupied Territory

Kaisha Esty

It was the middle of spring in 1865, a month after Confederate general Robert E. Lee's surrender in Appomattox, Virginia. Susan was in the final days of her pregnancy. She was a woman of color residing on a plantation near Salisbury, North Carolina, owned by her former enslaver, George Lyerly.[1] Like many other freedpeople, Susan likely felt immeasurable joy knowing that her baby would be born free. The threat of routine family separation that plagued enslaved motherhood was, for the most part, behind her.[2] Susan could expect to negotiate her time and labor for a wage. She might commit herself to familial and collective duties as a wife, mother, and community member. As an emancipated woman, the many horrors inherent to the market in the sale and exploitation of human flesh and labor should no longer have been part of her lived reality.

But Susan's dreams of freedom were viciously interrupted when she was raped by a Union soldier.[3] The terror occurred on or about May 10, 1865. Private Adolph

I would like to extend my gratitude to co-organizers Christopher Phelps and Leon Fink for the invitation to contribute to this timely special issue. In addition to the feedback from my co-contributors, I wish to also thank Beryl Satter, Ashraf Rushdy, Kidada E. Williams, Cheryl Hicks, Kali Gross, Alexandria Russell, Miya Carey, Nakia D. Parker, and Ashleigh Lawrence Sanders for their penetrating and invigorating comments on earlier drafts.

1. Susan's testimony names George "Larley" as the owner of the plantation where she lived. This is likely a misspelling. The 1860 US Federal Census—Slave Schedule identifies a person called George Lyiely (more commonly spelled as "Lyerly" or "Lyrely") who owned a plantation in Salisbury, Rowan County, NC. See Records of the Judge Advocate General's Office (Army), Entry 15, Court Martial Case File, file MM2407, Record Group 153, National Archives and Records Administration (hereafter cited as RG 153, NARA); US Federal Census, George Lyrely, 1860, Salisbury, Rowan, NC, p. 529, Family History Library Film 803912; George Lyrely, 1870; Providence, Rowan, NC, Roll M593_1158, p. 548A.

2. In the wake of emancipation, formerly enslaved families confronted new systems of oppression, such as forced apprenticeships, that undermined parental authority. See Zipf, *Labor of Innocents*.

3. MM2407, NARA, RG 153.

Labor: Studies in Working-Class History, Volume 19, Issue 1
DOI 10.1215/15476715-9475702   © 2022 by Labor and Working-Class History Association

Bork of the 183rd Ohio Volunteers and four other soldiers had visited Lyerly's plantation. Along with several other Black women, Susan recalled standing on a porch and watching as the soldiers roamed around the plantation grounds asserting their power. Presuming the availability of the labor of the Black female onlookers, a soldier ordered them to prepare some dinner. Unable to help due to her condition, Susan left the company of the other women and headed over to her cabin. There she found three of the soldiers. She waited until they departed before entering her home, shutting the door behind her.

When Susan was done gathering her things, she confronted Bork at her door. Addressing her as "Aunty," Bork showed that he did not view Susan as a person. He asked if she had any Confederate money. She told him that she didn't but that her "old man" did and that he could have it.[4] He then asked her if she wanted to *make* some money. Seeking clarification, Susan asked Bork, "What sort," to which he responded: "Confederate."[5] She refused Bork's offer, knowing that Confederate currency "was no account."[6] In doing so, Susan refused to participate in the games that men who rape deploy in their assaults.[7] Bork then threatened Susan at gunpoint, telling her that whether "you want to make money or not you will have to."[8] Susan, who had been holding the child of another woman on her lap, got up and laid the child down. Knowing Bork's intentions, she fearfully began removing her clothes. Susan pleaded as Bork—the supposed enforcer of her emancipation—raped her. In a testimony before a General Court Martial, Susan asserted that she neither consented nor accepted any money from Bork. "I told him to let me alone," Susan testified, "that he hurt me."[9] In offering further "proof" that she did not consent, Susan emphasized her marital status as an indication of her sexual respectability. "I am a married woman," she stated. "I was married by a colored exhorter."[10] At the close of the trial, Bork was sentenced "to be shot to death with musketry," a sentence later mitigated to five years of hard labor.[11] Susan's experience transpired under the assumption that African American women were always prepared to negotiate sex in addition to, or as part of, their (nonsexual) labor.

4. MM2407, NARA, RG 153.

5. MM2407, NARA, RG 153.

6. MM2407, NARA, RG 153.

7. Early American historian Sharon Block makes the excellent point that "social and economic power relations underwrote sexual power, not only in the ability to evade legal punishment but also through the very commission of sexual coercion. . . . In other words, men could commit rape not just as an act of power—they could use their power to define the act." Block, *Rape and Sexual Power in Early America*, 54.

8. MM2407, NARA, RG 153.

9. MM2407, NARA, RG 153.

10. MM2407, NARA, RG 153.

11. Bork was also on trial for "assault with intent to kill" another soldier. In a broader military court culture that repeatedly failed to recognize the humanity of Black female victims, the severity of the initial sentence was most certainly due to this second charge. MM2407, NARA, RG 153.

The Constraints of Consent

Scholars of nineteenth-century American liberalism have rightly exposed how the concept of consent as stipulated in relation to the "social contract" has been anything but universal in its historical application.[12] As the feminist scholar Pamela Haag argues, "The deployment of consent or violence in one type of relationship necessarily affects and is modified with reference to other social 'contracts' inherent to citizenship and labor."[13] Had Susan been sexually assaulted six months earlier, the outcome would have been different. Before the completion of Union general George Stoneman's raid on Salisbury, North Carolina, in early 1865, Susan's sexual assault would not have been prosecuted as an injury on her person, if appealed at all.[14] Sexual access to enslaved women was foundational to the accumulation of white capital and the culture of slavery as a whole.[15] The sexual availability of enslaved women was built into the definition and exploitation of their labor. Their enslaved status was rooted in the negation of their capacity to give consent.[16] Any power for legal redress would have rested in the proprietary rights of Susan's owner.[17]

The Emancipation Proclamation and the Lieber Code, each issued in 1863, marked a major turning point as much in the lives of African American women as in the American Civil War. The Lieber Code acknowledged Black women as victims of sexual violence for the first time in US history.[18] Still, this new legal recognition existed in tension with the everyday reality evident in Susan's case. For Black women, the right to refuse unwanted sex remained elusive even after the end of slavery. How does one account for a history of sexual violence against African American women of liminal status on shifting legal ground?

Refugee and freedwomen's testimonies of sexual violence must be read as part of a contestation over labor and sexual consent in the mid-nineteenth-century United States. In their petitions before the military courts, fugitive and refugee enslaved women and girls asserted themselves foremost as sexually sovereign, especially as respectable, morally sound, and virtuous women and girls. These women and girls understood the racist and sexist structure of southern rape laws. Victorian

12. As a concept in Western liberalism, the idea of consent has traditionally affirmed notions of individual proprietary rights as part of the social contract. Feminist critiques of contract theory have underscored how consent has historically served as a mechanism of white patriarchal supremacy. With such rights demarcated within the parameters of the law, consent thus must be understood as an instrument of subjectivity and its attendant freedoms, as well as an aide of imperial conquest, Indigenous dispossession, colonialism, slavery, and capitalist exploitation. See Pateman, *Sexual Contract*; Haag, *Consent*.

13. Haag, *Consent*, xviii.

14. Fordney, *George Stoneman*, 113.

15. Black feminist scholar Adrienne Davis offers the crucial language of the "sexual economy of American slavery" to describe enslaved women's systemic sexual exploitation within the institution. See Davis, "Don't Let Nobody Bother Yo' Principle."

16. Hartman, *Scenes of Subjection*, 105.

17. For example, see Morris, *Southern Slavery and the Law*; Edwards, "Status without Rights," 369; Bardaglio, "Rape and the Law in the Old South," 760.

18. See Feimster, "What if I Am a Woman?"

sexual morality, combined with narrow rape laws centered on the premise of (white) female chastity, determined the most "acceptable" representation of female sexual sovereignty.[19] The laws that previously prohibited Black testimony against a white assailant, and the cultural values that made no distinction among Black women's non-sexual and sexual labor, ensured that only white middle-class women could be considered "chaste." Black women were considered "unrapable" because any violence done to their person was either legally sanctioned or culturally beneath notice. The testimonies of Black women and girls in these courts-martial attempted to overturn all these legal and cultural attitudes. Through the language of sexual respectability, Black women in occupied territory who were not sex workers argued that sexual assaults interfered with their ability to be productive as women, wives, and mothers. Grasping the power offered them by the Lieber Code, these formerly disempowered women created a rupture in what feminine virtue meant and who could be said to possess it.

In the perilous and jagged transition from slavery to emancipation, fugitive and refugee enslaved women and girls embarked on a fight to renegotiate assumptions around their labor. This article illuminates some of their stories. Ushering in their own meanings of consent that drew sharp distinctions between their (nonsexual) labor and sexual availability, African American women and girls asserted their right to withhold consent on their own terms.[20] Using testimonies of wartime rape of Black women and girls by Union soldiers and other military personnel, this article explicates the ways Black women and girls fought for sexual autonomy, and sometimes won acknowledgment of it, regardless of their class, status, or statelessness.[21]

Race, Sexual Violence, and the Civil War Military Record

Even by a conservative estimate, at least 250 Union soldiers faced military courts-martial on charges of sexual assault during the Civil War. Scholars E. Susan Barber and Charles F. Ritter have counted around 450 cases.[22] Both historically and contemporarily, sexual violence is heavily underreported, with even fewer cases making it to legal proceedings. The confirmed incidents of Union-perpetrated sexual violence during the Civil War may be inferred to represent but a small fraction of a larger

---

19. See Freedman, *Redefining Rape.*

20. In a meeting with Secretary of War and Major-General William T. Sherman on January 12, 1865, twenty African American ministers and church officers expressed their understanding of slavery. They stated, "Slavery is, receiving by *irresistible power* the work of another man, and not by his *consent.*" Invoking the language of consent, these figures demonstrated that African Americans held their own meanings of consent. It bears highlighting that the voices in this interview represent an African American male perspective. The systemic intimate abuses that marked Black women's experiences in slavery demonstrated the gendered nature of the institution. As such, meanings of slavery and freedom should be analyzed along gendered lines. See Berlin et al., *Freedom;* and for an excellent discussion of gendered meanings of liberation, see Threadcraft, *Intimate Justice.*

21. Glymph, *Women's Fight,* 247.

22. Thomas P. Lowry estimates around 250 prosecuted cases, whereas an ongoing project by scholars E. Susan Barber and Charles F. Ritter have measured at least 450 cases. Lowry, *Sexual Misbehavior in the Civil War;* Barber and Ritter, "Physical Abuse . . . and Rough Handling," 51.

phenomenon. With the number of cases in the Union army court record, the over-representation of Black women and girls as victims and white Union servicemen as perpetrators underscores two essential points.[23] First, it demonstrates that stereotypes of African American women's sexual availability were not confined to the white South. White and northern Union soldiers' sexual expectations of Black women and girls were remarkably reflective of the attitudes of their white southern and pro-Confederate counterparts. Second, the fact that such an historical record of Black women's and girls' testimonies of sexual violence during the Civil War exists shows the huge importance of legal developments that empowered them to pursue justice.[24]

Sexual violence cases involving African American female victims reflect the arbitrary and racialized nature of record-keeping during wartime in the mid-nineteenth-century. In some instances, Black female victim's names are not identified. Unnamed women are sometimes referred to as "a woman of color" or "a Negro" woman." This was most prevalent in courts-martial that did not feature the testimonies or firsthand accounts of Black women. Union military courts often showed greater concern with the conduct of soldiers than with the harm suffered by the victim, meaning that statements invoking the voices of survivors themselves were not always a priority. It is also possible that some of these women and girls chose to remain anonymous due to fear of retaliation. Depending on the outcome of these trials, many survivors could expect to live and work within the vicinity of their assailants.

In addition to the erasure of Black women's personhood, the record is problematic in its repeated reformulation of Black girls as women. Born in enslavement, many victims could not accurately recall their age. Few courts took this unique context into account in their treatment of younger victims. Where prepubescent girls may have received sympathy, adolescent girls were more systemically "adultified." The violence of "adultification" in the court environment dehumanized and further traumatized Black girls by diminishing their childhood innocence and undeveloped maturity.[25]

Despite these limits, though, Union courts-martial and commissions give a rare insight into the environment that refugee and freed female sexual violence victims navigated in their struggle for sexual autonomy. They offer a useful site for investigating the complexity of the interactions between contraband, fugitive, and refugee women and the Union army. These women often conducted nonsexual labor in the company of soldiers, increasing their vulnerability to sexual attacks from soldiers. Black women and girls were compelled to seek justice from military courts, the same entity whose representatives were responsible for their ill-treatment.

23. Many of these cases involved Black female victims. Acknowledging this point, Barber and Ritter also emphasize that "no woman was safe from wartime sexual predation. The female victims came from all economic and social strata of Southern society." Barber and Ritter, "Physical Abuse . . . and Rough Handling," 57–58.

24. Feimster, "What if I Am a Woman?"

25. Epstein, Blake, and Gonzalez, "Girlhood Interrupted," 6.

Testimonies of Sexual Violence

African American women's and girls' testimonies of sexual violence during the Civil War and the emancipation era challenged cultural and legal assumptions around sexual consent in mid-nineteenth-century America. The battlefield of this rupture manifested primarily in relations of labor involving fugitive and refugee women and girls, and military personnel. During the first part of the Civil War, fugitives, "contraband," and refugees were mainly African American men. However, by 1863, with the passage of the Emancipation Proclamation, greater numbers of African American women, children, and elderly people flocked to Union lines. "Attaching themselves to the rear of columns on the move," formerly enslaved people established make-shift communities.[26] Thousands of men, women, and children contributed to the war effort through noncombatant military labor. Refugee women and girls took on roles as officer's servants, laundresses, cooks, nurses, and plantation field hands, though it was not uncommon for Black women to engage in more physically grueling labor like hoisting wheelbarrows, digging ditches, building roads and bridges, clearing canals, and burying the dead.[27] As historian Thavolia Glymph notes, "For them, it was an opportunity to work for their own freedom and for Union victory."[28]

Scholars of sexual violence during the Civil War underscore the significance of groundbreaking wartime legislation in creating an avenue for Black female rape survivors to seek justice. Clauses within legislation such as the Enrollment Act of March 1863 pried open a door. In Section 30 of this act, the US military acquired "jurisdiction over common-law felonies," including rape, "when committed by US military personnel."[29] Thus, in language aimed at regulating the sexual conduct of Union soldiers, the government set in motion an unprecedented, albeit incidental, recognition of Black women and girls within the category of sexual assault victims. In a social and legal culture that narrowly defined rape as an assault on a chaste white woman, and rendered Black, especially enslaved women, unrapable, such legislation was innovative in its implications.

The introduction of President Abraham Lincoln's "General Order No. 100: Instructions for the Government of the Armies of the United States in the Field," also known as the Lieber Code, fortified both the Emancipation Proclamation and section 30 of the Enrollment Act. Issued on April 24, 1863, the Lieber Code further outlined the terms of conduct during warfare. In article 37, section 2 of the Lieber Code, the US government promised to protect the "religion and morality; strictly private property; the persons of the inhabitants, especially those of women: and the sacredness of domestic relations" in Union-occupied territory.[30] In addition, articles 44 and 47 each invoked rape—among "all wanton violence"—as a punishable crime when commit-

26. McCurry, *Women's War*, 7.
27. Glymph, "Noncombatant Military Laborers in the Civil War," 25.
28. Glymph, "Noncombatant Military Laborers in the Civil War," 25.
29. Barber and Ritter, "Physical Abuse . . . and Rough Handling," 56.
30. Lieber, "Instructions for the Government of Armies of the United States in the Field."

ted by Union soldiers against "persons in the invaded country."[31] As historian Crystal N. Feimster emphasizes, these three articles collectively "conceived and defined rape in women-specific terms as a crime against property, as a crime of troop discipline, and a crime against family honor."[32] The absence of the language of crimes committed against specifically *white* women meant that African American women and girls gained access to the protections of the Lieber Code.

Amid these legal developments, as well as Black women's noncombatant military labor, refugee women and girls in Union territory navigated what historian Stephanie McCurry describes as a "different and more forbidding landscape than the men."[33] Many Union soldiers were volunteers from predominantly small white rural regions in the North. Most had little prior interaction with African American women. With ideas of Black women drawn from cultural stereotypes rooted in slavery, Union soldiers who committed acts of sexual violence on refugee and freedwomen abused their power and mistreated Black women with the belief that sex could be freely solicited as part of their labor. This contrasted sharply with Union soldiers' treatment of Confederate women, though it is not to suggest that white women were spared Union-perpetrated sexual violence. As historian Drew Gilpin Faust argues, "Most Yankee soldiers were reluctant to harm white southern women, particularly those who seemed to be ladies of the middle or upper class."[34] Class and race therefore contributed to laboring Black women's sexual vulnerability in Union-occupied territory. Though Union soldiers were supposed to represent the enforcers of emancipation, some directed their aggression toward Confederate property, including human "contraband." "In all likelihood," Faust continues, "black women served as the unfortunate sexual spoils when Union soldiers asserted their traditional right of military conquest."[35] Whether in the officers' quarters in a camp, a cabin on a plantation leased by the federal government, or in the homes of Black families living in occupied territory, "contraband," fugitive and refugee women and girls were uniquely situated as targets of the kinds of gender violence that too often accompanies war.

It is crucial to stress that amid the uncertainty of war, refugee and freed women and girls in occupied territory did not wait for their legal status to be defined in order to protect their dignity and bodily integrity. As a class of poor, uneducated, and stateless workers, these women and girls launched arguments that hinged on their moral authority to compel the state to punish those soldiers who violated their person. Constructing their freedom from the ground up in the midst of war, African American women and girls were clear about what it meant for them to live, work, and provide for themselves and their families free from the constant threat of rape and sexual assault.

31. Lieber, "Instructions for the Government of Armies of the United States in the Field."
32. Feimster, "Rape and Justice in the Civil War."
33. McCurry, *Women's War*, 7.
34. Faust, *Confederate Women and Yankee Men*, 199.
35. Faust, *Confederate Women and Yankee Men*, 200.

The well-known Port Royal Experiment offers a powerful case in point. Introduced in late 1861, this vast and profitable labor program put ten thousand former slaves to work the land on South Carolina's abandoned Sea Islands. "Contraband" and refugees picked and ginned cotton—valued at a premium rate from this region. They produced and distributed manure. Potatoes and corn that they harvested formed part of their main diet. Months without pay for Black soldiers meant that their wives had to help support their families. These women washed "for the officers of the gunboats and the soldiers" and made "cakes and pies which they sold to the boys in camp."[36] While the Port Royal Experiment was touted as assisting African Americans' self-determination, expectations around their labor—defined in slavery—were readily adopted by the federal government. For example, Charles Francis Adams Jr., a member of the prominent political family, was reluctant to dissociate emancipated African Americans from their previously enslaved status. As a Union soldier in 1862, Adams penned a letter in which he reflected: "The scheme, so far as I can see it, seems to be for the Government, recognizing and encouraging private philanthropy and leaving to it the task of educating the *slaves* to the standard of self-support, to hold itself a sort of guardian to the *slave* in his *indefinite state of transition*, exacting from him that amount of labor which he owes to the community and the cotton market."[37] Calling refugees "slaves" and describing their transition to self-determined labor as disruptive to the market and deficit in nature, Adams's language revealed the logic that undergirded government policy towards former slaves. By 1862, the US Treasury projected upward of 2.5 million pounds of ginned cotton from the hands of refugees.[38]

Government agents viewed Black women at Port Royal with suspicion and contempt. "The women, it is said," wrote E. L. Pierce in a report, "are easily persuaded by white men . . . a facility readily accounted for by the power of the master over them, whose solicitation was equivalent to a command."[39] In stating this, Pierce acknowledged the cultural presumption that sex constituted part of the labor expected of Black women. However, rather than criticizing white men who exploited the sexual vulnerability of Black women, Pierce consigned Black women's sexuality to pathology. "They have been apt to regard what ought to be a disgrace as a compliment, when they were approached by a paramour of superior condition and race," he concluded.[40]

Yet multiple sexual assault charges brought against Assistant Surgeon Charles F. Lauer in Beaufort, South Carolina, in 1863, proved that for many Black women, white men who abused their power were a nuisance and a danger in their working

---

36. Taylor, *Reminiscences of My Life Camp*, 16.

37. "Letter from Charles Francis Adams, Jr., to Henry Adams, Milne Plantation, Port Royal Island, Monday, April 6, 1862," in Ford, ed., *Cycle of Adams Letters, 1861–1865*, 128.

38. US Department of the Treasury and Edward Lillie Pierce, *Negroes at Port Royal*, 7.

39. US Department of the Treasury and Edward Lillie Pierce, *Negroes at Port Royal*, 13.

40. US Department of the Treasury and Edward Lillie Pierce, *Negroes at Port Royal*, 13.

lives. Laundresses Sarah and Jane were among several women who testified against Lauer for offences committed on the Milne plantation on Port Royal Island.[41] They asserted that Lauer sexually abused them under the pretense of a medical examination. In his defense, Lauer ascertained that he conducted an examination of their genitalia because he suspected they had contracted a venereal disease.[42] In doing so, Lauer brought the possibility that Sarah and Jane were sex workers into the military court's line of sight.

Captain S. S. Metzger, a witness for the prosecution who was present during Jane's examination, corroborated Lauer's challenge to Jane's virtue. In his testimony, Metzger confirmed that Jane initially resisted the examination. He went on to imply that Jane was a prostitute, noting the "general impression" being that "some of the members of the regiment had been diseased by her."[43] In a court environment that evaluated the sexual reputation of women to determine whether they were "true" victims of sexual assault, Lauer's view clearly aligned with this presumption. The belief that Jane was a prostitute—or at least sexually active—appeared to have forfeited her right to withhold consent to an invasive "medical" procedure. Lauer exploited this gray area in his assault.

Eda and Rebecca were among the women who testified to Lauer's violence and sexual harassment.[44] Eda told the court that Lauer visited her home on three nights trying to "knock" her. To avoid any further harassment, she told the court that she started sleeping in the cotton fields.[45] She described how the doctor punched her when she refused his advances. Similarly, Rebecca testified that the doctor approached her as she sat on a bench, asking if she "would do it." "I said no," she stated, "He asked why. I told him I didn't want to do it and then went into the house. He followed me. When I said again I wouldn't do it, he slapped me."[46] Rebecca's experience descended into further violence and a failed attempt to get immediate help. "He kicked me twice in the stomach and boxed me on the face," she continued.[47] Rebecca escaped and reported Lauer to Captain Nesbitt, who "said he didn't think the doctor would do such a thing."[48] In the moment of terror, the presumed respectability of the doctor as indicated by Nesbitt overshadowed Rebecca's claims. Substantiating Rebecca's account, Sarah spoke as a witness. "I am well-acquainted with him [Dr. Lauer]. I used to do his laundry," Sarah testified. "I heard him trying to get her to go to his tent. She didn't want to. He slapped her and I said to him. 'Doctor . . . when a woman did not give it up to him, he should leave her alone instead of striking her.'"[49] The tes-

41. NN624, NARA, RG 153, as quoted in Lowry, *Sexual Misbehavior in the Civil War*, 138–39.
42. See Barber and Ritter, "Dangerous Liaisons," 8.
43. As quoted in Hedger, "Broken Promises," 8; and Lowry, *Story the Soldiers Wouldn't Tell*.
44. NN624, NARA, RG 153, as quoted in Lowry, *Sexual Misbehavior in the Civil War*, 138–39.
45. NN624, NARA, RG 153, as quoted in Lowry, *Sexual Misbehavior in the Civil War*, 138–39.
46. NN624, NARA, RG 153, as quoted in Lowry, *Sexual Misbehavior in the Civil War*, 138–39.
47. NN624, NARA, RG 153, as quoted in Lowry, *Sexual Misbehavior in the Civil War*, 138–39.
48. NN624, NARA, RG 153, as quoted in Lowry, *Sexual Misbehavior in the Civil War*, 138–39.
49. NN624, NARA, RG 153, as quoted in Lowry, *Sexual Misbehavior in the Civil War*, 138–39.

timony of these Black women in court was disruptive. Union officials were compelled to listen to refugee Black laundresses scold a white doctor about sexual consent. As stateless, noncombatant military laborers who may or may not have engaged in sex for pay, including survival sex, these women were clear about asserting control over the borders around their own bodies. They upended so many existing beliefs about race, class, respectability, and sexual consent.

Like Lauer, Union soldiers and military personnel who sexually assaulted formerly enslaved women not only upheld ideas about the availability their sexual labor, but also deployed racist arguments that reinforced Black women's legal marginalization. Within months of the hard-fought Battle of Stones River campaign, which pushed the Confederate army from its post in Murfreesboro, Tennessee, Harriet Elizabeth McKinley and Matilda McKinley brought rape and attempted rape charges against Privates Perry Pierson and William Lindsey of the Indiana Volunteer Infantry.[50] Harriet was living on the plantation of her former owner, Joseph R. McKinley, when Pierson raped her. When Harriet was first called before the military tribunal, Pierson objected to her testimony on the ground that she "was not a qualified witness, being a colored woman."[51] Taking Pierson's charge of Harriet's social inferiority seriously, the commissioners cleared the court for deliberation. The mere existence of Harriet's body in a courtroom caused debate.[52]

The commission rejected Pierson's attempt at legal obstruction, but that was only Harriet's first challenge. Despite confidently recalling her experience with details attesting to her sound-mindedness and credibility as a witness to her own body, the court repeatedly asked whether or not she consented. Harriet was compelled to perform her trauma. She insisted that she screamed throughout the entire assault and told the court explicitly that she did not consent to the act. Harriet was also was forced to disclose that she was unmarried and a virgin. Pierson was found guilty. He was sentenced to a year of hard labor and deprived of pay for four months.[53]

Harriet and Matilda each offered testimonies that emphasized their militant protection of their sexual and bodily integrity. Matilda, who accused Lindsey of attempted rape, testified that she was prepared to have her throat cut when Lindsey threatened that as an alternative to sex.[54] Similarly, after Harriet professed her sexual innocence before the court, she added that when Pierson penetrated her, she "hollered so that you might hear me for two miles."[55] By stating that she was a virgin and emphasizing her pain, Harriet defied the stereotype of enslaved female promiscuity and availability for illicit sex as well as the common ideological belief that African Americans were less susceptible to pain.[56] She asserted her bodily violation before the

50. MM746, NARA, RG 153.
51. MM746, NARA, RG 153.
52. Esty, "Crusade against the Despoiler of Virtue."
53. MM746, NARA, RG 153.
54. MM746, NARA, RG 153.
55. MM746, NARA, RG 153.
56. For more on slavery and discourses of pain see Clark, "'Sacred Rights of the Weak.'"

Union army despite her liminal status and demonstrated her sense of self-ownership. Formerly enslaved women made the best of a legal culture that invited them to testify within the narrow script of the (white) chaste female victim while equally subjecting them to suspicion and condescension because of their race.

Harriet and Matilda's defense of their chastity and sexual self-possession brings into view the fact that formerly enslaved women and girls adhered to their own codes of sexual ethics in defiance of white assumptions about their sexuality. Testifying in military courts enabled Black women and girls to define these sexual and moral values and, relatedly, their meaning of sexual consent. This was especially evident in cases involving violence against Black girls. It is important to stress that Black girls were not spared the violence of rape and sexual assault. Like Black women, prepubescent and adolescent girls faced sometimes hostile military courts that compelled them to recount in excruciating detail the horrors of their trauma, often with the assailant present. If their apparent young age promised to sever the suspicion that illicit sex occurred, their race and gender also subjected them to the violence of "adultification."[57] As a form of dehumanization, Black girls struggled with the violence of "adultification" in myriad ways. At the level of their assaults, perpetrators either approached them as mature women or later attempted to justify their attacks with arguments that Black girls were actually women who consented to illicit sex.[58] Additionally, Black girls were further traumatized by "adultification" within the court environment, from modes of questioning to the ways that their cases were recorded. In the mid-nineteenth-century US, the legal age of sexual consent was set between ten and twelve across most states. But, as historian Wilma King notes, "enslaved girls, who had no legal protection against sexual violence, were assumed to be experienced without concern about whether or not they were sexually active."[59] While ascribing moral meaning to age helped to underline the innocence and victimhood of African American girls, their race, status, and the labor they were compelled to perform nevertheless depicted Black girls as fair game, like Black women.

Thus, Black girls experienced sexual violence as part of the normalized conditions of violence that Black women experienced. Their testimonies and statements offered repeated markers of their sexual innocence as well as the moral and cultural values that they developed from their enslaved upbringing. In Wilmington, Virginia, an unnamed sixteen-year-old described her terrifying experience of sexual assault by five men, one of whom was John Murray of the 117th New York Infantry. She did not testify in court but evidently shared with a nearby witness, who testified that "they tried to take my maidenhead"—an expression that underlined the scale of the soldiers' crime.[60] Jennie Green did not know her age when she was raped by Lieutenant Andrew J. Smith of the Eleventh Pennsylvania Cavalry in City Point, Virginia, in

57. Epstein, Blake, and Gonzalez, "Girlhood Interrupted."
58. Epstein, Blake, and Gonzalez, "Girlhood Interrupted."
59. King, "'Prematurely Knowing of Evil Things,'" 174.
60. Lowry, *Sexual Misbehavior in the Civil War*, 131.

1864. She was an enslaved girl who transitioned to fugitivity when she followed Union soldiers to federal lines sometime in late spring 1864. Yet Jennie carried with her a clear sense of right and wrong. Despite her young age, lack of formal education, and liminal legal status in a country in the throes of a Civil War, she sought sexual justice.

Like most refugee and freed women and girls who were sexually assaulted by Union soldiers, Jennie's experience occurred as she was providing nonsexual labor. She was working as an officer's servant in a military camp. In her testimony, Jennie explained that she had entered Smith's quarters to deliver his supper. When she turned to leave, he grabbed her arm and locked the door behind her. She described how Smith forced her on the ground and proceeded to rape her. Testifying to her sexual innocence as well as her sense of sexual sovereignty, even as a young girl, Jennie stated, "He did the same thing that married people do. . . . That was what hurt me. I did not give my consent to have that done."[61]

One should not rush over the precise language Jennie used in her testimony. For an enslaved girl, barely weeks off the plantation, to use the language of "consent" in this context speaks volumes about the kind of consciousness that would assertively seek redress in a military court. What Jennie said to the court reveals to what extent she possessed a moral code and set of principles in enslavement that permitted her to make claims about her power, privilege, and self-ownership in court. The term *consent* belies the assumed consciousness of an enslaved girl. The notion of power, privilege, and self-ownership inherent in the language of consent was incongruous to the logic of slavery. Jennie not only affirmed that she did not consent to have sex but also defined her understanding of sexual intercourse as a practice that should be reserved for "married people." In a society where marriage between enslaved couples held no legitimacy under the law, the fact that Jennie framed sex as part of a marital union sheds light on the ways that sexual respectability operated as a subversive script in the testimonies of fugitive and refugee women and girls.

By the summer of 1864, Jennie was at the center of a high-profile rape case. The surviving record of her case reveals the kind of inconsistencies that spoke to her struggle with systemic "adultification." In one statement, she is described as "a young negro girl"; in another, Jennie is presented before the court-martial as a "colored woman."[62] Nellie Wyatt, an African American woman who testified as a witness for the prosecution, corroborated Jennie's youth and sexual innocence. She explicitly asserted that Jennie was "nothing but a child."[63] Wyatt went further in her defense of Jennie's challenged childhood by arguing that it was precisely because of Jennie's young age that Smith took advantage of her. Understanding that Smith might just as easily have attempted an attack on her, Wyatt testified, "I got off by being married."[64]

---

61. NN2099, NARA, RG 153.
62. NN2099, NARA, RG 153.
63. NN2099, NARA, RG 153.
64. NN2099, NARA, RG 153.

Smith was convicted with the endorsement of General Benjamin Butler. The recommendation for his sentence consisted of years at hard labor combined with the loss of rank and position. A known enforcer of the Lieber Code's policy regarding the conduct of Union soldiers, General Butler expressed his disgust. "A female negro child quits slavery, and comes into the protection of the Federal government, and upon first reaching the limits of the Federal lines receives the brutal treatment from an officer, himself a husband and a father, of violation of her person," Butler wrote. "Of this the evidence is conclusive."[65] Butler's response revealed that some white Union officials were open to an inclusive understanding of sexual consent. Lincoln, however, was unconvinced that Jennie had accurately identified her assailant. After Smith had spent a short period in a penitentiary, the president issued repeated orders for his release. While Jennie likely never received full sexual justice, her self-presentation as a moral subject, assertion of sexual sovereignty and insistence on sexual consent attests to the subversive potential of her testimony.

Jennie's case shows that Black female servants working for Union officials were especially vulnerable to sexual assault. Accessing the private space of officials' quarters made inappropriate contact much easier to execute. In addition, the threat of losing their provisions offered a potential reason to remain silent, while the authority of Union officials often masked their predatory behavior. Many Black women testified with arguments that demonstrated their demands not only around the question of consent, but also for a safer working environment. On April 22, 1865, at a contraband camp on the south side of the Cape Fear River, Julia Jennison told a tribunal that she had explicitly told William McManus of the Thirty-Third New Jersey Infantry that she did not want to sleep with him. Working as a servant in the officers' quarters, Jennison recalled that she was in one of the officers' rooms, making the bed, when McManus accosted her. "He asked me if I would sleep with him. I told him no. He said I got to do it. I told him I wouldn't."[66] McManus then attacked Jennison, and she fought back. As she tried to protect herself, McManus punched her in the eye and stated, "Jeff Davis had but one eye and why couldn't [she] have?"[67] Jennison's case clearly highlighted the assumption that sex formed part of the service that Black women owed to Union soldiers.

The routine assertion of one's moral authority within the overlapping frameworks of Protestant Christianity and Victorian sexual morality was undeniably strategic. In asserting their identities as married women, for example, refugees made explicit claims to their sexual respectability as evidence of the absence of their consent. In the mid-nineteenth century, marriage constituted the cornerstone of a moral, civilized society.[68] For African Americans, this notion held consequences that affected their material lives. Slaveholders prohibited legal marriage among enslaved couples, while abolitionists pointed to the lack of legitimate marriage as the main cause of sex-

65. NN2099, NARA, RG 153.
66. OO1056, NARA, RG 153.
67. OO1056, NARA, RG 153.
68. See Stanley, *From Bondage to Contract*.

ual immorality within the enslaved community. For white Americans on both sides of the slavery debate, the idea that African Americans simply didn't value the covenant of marriage was commonplace.

Black women's self-presentation as wives did more than simply convey that they valued chastity, or even that they sought participation in conventions set by white American society. As wage earners as well as wives, refugee women brought attention to their uniquely situated racialized sexual oppression. The mention of husbands exposed the fact that even after emancipation, they could not expect the kind of patriarchal protection available to white women. For example, a woman addressed as Mrs. Cornelius Robinson was introduced as the "wife of a loyal colored citizen" when she appeared in court in February 1865. She was the mother of a five-day-old infant when George Hakes of the Sixth Michigan Cavalry raped her at her home, roughly two miles from Winchester, Virginia.[69] In her account, Mrs. Robinson stated that Hakes entered her family home and ordered her husband on an errand to buy some sheepskin. When Mr. Robinson left, Hakes pushed Mrs. Robinson into the bedroom and assaulted her: "He said if I did not give up to him he would shoot me. I said, 'Then you'll have to shoot me.'"[70] While the horror of the assault was central in Robinson's testimony, her husband's absence augmented both her defenselessness and the magnitude of the crime. Framing her assault as a violation of her individual self and the sanctity of her marriage, Robinson's testimony stood in accordance with the Lieber Code's definition of rape as "a crime against family honor."[71]

Refugee and freedwomen also emphasized their chastity and marital status as a form of sexual resistance and an assertion of their sexual autonomy, both individually and in relation to their husbands. On a Saturday night in March 1865 in Central Knob, near Chattanooga, Tennessee, a Black Union soldier entered the home of Mrs. Sarah Beuford and "did by force try to have dealings of a carnal nature."[72] Beuford was awakened by a knocking at her door. Her visitor, Private John Lewis of the Sixteenth United States Colored Infantry (USCI), introduced himself as a patrol guard on a routine check. This puzzled Beuford, because two guards had already passed by earlier before she went to bed. Lewis used his authority to gain access to Beuford's home, and in doing so he established an expectation for Beuford's deference and service. He asked for some bread, and she explained that she hadn't had any for several days. He stole some meat from a pig that she had killed earlier that morning. Shortly thereafter, Lewis's pillaging evolved into the threat of rape. He informed Beuford that he'd thought she was "an old woman"—an ominous comment gesturing to his sexual interest.[73] Slapping her on the shoulder, he asked if she "had nothing else to give him."[74] "I asked what he meant and he said I know what," Beuford later recalled, "I

69. Lowry, *Sexual Misbehavior in the Civil War*, 126.

70. Lowry, *Sexual Misbehavior in the Civil War*, 126.

71. Feimster, "Rape and Justice in the Civil War."

72. MM2774, NARA, RG 153.

73. MM2774, NARA, RG 153.

74. MM2774, NARA, RG 153.

asked him about a hundred times what he meant and he said I know."[75] By insisting that Lewis name his intentions, Beuford refused the terms of secrecy that empowered and protected sexual predators. Thus, when Lewis asked for "some skin," Beuford replied that it was "a pretty question to ask a married woman."[76]

Offering $40, Lewis attempted to recast his sexual affront into an illicit, consensual exchange. He promised Beuford that her husband wouldn't find out about the encounter. In a court-martial testimony, Beuford was clear in her response to Lewis. She underscored that her chastity was a self-governing virtue and a reflection of her identity as a Christian and a wife. "I told him if my husband would not know it God would and that if I had done the like I could not be depended on by my husband," she declared. "[I] said I was a lady before my husband's face and behind his back."[77] In a legal culture where rape laws and statutes scrutinized the chastity, reputation, and character of sexual assault victims, Beuford was aware that her credibility as a respectable woman was also on trial.[78] She told the court that Lewis held her at gunpoint and threatened to have her gang-raped by "thirty of the boys."[79] "I told him if they come, I would have more Company to go to the Lieutenant with and asked if he had any objection," she stated.[80] Beuford succeeded in scaring Lewis off. Risking her life in the pursuit of sexual justice, she followed Lewis back toward the military camp where he was stationed, undeterred by his attempts to shoot at her.[81] The next day, she reported Lewis to Lieutenant John Scott, commander of Company C.[82] At the close of the trial, Lewis was found guilty of three charges, including assault and attempted rape.[83]

The resistive tension between Lewis's solicitation of "some skin" and Mrs. Beuford's riposte as a married woman is emblematic of the sexual precarity of African American women and girls in the transition from slavery to emancipation. Beuford's self-identification as a married woman was strategically encoded in the protections of a female liberal subject-position. That Lewis was an African American

75. MM2774, NARA, RG 153.

76. MM2774, NARA, RG 153.

77. MM2774, NARA, RG 153.

78. Freedman, *Redefining Rape*, 21–22.

79. MM2774, NARA, RG 153, RG 153.

80. MM2774, NARA, RG 153, RG 153.

81. Between 1863 and 1865, the town of Chattanooga, Tennessee, was under military occupation by the Union army. Ideally located near the Tennessee River and railroad connections, Chattanooga "retained the appearance of an armed camp" with an "important supply base." This attracted a number of freedpeople who set up residence within the vicinity of the town. Govan and Livingood, "Chattanooga under Military Occupation, 1863–1865," 23.

82. MM2774, NARA, RG 153. African American soldiers generally received harsher sentences for the same crime committed by white soldiers. Private John Lewis's conviction was the result of three charges. The first charge was "Disobedience of Orders"; the second charge was "Pillaging"; and the third charge was "Assault and Attempt to Commit Rape." Private Lewis was sentenced to one year of hard labor in a military prison, and the loss of pay and allowances for the duration of that time.

83. MM2774, NARA, RG 153.

soldier, added to Black women and girls' dangerously confounding relationship to representatives who were at once their assailants and protectors. Living within the vicinity of a military base, Beuford may easily have been a Black soldier's wife—a point that augments Lewis's dishonor as a soldier and community member. As noted, notions of the safeguard of marriage were not readily available to Black women, including Beuford, a free(d)woman living in Union-occupied Tennessee in early 1865.[84] But the assertion of her identity as a married woman combined with her use of the language of sovereignty and inverted dependency—"I could not be depended on by my husband"—demonstrates how Black women like Beuford self-fashioned a position that claimed the prerogatives usually limited to the (white) female liberal subject.

African American women were intentional about spotlighting their respectability and moral character in military courts and commissions by differentiating themselves from sex workers in a society where prostitution was often publicly visible and not explicitly illegal. Presenting themselves as "not that kind of woman" emphasized their understanding of a distinction between women who engaged in illicit sex and those who chose the path of chastity, modesty, and Christian morality. Using gendered conventions of modesty and respectability, Black women sought to dismantle the assumption that their labor was indivisibly nonsexual and sexual.

Of course, in emphasizing their sexual respectability, refugee and freedwomen reinforced the problematic belief that women who had any past sexual experience outside of marriage did not deserve justice. In the early nineteenth century, prostitutes and other women of so-called "lost virtue" were often removed from consideration as victims of rape and sexual assault. "Virtuous" women were believed to be the true victims, as their lifestyles did not conform to the kind that invited male sexual attention.

Still, the precarious nature of life for African American women meant that their virtue was continuously challenged by men who sought illicit sex. Black women and girls contended with real as well as scam enticements of payment before, during, and after sexual affronts and violence. Detractors' efforts to recast an assault through offerings of money and gifts spoke to the common attitude that Black women were always prepared to negotiate sex as part of a labor transaction. In a court-martial on March 14, 1865, Laura Ennis similarly testified that Charles Clark attempted to bribe her with coffee and sugar in exchange for her silence after he attacked her.[85] Sarah Beuford told the military court that she refused John Lewis's offerings of money, gloves, and shoes after his attempted assault.[86] Women, Black or white, explicitly framed solicitations for sex in exchange for payment as an insult to their character. On

---

84. Mrs. Sarah Beuford's status is not explicitly referenced in the court-martial record. It is possible that she was a free or freed person. I draw the distinction on the basis of her legal status prior to Andrew Johnson's emancipation notice in Tennessee, delivered in October 1864.

85. OO654, NARA, RG 153.

86. MM2774, NARA, RG 153.

September 12, 1863, Mrs. Ellie Farnan and her daughter beat up a drunken Private William Van Buren of Company B, 212th Illinois, after he tried to accost them. He had offered to exchange money for "some skin," and Mrs. Farnan and her daughter reportedly took this offer as an "insult and abuse." In a statement offered by a witness for the prosecution, Mrs. Farnan apparently said to Van Buren: "You god damned old son of a bitch, you had the impudence to offer a decent woman like myself a dollar and my girl, that I'm raising, three [dollars]."[87]

Indeed, not all Black women and girls were able to, or even desired to, define sexual consent within the frame of respectability. Some pushed for more sophisticated understandings of sexual consent in ways that deviated from the legal script of the virtuous female victim. In 1865, in Clarksville, Tennessee, a fourteen-year-old noted on record as "Rachel, a Negro Girl" told a court-martial that Private John Locker had attempted to rape her. Rachel was staying at a known "house of ill fame" when Locker met and attacked her. According to the court proceedings, Locker was intoxicated and initially groped Rachel on her bosom. Witnesses differ in their accounts of how much Rachel resisted this act, but Rachel testified that she told Locker "to quit."[88] She became more vocal in her resistance when Locker progressed with an attempt to penetrate her. Once again, Rachel, like other Black girls who sought sexual justice, was treated with the presumption of her fully developed maturity—regardless of whether she was sexually active or not. Interestingly, when the defense asked Rachel, "Why would you not permit the accused to have carnal knowledge of you?" she responded: "Because he was not of my color."[89] Rather than appealing to ideals of chastity, Rachel, who was likely a sex worker, invoked her own notion of sexual respectability. To be sure, the defense asked if "color was the only object," to which Rachel said yes.[90] Perhaps the taboo of interracial sex was where Rachel drew the line. What is compelling about this case is that Rachel claimed moral authority on her terms, and when the borders of her body were violated, she pursued full legal recognition and justice.

Conclusion

In their refusal to be reconstituted as sexually available laborers in the crucial period of Civil War and emancipation, fugitive, refugee and freed women and girls embarked on a contestation over labor and sexual consent. Intervening in, and weaponizing, nineteenth-century ideals of sexual respectability, refugee and freed women's and girls' testimonies resisted the persistence of cultural assumptions that sex could be negotiated as part of, or in addition to, their nonsexual labor. Survivors of sexual violence were especially positioned to intervene in existing definitions of Black women's

87. NN854, NARA, RG 153. See also Lowry, *Story the Soldiers Wouldn't Tell*, 124. Mrs. Farnan's race is not listed in the military record.
88. OO857, NARA, RG 153.
89. OO857, NARA, RG 153.
90. OO857, NARA, RG 153.

labor, and many seized the opportunity to shape this reformulation. Married women also challenged the attitude that African American marriage was a mere inconvenience that a man wanting sex could easily evade or ignore. Their deployment of the language of chastity and assertion of their marital status subverted the legal premise of the chaste white female sexual assault victim. As a result, stateless working women and girls ushered in more sophisticated meanings of sexual violence and consent in mid-nineteenth-century America.

But appeals to chastity neither guaranteed these women and girls sufficient sexual justice or protection. The window of recognition that wartime legislation offered them was not sustainable. Enforced to regulate the conduct of Union military personnel, legislation such as the Lieber Code acknowledged Black women and girls as rape victims within the specific context of war. The period of Reconstruction introduced a formal rights framework for freedwomen to define their sexual autonomy as citizens. To be sure, neither citizenship nor education, literacy, or middle-class status were ever prerequisites for Black women and girls to assert their moral agency, dignity, and desire for sexual ownership. Their struggle for sexual sovereignty joined a long-standing tradition of sexual resistance fashioned by enslaved women—the most marginalized and nontraditional political actors. As citizens, freedwomen gained access, at least in theory, to a model of female citizenship. But as Reconstruction came to a close, the resurgence of southern white male political power unleashed a nadir of extreme racial and sexual terror. Working-class, middle-class, and educated African American women within the Black Baptist community would deploy strategies of sexual resistance similar to those used by their fugitive and refugee forebears in what historian Evelyn Brooks Higginbotham has defined as a "politics of respectability."[91] The shifting legal ground and character of the state that Black women and girls confronted reveals their fraught historical relationship to notions of sexual consent within the framework of Western liberalism. Their strategies speak to the ultimately burdened ways that African American women were compelled to seek sexual freedom in the mid- to late nineteenth-century United States. ◪

KAISHA ESTY (PhD, Rutgers University) is an assistant professor of African American Studies, History, and Feminist, Gender, and Sexuality Studies at Wesleyan University. She is a historian of Black women, sexuality, and slavery and its aftermath in the nineteenth-century US. Her current book project, tentatively titled, *Weaponizing Virtue: Black Women and the Struggle for Sexual Autonomy* is an intimate history of enslaved and freed women's lives and labor under US expansion and imperialism.

91. Higginbotham, *Righteous Discontent.*

References

Barber, E. Susan, and Charles F. Ritter. "Dangerous Liaisons: Working Women and Sexual Justice in the American Civil War." *European Journal of American Studies*, document 2.3, March 31, 2015. http://journals.openedition.org/ejas/10695 (accessed April 30, 2019).

Barber, E. Susan, and Charles F. Ritter. "Physical Abuse . . . and Rough Handling: Race, Gender and Sexual Justice in the Occupied South." In *Occupied Women: Gender, Military Occupation and the American Civil War*, edited by LeeAnn Whites and Alecia P. Long, 49–64. Baton Rouge: Louisiana State University Press, 2009.

Bardaglio, Peter W. "Rape and the Law in the Old South: 'Calculated to Excite Indignation in Every Heart.'" *Journal of Southern History* 60, no. 4 (1994): 749–72.

Berlin, Ira, Thavolia Glymph, Julie Saville, Leslie S. Rowland, Steven F. Miller, and Joseph Reidy, eds. *Freedom: A Documentary History of Emancipation 1861–1867: Selected from the Holding of the National Archives of the United States*. Series 1, vol. 3: *The Wartime Genesis of Free Labour in the Lower South*. New York: Cambridge University Press, 1991.

Block, Sharon. *Rape and Sexual Power in Early America*. Chapel Hill: University of North Carolina Press, 2006.

Clark, Elizabeth B. "'The Sacred Rights of the Weak': Pain, Sympathy, and the Culture of Individual Rights in Antebellum America." *Journal of American History* 82, no. 2 (1995): 463–93.

Davis, Adrienne D. "'Don't Let Nobody Bother Yo' Principle': The Sexual Economy of American Slavery." In *Black Sexual Economies: Race and Sex in a Culture of Capital*, edited by Davis and the BSE Collective, 15–38. Champaign: University of Illinois Press, 2019.

Edwards, Laura F. "Status without Rights: African Americans and the Tangled History of Law and Governance in the Nineteenth-Century U.S. South." *American History Review* 112, no. 2 (2007): 365–93.

Epstein, Rebecca, Jamilia J. Blake and Thalia González. *Girlhood Interrupted: The Erasure of Black Girls' Childhood*. Washington, DC: Georgetown University Law Center, Center on Poverty and Inequality, 2017.

Esty, Kaisha. "A Crusade against the Despoiler of Virtue: Black Women, Sexual Purity and the Gendered Politics of the Negro Problem, 1839–1920." PhD diss., Rutgers University, 2019.

Faust, Drew Gilpin. *Confederate Women and Yankee Men*. A UNC Press Civil War Short excerpted from *Mothers of Invention: Women of the Slaveholding South in the American Civil War*. Chapel Hill: University of North Carolina Press, 2012.

Feimster, Crystal. "Rape and Justice in the Civil War." *New York Times*, "Opinionator," April 26, 2013. https://opinionator.blogs.nytimes.com/2013/04/25/rape-and-justice-in-the-civil-war/.

Feimster, Crystal. "'What if I Am a Woman?': Black Women's Campaigns for Sexual Justice and Citizenship." In *The World the Civil War Made*, edited by Gregory Downs and Kate Masur, 249–68. Chapel Hill: University of North Carolina Press, 2015.

Ford, Worthington Chauncey, ed. *A Cycle of Adams Letters, 1861–1865*. Vol. 1. Boston: The Riverside Press Cambridge, 1920.

Fordney, Ben Fuller. *George Stoneman: A Biography of the Union General*. Jefferson, NC: McFarland & Company, 2008.

Freedman, Estelle B. *Redefining Rape: Sexual Violence in the Era of Suffrage and Segregation*. Cambridge, MA: Harvard University Press, 2013.

Glymph, Thavolia. "Noncombatant Military Laborers in the Civil War." In "Civil War at 150: Mobilizing for War," special issue, *OAH Magazine of History* 26, no. 2 (2012): 25–29.

Glymph, Thavolia. *The Women's Fight: The Civil War's Battles for Home, Freedom, and Nation*. Chapel Hill: University of North Carolina Press, 2020.

Govan, Gilbert E., and James W. Livingood. "Chattanooga under Military Occupation, 1863–1865." *Journal of Southern History* 17, no. 1 (1951): 23–47.

Haag, Pamela. *Consent: Sexual Rights and the Transformation of American Liberalism*. Ithaca, NY: Cornell University Press, 1999.

Hartman, Saidiya. *Scenes of Subjection: Terror, Slavery, and Self-Making in Nineteenth-Century America*. New York: Oxford University Press, 1997.

Hedger, Kellie J. "Broken Promises: Rape, Race, and the Union Army." Master's thesis, Central Washington University, 2015.

Higginbotham, Evelyn Brooks. *Righteous Discontent: The Women's Movement in the Black Baptist Church, 1880–1920*. Cambridge, MA: Harvard University Press, 1994.

King, Wilma. "'Prematurely Knowing of Evil Things': The Sexual Abuse of African American Girls and Young Women in Slavery and Freedom." *Journal of African American History* 99, no. 3 (2014): 173–96.

Lieber, Francis. "Instructions for the Government of Armies of the United States in the Field." Prepared by Francis Lieber, LLD, originally issued as General Order No. 100, Adjutant General's Office, 1863. Washington, DC: Government Printing Office, 1898. *The Avalon Project*, Yale Law School. https://avalon.law.yale.edu/19th_century/lieber.asp (accessed April 30, 2021).

Lowry, Thomas P. *Sexual Misbehavior in the Civil War: A Compendium*. Bloomington, IN: Xlibris, 2006.

Lowry, Thomas P. *The Story the Soldiers Wouldn't Tell: Sex in the Civil War*. Mechanicsburg, PA: Stackpole Books, 2012.

McCurry, Stephanie. *Women's War: Fighting and Surviving the American Civil War*. Cambridge, MA: Belknap Press of Harvard University Press, 2019.

Morris, Thomas D. *Southern Slavery and the Law, 1619–1860*. Chapel Hill: University of North Carolina Press, 1996.

Pateman, Carole. *The Sexual Contract*. Cambridge, UK: Polity Press, 1988.

Stanley, Amy Dru. *From Bondage to Contract: Wage Labor, Marriage, and the Market in the Age of Slave Emancipation*. New York: Cambridge University Press, 1998.

Taylor, Susie King. *Reminiscences of My Life Camp, with the 33D United States Colored Troops Late 1st S.C. Volunteers*. Boston: Published by the author, 1902.

Threadcraft, Shatema. *Intimate Justice: The Black Female Body and the Body Politic*. New York: Oxford University Press, 2016.

US Department of the Treasury and Edward Lillie Pierce. *The Negroes at Port Royal: Report of E. L. Pierce, Government Agent, to the Hon. Salmon P. Chase, Secretary of the Treasury*. Boston: R. F. Wallcut, 1862.

Zipf, Karin L. *Labor of Innocents: Forced Apprenticeship in North Carolina, 1715–1919*. Baton Rouge: Louisiana State University Press, 2005.

Shouting Abuse, Harmless Jolly, and Promiscuous Flattery: Considering the Contours of Sexual Harassment at Macy's Department Store, 1910–1915

Mara Keire

As the white slavery scare peaked in the United States in the early 1910s, Americans speculated about why women entered prostitution. Writers and reformers feared that men were coercing girls into sex work. The Progressives warned about various danger zones where vulnerable young women might meet predatory men, including everywhere from railway stations to dance halls and employment offices, but department stores consistently figured among the most menacing sites for corrupting women's morals.[1] Theodore Dreiser set the tone in his 1900 novel *Sister Carrie* when he memorably described the temptations of all the lovely items on display.[2] The allure of ribbons and fancy shirtwaists did not pose the only danger. Stores also could not control the character of their customers. Many department stores were located within blocks of their city's red-light district.[3] Popular movies like George Loan Tucker's *Traffic in Souls* (1913) showed pimps and madams wandering into stores to entice girls with promises of greater earnings, while others, including Ulysses Davis's *The Kiss* (1914), depicted wealthy libertines seducing girls with food and drink. Some reform-

Many people have enriched this article through their insightful comments, including Christopher McKenna, Oenone Kubie, Christopher Phelps, Leon Fink, Vanessa May, Jennifer Fronc, Catherine Sloan, Joseph Spillane, Ann Schofield, Heather Gold, Sasha Rasmussen, Lizzie Evens, Mia Liyange, Emma Day, Sage Goodwin, Lynne Foote, Tabitha Clayton, and the participants in University of Edinburgh's History of Gender and Sexuality Seminar and the Workshop on Class and Consent at Georgetown University.

1. MacLean, "Two Weeks in Department Stores," 736; Addams, *New Conscience and an Ancient Evil*, 64–68; Malino, "Faces across the Counter," 277; Berebitsky, *Sex and the Office*, 42.

2. Dreiser, *Sister Carrie*, 22–23. See also Benson, *Counter Cultures*, 134–35; Vapnek, *Breadwinners*, 78.

3. Bowen, *Department Store Girl*; Peiss, *Cheap Amusements*, 38; Gilfoyle, *City of Eros*, 201–2, 205; Remus, *Shopper's Paradise*, 164–73.

Labor: Studies in Working-Class History, Volume 19, Issue 1
DOI 10.1215/15476715-9475716   © 2022 by Labor and Working-Class History Association

ers, however, warned that saleswomen faced more than external pressure; they also feared that male managers forced women to protect their jobs through sexual service.[4]

In 1913, worried about the reputation of departments stores in general and Macy's in particular, the Straus brothers—Percy, Jesse, and Herbert—commissioned New York City's premier anti-vice association, the Committee of Fourteen, to investigate why shopgirls might "go wrong."[5] They were not particularly concerned with "the question of whether there are immoral girls in [Macy's], or temptations to immorality, or lack of direct protection from temptations to immorality." Rather, they professed to seek information on how to "improve the general condition" for women workers.[6] In pursuit of this goal, the Fourteen and Macy's hired three women—Faith Habberton, Marjorie Sidney, and Natalie Sonnichsen—to go undercover at Macy's Herald Square store and to report women's experiences as department store employees.[7] From six months of accumulated reports, the Committee of Fourteen drew their conclusions and made their judgment, only occasionally consulting the investigators.[8] The resulting *Department Store Investigation* (1915) was an anodyne pamphlet that exonerated the owners and blamed individual workers.[9] The Committee of Fourteen saw no evidence that department store labor caused women to enter into prostitution or that managers pushed shopgirls into supplementing their wages by catering sexually to male customers. Finally, they saw no proof that male managers demanded women clerks have sex in order to stay in their jobs or to earn promotions. To use a modern and legalistic framework, the Committee of Fourteen cleared Macy's and its male managers of quid pro quo sexual harassment.

In contrast to the rather toothless pamphlet the Committee of Fourteen produced, the unedited reports from the three women investigators offer a more complicated story of power dynamics—sexualized or not—at Macy's. Although Habberton, Sydney, and Sonnichsen reported to the Committee of Fourteen, they were not "bourgeois women reformers."[10] They were working women previously employed in Bamberger's welfare office, on the stage, and as a freelance journalist. Expected to

4. US Congress, *Wage-Earning Women in Stores and Factories*, 28–36; Bowen, *Department Store Girl*; Kessler-Harris, *Out to Work*, 103; Johnson, "'The Rest Can Go to the Devil,'" 34–35.

5. On the three brothers, see Grippo, *Macy's*, 95–96. On department stores' image problem, see Johnson, "'The Rest Can Go to the Devil,'" 35–36; Benson, *Counter Cultures*, 136.

6. John P. Peters to Percy Straus, draft, n.d., file 1, box 39, Committee of Fourteen Records, New York Public Library (hereafter cited as C14DSI). The department store investigation records are in one archive box with five folders. Folders 1 and 2 contain respectively the administrative details and the report and report drafts. The next three folders are each dedicated to one of the three investigators. Unfortunately, the material in these files is not always clearly dated, numbered, or collated chronologically.

7. For an anonymized description of the women investigators and their backgrounds, see *Department Store Investigation: Report of the Sub-committee* (New York, 1915), printed pamphlet, pp. 7–8, file 2, C14DSI.

8. Faith Habberton to Frederick H. Whitin, February 27, 1914, file 1; Natalie Sonnichsen to Whitin, January 7, [1913], file 5, both C14DSI.

9. *Department Store Investigation*. On the report and the response to it in the popular press, see Johnson, "'The Rest Can Go to the Devil,'" 47.

10. Johnson, "'The Rest Can Go to the Devil,'" 32.

blend in on the shop floor, Habberton, Sydney, and Sonnichsen more closely resembled the clerks with whom they labored than the men to whom they reported.[11] They and most of the workers they talked to considered a job at Macy's a pretty good one. Salesclerks had few complaints about their earnings and thought that overall Macy's was more "refined" than other department stores.[12] Workers did, however, protest the power that buyers, an increasingly vestigial title for section heads, had over individual departments. Buyers set the tone and made the rules that governed the management of their domain. Salesclerks had few ways to challenge how buyers ran a department.[13] Nor could they easily protect themselves from retaliation. Habberton described how, when one woman complained to Macy's management about men using offensive language, the buyer removed all the chairs in the department.[14] In other words, buyers could actively encourage or passively condone what feminist lawyer Catharine MacKinnon called a hostile work environment: a shop floor culture that sexualized women and diminished their status and opportunities.[15] In the over six hundred pages that comprised their collected reports, Habberton, Sydney, and Sonnichsen exposed the micropolitics of power that made particular departments difficult places to work.

By examining these ordinary interactions, this article contributes to the historiography on sexual harassment and on women's labor. The best histories of workplace harassment in the United States have focused predominantly on the period since the 1964 Civil Rights Act. From Linda Hirshman's *Reckoning* to Gillian Thomas's *Because of Sex* and Carrie N. Baker's *The Women's Movement against Sexual Harassment*, these works have used a legal framework to document how men have abused women at work and to trace the fight for better treatment.[16] Understandably, these books have tended to highlight interactions extreme enough to reach the courts or make the news. This article, by contrast, expands the chronological framework for considering the history of sexual harassment while illuminating the banal. The women here never pursued court cases, never went to the press, and in most cases never complained to management. Instead, they chose to ignore harassing men, play along, yell back, quit, or on rare occasion appeal to management.

---

11. *Department Store Investigation*, 7–8; "Committee of Fourteen: Report of a Department Store Investigation" (typescript), n.d., file 2, C14DSI; Sonnichsen to Whitin, December 24, 1913, file 1, C14DSI. When the investigation ended, Macy's hired Marjorie Sydney to work in their welfare office. See Hower, *History of Macy's*, 388.

12. "Committee of Fourteen," 8; Habberton, August 29, 1913, p. 4, file 3; Sydney, November 1–8, 1913, p. 2, file 4, both C14DSI.

13. Benson, *Counter Cultures*, 48–52, 58–62. By 1920, only 1–2 percent of buyers were women. See Malino, "Faces across the Counter," 217–18.

14. Habberton, n.d., p. 2, file 3, C14DSI. Chairs were a contentious issue. See Benson, *Counter Cultures*, 140; Vapnek, *Breadwinners*, 80.

15. MacKinnon, *Sexual Harassment of Working Women*.

16. Hirshman, *Reckoning*; Thomas, *Because of Sex*; Baker, *Women's Movement against Sexual Harassment*.

In the historiography on department stores in the late nineteenth and early twentieth centuries, scholars have tended to characterize these sorts of interactions within the interpretative framework of workplace culture and laboring women's resilience. Like other histories written in the 1980s, Susan Porter Benson's 1986 book *Counter Cultures: Saleswomen, Managers, and Customers in American Department Stores, 1890–1940* and Sarah Smith Malino's 1982 dissertation "Faces across the Counter: A Social History of Female Department Store Employees, 1870–1920" emphasized women's agency and their ability to create meaningful relationships within oppressive capitalist structures.[17] Benson discussed some of the sexualized bullying that salesclerks experienced, but it was only in 2007 that Val Marie Johnson elaborated on that harassment in her article "'The Rest Can Go to the Devil': Macy's Workers Negotiate Gender, Sex, and Class in the Progressive Era." One of the few historians who has used the Committee of Fourteen's investigation, Johnson argued that "workingwomen both adapted and subverted patriarchal and classist tools as they navigated a range of sensual adventure, sexual regulation, and everyday survival concerns."[18] While women's agency remains important in this article, I incorporate the insights of the more recent histories of sexual harassment to consider the detrimental impact of men's actions on women's experiences working in department stores in the early twentieth century. I am particularly concerned about how male managers with higher status used their power and the degree to which women clerks could respond. In so doing, I aim to add more nuance to labor history's portrayal of gendered power in the workplace.

I have organized this article into four sections, alternating between general discussions of department stores and their workplace culture and specific case studies detailing the harassment by two individual men: the head of the Bureau of Investigation and the floorwalker in Carpets and Rugs. The first section examines the scale and scope of department stores and the implications of a decentralized responsibility. The next section addresses the behavior of Mr. Schonfeld, head of the Bureau of Investigation, who had a reputation as a man who bullied the tracers working for him. The third section describes the sexualized elements of Macy's workplace culture and what the shop clerks regarded as acceptable behavior. The fourth section centers on Leon Dringer, a floorwalker with a citywide reputation as a "lady killer" who overstepped workplace norms and made his department a distressing place for women. Sexual harassment existed at Macy's along a continuum; it affected women to varying degrees. In seeking causal explanations, however, everyone from the lowliest clerks to the Strauses themselves placed the onus of blame on women while making excuses for men perpetuating hostile work environments.

17. Benson, *Counter Cultures*, 253–58, 265–66; Malino, "Faces across the Counter," iv.
18. Johnson, "'The Rest Can Go to the Devil,'" 33.

Figure 1. Macy's Herald Square Building, 1907. Photograph by Irving Underhill.
Prints and Photographs Division, Library of Congress, Washington, DC.

Department Stores at the Turn of the Century

At the turn of the century, department stores were among the biggest capitalist ventures in the United States. Marshall Field and Macy's Herald Square store each comprised over 1 million square feet of floor space. Susan Porter Benson observed that "four factories of Ford's Highland Park plant would have fit comfortably inside either store."[19] She also noted that department stores employed staggeringly large workforces. "By 1898 Macy's had three thousand employees, putting it in a class with such manufacturing giants as the Merrimack Mills in Lowell, Massachusetts, the Waltham Watch Company, and Carnegie Steel's J. Edgar Thompson plant."[20] Thirteen years later, Macy's workforce had expanded to approximately 5,200 workers.[21] Department stores hired a large number of women in mixed-sex workplaces. In 1913, the National Civic Federation determined that nineteen firms across the nation employed thirty-three thousand workers, of which two-thirds were women.[22] Unlike factories, however, department stores were located in their city's central business districts and were

19. Benson, *Counter Cultures*, 32.
20. Benson, *Counter Cultures*, 34.
21. Malino, "Faces across the Counter," 15.
22. Howard, *From Main Street to Mall*, 49.

Figure 2. A busy shop floor showing customers and salesclerks. "View of Interior of Store, Elliott-Taylor-Woolfenden Col, Detroit, Mich.," *Dry Goods Economist* 67, no. 3 (August 1913): 2.

open to the flow of tens of thousands of customers.[23] In addition to large workforces, expansive physical spaces, and freely moving customers, department store managers also oversaw the purchase, display, and sale of millions of dollars of merchandise.[24] To address the large scale of their organization, store owners created a hierarchical but decentralized management structure that made individual departments the foundational unit of their enterprise.

By 1900 Macy's had over fifty departments. That number increased when they moved uptown from their cramped Fourteenth Street store to the palatial building at Thirty-Fourth Street and Broadway. Departments included everything from leather goods, motorists' clothing, photographic supplies, ladies' dresses, clocks and bronzes, solid gold jewelry, boys' hats, cutlery, artists' materials, cakes and pies, to baby carriages.[25] While some contemporary critics considered this new type of store overwhelming, customers found the scope of offerings appealing. Rather than shopping at multiple venues scattered across Manhattan, they could go to one store and buy most everything they needed in one trip.

Specialized departments required specialized knowledge of the products on sale. Heads of departments, and the salesclerks within them, hoarded knowledge, protecting their positions and reinforcing their association with a particular part of the store.[26] Department heads thus served as informational chokepoints.[27] Salesclerks learned at the direction of their managers, while, in the words of business historian Ralph Hower, the Strauses "were obliged to depend more and more upon departmental heads to handle relations with the rank and file."[28] Each department functioned much like an independent fiefdom, yet coordinating those fiefdoms required managerial oversight.[29]

23. Benson, *Counter Cultures*, 34.

24. Malino, "Faces across the Counter," 16.

25. Hower, *History of Macy's*, 330, 360. In the 1880s, most stores only had fifteen small departments, but by 1910 many offered up to 125. Leach, *Land of Desire*, 34.

26. Habberton, August 7, 1913, pp. 1–3, file 3, C14DSI; Benson, *Counter Cultures*, 245–51.

27. Benson, *Counter Cultures*, 153–54.

28. Hower, *History of Macy's*, 387.

29. Benson, *Counter Cultures*, 10.

Large department stores contained multiple tiers of management. The owners delegated to the general superintendent, who received support from assistant superintendents, who directed floor managers. Floor managers cooperated with buyers, who both oversaw the stocking of merchandise and the personnel in their departments. Departmental personnel fulfilled a range of roles from the higher-status floorwalkers and aisle managers to the salesclerks, who made up the majority of the stores' workforces. Wrappers who bundled up purchases and cash girls who processed payments were the youngest and had the lowest status of all the departmental workers. The shipping division comprised drivers, packers, and their assistants. At Macy's, the Bureau of Investigation, which was in the basement with shipping, processed complaints and had a corps of tracers who tracked down information on missing items, unfulfilled orders, improperly filed checks, and other logistical issues.[30] Macy's also employed welfare officers, a doctor, and nurses.[31] Almost all of the workers, other than the Black men who operated the elevators, were white. While Macy's management did recruit ethnic employees, they usually hired the Americanized first generation as salesclerks. The "roughest sorts" Macy's kept out of sight in the basement departments.[32]

The combination of strict managerial hierarchies and minimal departmental oversight made workers vulnerable to the people running their department. Salesclerks repeatedly heard that everything must go through their department heads.[33] As Habberton noted, "The average girl knows of no management but that of her Aisle Manager and Section Manager. In all matters relating to her personal rights the wishes of the management are practically unknown to her."[34] At the end of the investigation, Habberton concluded that "the general management does not exist for the shopgirl—it is all department management."[35] Sidney, Sonnichsen, and Habberton all documented salesclerks' limited options when dealing with a difficult department head: they could stay quiet and take the abuse, they could yell back, and they could quit. When they did complain, they expected retaliation ranging from smeared reputations to the removal of seats or delay of the dismissal bell. Without a union to guide and protect them, clerks did not know to whom they could safely complain.[36]

30. Sonnichsen, October 27, 1913, p. 2, and November 2, 1913, p. 1, file 5, C14DSI. See also Benson, *Counter Cultures*, 47.

31. Habberton, August 28, 1913, p. 3, file 3, C14DSI.

32. "Extracts in re Greenhut-Seigel-Cooper's," 3; "Committee of Fourteen," 2, both file 2, C14DSI. In 1888, results from a national study showed that under 15 percent were immigrants, while 71 percent of the native-born women with at least one immigrant parent; 55 percent had two foreign-born parents. See Malino, "Faces across the Counter," 228.

33. A 1903 list from Seigel-Cooper's shows a typical set of rules. See Malino, "Faces across the Counter," 127.

34. Habberton, [August 1913], n.p., file 3, C14DSI.

35. "Miss Habberton's Summary," p. 11, n.d., file 3, C14DSI.

36. On the opacity of upper management, see Benson, *Counter Cultures*, 138. On attempts to unionize, see Benson, *Counter Cultures*, 269–70.

Over the course of their time at Macy's, the investigators noted that women reported bad behavior to Mr. Wells, the assistant superintendent; Mr. Byrnes, the general superintendent; and Percy Straus. No women went to Miss Kenyon, the welfare officer hired to field women's complaints about men acting inappropriately. Habberton asked multiple women how to protest sexualized interactions within a department, but no one mentioned Kenyon. "Not one of the twenty-five have the faintest idea that she is there to 'protect the younger girls,' or 'to improve the moral tone of the store.'"[37] To make the complaints process more transparent, Habberton suggested that "it would be perfectly simple to inform each new employee that all complaints and questions of a certain nature were to be handled by Miss Kenyon, and that it was a part of her business to see that the person complaining did not 'get hit back.'"[38] She also suggested signs in the stairways and information slips in pay packets, but Macy's management did not act on any of these proposals.[39]

The combination of a hierarchical structure and the fragmentation of the workforce into tightly defined and strictly controlled departments meant that workers had little recourse for challenging a hostile work environment. Clerks did not know the function of the Welfare Office beyond the boring lectures it offered.[40] Department stores only instituted personnel departments in the late 1920s; complaints procedures before then were particularly opaque.[41] Profitability and the efficient running of a department usually mattered more than worker morale. Owner Percy Straus hired the Committee of Fourteen as much to perform reputational due diligence as to uncover the causes of women's sexual vulnerability. In this way, the Fourteen served as narrative gatekeepers that legitimized the structural inequalities at Macy's. The next three sections consider different types of workplace interactions and what they meant for women clerks.

Shouting Abuse

The first case study involves Mr. Schonfeld, who ran Macy's Bureau of Investigation.[42] Those working under him considered Schonfeld a bully who relished arbitrarily exercising power. He was a boss who deliberately delayed ringing the bell that ended the workday for his department.[43] Natalie Sonnichsen observed his negative impact on the sub-basement where they worked. "Everybody is always in a state of irritation and very small things start abuse and fights. Mr. Schonfeld gives the tone to this by his own lack of restraint. Any slight mistake rouses him and he begins to abuse."[44] Yet the superintendent did not fire him, instead castigating him now and then when

37. Habberton, July 2, 1913, pp. 10–11, C14DSI.
38. Habberton, September 9, 1913, pp. 2–3, file 3, C14DSI.
39. "Miss Habberton's Summary," 9; Habberton, October 18, 1913, p. 8, both file 3, C14DSI.
40. Habberton, July 29, 1913, p. 2, file 3; Sidney, October 13–15, 1913, pp. 9–11, file 4, both C14DSI.
41. Benson, *Counter Cultures*, 52.
42. Sonnichsen, November 2, 1913, p. 1, file 5, C14DSI.
43. Sonnichsen, November 2, 1913, p. 3, file 5, C14DSI.
44. Sonnichsen, November 2, 1913, p. 4, file 5, C14DSI.

one of Schonfeld's tracers complained. Schonfeld received at least two "calls," reprimands from upper management, in the six months during the investigation.[45] As an employee of almost eighteen years, Schonfeld had no doubt received multiple calls, but he responded by temporarily moderating his verbal imprecations and by retaliating.[46] His actions drove out multiple workers who left Macy's rather than tolerate his abuse.[47]

Yet when Frederick Whitin, the general secretary of the Committee of Fourteen, typed up a fourteen-page, typewritten, internal, and unexpurgated report summarizing the investigation's findings, he never alluded to Schonfeld as causing problems for women employees.[48] Whitin probably omitted Schonfeld because he did not directly lead any department store girls into prostitution, but also because of the banality of the interactions. Schonfeld was notable, but not singular. Other managers also shouted abuse at their workers. It is the record of his interactions with workers and management that makes Schonfeld exceptional. The investigative reports made explicit how the exercise of power worked within Macy's hierarchical departments. Schonfeld did not harass his workers sexually, but he bullied them, exposing a continuum of gendered microaggressions and worker abuse that senior management tolerated.

From the beginning of her initial employment, Schonfeld raised red flags for Natalie Sonnichsen. When she started her job as a tracer on October 27, 1913, he warned her "not to tell any of the girls" her salary, as that "might create jealousy and ill-feeling."[49] A seemingly benevolent comment, it foreshadowed other ways in which Schonfeld tried to isolate the five women tracers and the unknown number of men.[50] Schonfeld also asked Sonnichsen where she lived, not for sexual purposes as salesmen elsewhere did, but because her proximity to Macy's meant a short commute. "You don't live far, so you can easily work after 6. You should be willing to work an extra half hour for the training we are giving you."[51] Like many other managers, Schonfeld expected gratitude and recompense for on-the-job training. Macy's and most other companies in those years did not pay much overtime—even during the pre-Christmas rush—but of all the managers described in the investigation, Schonfeld was the one who purposely used his control of workers' time as a way to assert performatively his power over them.[52] But his abuse went further than eking out extra hours from employees.

45. Habberton, July 2, 1913, p. 12, file 3; Habberton, September 26, pp. 11–12, file 3; Sonnichsen, December 1, 1913, pp. 2–3, file 5; all C14DSI.

46. Sonnichsen, November 2, 1913, p. 9; Sonnichsen, November 14, 1913, p. 4; Sonnichsen, November 18, 1913, pp. 3–4; Sonnichsen, December 1, 1913, pp. 2–3; all file 5, C14DSI.

47. Sonnichsen, 2 November 13, p. 3, file 5, C14DSI.

48. "Committee of Fourteen."

49. Sonnichsen, November 2, 1913, p. 1, file 5, C14DSI.

50. Sonnichsen, November 2, 1913, p. 3, file 5, C14DSI.

51. Sonnichsen, November 2, 1913, p. 12, file 5, C14DSI.

52. Sonnichsen, November 2, 1913, p. 4, file 5, C14DSI; Malino, "Faces across the Counter," 137–39.

Three weeks into her job in the department, Sonnichsen had determined the broad contours of Schonfeld's harassment. Within an hour of joining the Bureau of Investigation, Sonnichsen witnessed him shouting at a male tracer. "Mr. Schonfeld began abusing him in a most vulgar and unrestrained way. Profanity poured out of his mouth—and the man stood quietly and listened to it."[53] When she asked the women tracers about his behavior, they assured her that while he "swears at the men . . . he only shouts at them."[54] By mid-November, however, Sonnichsen had witnessed him berate multiple people, including women, and he did more than just shout at them. Although she did not record the specifics, she used words like *rough*, *abusive*, and *vulgar*.[55] She described how one day, "Rose had two bad fights with him. Celia had a stormy session, and Dorothea came away in tears, saying that the next time he speaks to her that way, she will leave."[56] Schonfeld's verbal violence affected the whole department.

Sonnichsen soon experienced his abuse firsthand. She made friends with the other women tracers and chatted with them while working. When Schonfeld witnessed her speaking to them, he tried to end their conversation. "On Thursday I was reprimanded for my 'friendships' with the girls. Rose Kaiser to whom I was talking was yelled at by Schonfeld, and of course she answered him back, so there was a scene."[57] Later that day, Sonnichsen asked for a pass from a floorwalker to have a soda in the cafeteria with another tracer, Celia Shapiro. "We were just beginning to enjoy our sodas when Schonfeld jumped up. He demanded roughly what we were doing."[58] Taking their pass away, presumably to authenticate it with the floorwalker, he soon returned, but since they had not broken any rules, he could not send them back to the department. He did, however, watch them the entire time they drank their sodas. That afternoon "Celia received a terrific scolding."[59] The next day, Schonfeld "gave me a rough talk about keeping the rules and having no friendships."[60]

Clues exist that Schonfeld treated men and women differently, imbuing a gendered component to his harassment. While Schonfeld tried to keep women under his surveillance apart from each other, he kept the male tracers close to him. Sonnichsen observed that he always seemed to have a "war council" around his desk.[61] This favoritism influenced how men treated the women with whom they worked, encouraging men to shout at women in an abusive manner. During one exchange, Rose Kaiser called a male tracer a "dirty liar."[62] Sonnichsen did not give the cause of

53. Sonnichsen, November 2, 1913, p. 1, file 5, C14DSI.
54. Sonnichsen, November 2, 1913, p. 4, file 5, C14DSI.
55. Sonnichsen, November 18, 1913, pp. 2–3; Sonnichsen, November 2, 1913, p. 9, both file 5, C14DSI.
56. Sonnichsen, November 18, 1913, p. 3, file 5, C14DSI.
57. Sonnichsen, November 18, 1913, p. 3, file 5, C14DSI.
58. Sonnichsen, November 18, 1913, p. 3, file 5, C14DSI.
59. Sonnichsen, November 18, 1913, p. 3, file 5, C14DSI.
60. Sonnichsen, November 18, 1913, p. 2, file 5, C14DSI.
61. Sonnichsen, November 6, 1913, pp. 1–2, file 5, C14DSI.
62. Sonnichsen, November 2, 1913, pp. 4–5, file 5, C14DSI.

the accusation. Indeed, she rarely gave specifics concerning what people yelled about, except in one important instance. Early into her time at the Bureau of Investigation, Sonnichsen found Celia Shapiro in the bathroom. They discussed how Schonfeld had told Shapiro that she "was a freak and a joke to look at."[63] These examples suggest that Schonfeld may have held men and women to different standards.[64]

Schonfeld's workers adopted various approaches to deal with his bullying. Some like Shapiro and the nameless male tracer of the first day, stood there, taking the abuse silently. Others yelled back. When Schonfeld summoned Rose Kaiser to his desk, everyone in earshot listened to him scream at her—and heard her answer back. "As she is a girl of spirit she too raised her voice and shouted at him. The whole department heard and evidently admired Rose."[65] Historian Val Marie Johnson interpreted the Macy's shopgirls yelling back as a sign that "they simply refused to be disciplined by their superiors."[66] But department heads wielded power, and resistance carried consequences. One of the tracers told the story of Kittie Talsey, who left Macy's for Seigel-Cooper. "When she worked at Macy's she had Schonfeld terrorized so he did not dare to call her down. She could always answer him back so cleverly, that in his exasperation he forbade the girls to speak to her."[67] Talsey was not the only one to leave. Sonnichsen learned about the department's high turnover early in her tenure there.[68]

Some workers tried to complain to upper management about Schonfeld. Before Sonnichsen had even started working at Macy's, Faith Habberton had heard a rumor about a nasty buyer in the basement who "used language no girl should hear, just because he was mad." Evidently, "the girl walked straight up to Mr. Straus's office and told him." Habberton admired her gumption. "If a girl has acted decent she needn't be afraid to tell her boss anything if he's a gentleman. If he isn't, she shouldn't be working for him." Yet Schonfeld retained his job. Habberton wrote that "Mr. Straus couldn't put the fellow out because he was a buyer but gave him a 'call' and he always spoke respectfully to the girls after that."[69] Since no buyers worked out of the sub-basement, and Schonfeld was the main authority down there, Habberton was probably talking about Schonfeld. A later conversation between Sonnichsen and Shapiro supports this conclusion. When Sonnichsen asked why Schonfeld still had his job, Shapiro responded, "Hes [sic] been here almost eighteen years otherwise he'd never keep his job. The management doesn't know much about him or he wouldn't be where he is. Still, I suppose he keeps a job because he is such an old employee."[70]

63. Sonnichsen, November 2, 1913, p. 10, file 5, C14DSI.

64. Feminist philosopher Kate Manne discusses double versus different standards, Manne, *Down Girl*, 117, 269, 297.

65. Manne, *Down Girl*, 4–5.

66. Johnson, "'The Rest Can Go to the Devil,'" 41.

67. Sonnichsen, November 14, 1913, p. 4, file 5, C14DSI; Johnson, "'The Rest Can Go to the Devil,'" 41. Fiction from the period also addressed these pyrrhic victories; see Berebitsky, *Sex and the Office*, 68–70.

68. Sonnichsen, November 2, 1913, p. 3, file 5, C14DSI.

69. Habberton, July 2, 1913, p. 12; Habberton, September 26, 1913, pp. 11–12, all file 3, C14DSI.

70. Sonnichsen, November 2, 1913, p. 9, C14DSI.

Management did know about Schonfeld, but he was out of sight of customers and kept his department running with sufficient efficiency.[71]

Although Schonfeld moderated his conduct immediately after a call, he also took out his displeasure on his workers. After one reprimand, Sonnichsen noted that "he still loses his temper but he does not yell quite as much, and instead of sitting all day at his desk he shows more personal interest in the work of the department. He walks around and looks busy."[72] This performance covered his barely hidden anger. Schonfeld "has been very mean about ringing the 6 p.m. bell. He would wait some evenings until 6.20, while most of the girls sat with folded arms as they had finished and had nothing to do."[73] Schonfeld also anticipated complaints. When Sonnichsen reported to Mr. Wells, an assistant superintendent, that Schonfeld had refused to grant her a sick pass, then withheld it after she went above his head to get one, she realized that Wells seemed unfavorably disposed to her. "It struck me that Schonfeld had to be complaining about me. . . . I have been late only twice and yet Schonfeld told Mr. Wells that I often came late."[74] Schonfeld proactively undermined workers he thought might complain to management and punished the whole department when one employee sought redress for her treatment, illustrating how bullies navigated corporate bureaucracy to retain their power and continue their everyday practices of abuse.

Despite his casual cruelty, the poor department morale, and the high turnover of women workers, Schonfeld neither lost his job nor received mention in either the published report or the unexpurgated internal version. His abuse was gendered but not sufficiently sexualized to meet Progressive Era standards of danger. Without a critique of sex-based discrimination, neither the Committee of Fourteen nor Macy's upper management saw Schonfeld's harassment as anything other than an occasional annoyance. Decentralized management meant that Schonfeld could torment the tracers without lasting consequences for almost eighteen years.

Harmless Jolly

While upper management did not work to end Schonfeld's abuse of his workers, they did care about the sexualized banter men and women exchanged while at work. The members of the Committee of Fourteen and the owners of Macy's spent considerable time evaluating whether these casual, quotidian interactions signified women's immorality. Frederick Whitin, the general secretary of the Fourteen, and to a lesser extent Habberton, used these reports to judge whether the "smutty talk" and teasing touches were "harmless jolly" or something more sinister. The unedited investigators' reports showed that women clerks used a nuanced vocabulary to categorize their coworkers'

---

71. Owners and managers worked very hard to keep labor abuses out of the public eye; see Benson, *Counter Cultures*, 137.

72. Sonnichsen, December 1, 1913, pp. 2–3, file 5, C14DSI.

73. Sonnichsen, December 1, 1913, pp. 2–3, file 5, C14DSI.

74. Sonnichsen, December 1, 1913, p. 4, file 5, C14DSI. Mr. Wells was possibly William J. Wells, brought in to manage the Deposit Account Department in 1906; Hower, *History of Macy's*, 366.

behavior and whether they deemed it appropriate or not, but by the time the Fourteen published their findings on the department store investigation, they had thoroughly obscured the sophistication of the salesclerks' own vernacular. Instead, Whitin adopted a binary approach to evaluate whether the workplace structure itself caused women to "go wrong" or whether the blame lay with a few corrupt men and inherently immoral women. This section explores what salesclerks thought about their coworkers' actions, shows how the Committee of Fourteen interpreted their words and behavior, and evaluates how contemporary ideas about women's responsibility as moral gatekeepers intersected with Macy's shop floor culture.

All three investigators commented on the coarseness of the conversation within the store. Natalie Sonnichsen, who also investigated disreputable dance halls, considered the talk worse than any in the dives she visited.[75] While Habberton, Sidney, and Sonnichsen all referred to vile language, they did not transcribe what the salesclerks said to each other. They did, however, document how men addressed them. When she worked as a floorwalker, Habberton did not mind that the people hailed her as "42," the number pinned to her dress.[76] But when Schonfeld summoned Rose Kaiser by her surname without the honorific *Miss*, she pointed out the deliberate slight to Sonnichsen.[77] In the sub-basement, the male packers (who loaded delivery trucks) called the women tracers "dear," "sweetheart," and "chicken." The Committee of Fourteen concluded in the printed pamphlet that "the girls on the whole consider them decent; the talk being more or less harmless jolly"; however, Sonnichsen observed that most men respected Dorothea Schneider and "do not jolly much when she comes around. The packers are the one exception to this rule."[78] When Schneider and Sonnichsen entered their department, the men started catcalling. "They teased me . . . generally doing all in their power to make things uncomfortable."[79] These supposed endearments might seem more humanizing than referring to saleswomen by their numbers, but the diminishing address combined with the men's intention to discomfit the women entering their department distinguished the two types of interactions, particularly since the women tracers were likely following up a complaint about missing or mishandled merchandise. By the very nature of their job, they questioned the authority and competency of the male packers. The men responded with verbal reminders that they considered women sexual subjects, not workforce equals.

At the time, however, people interpreted men's sexualized interactions with women as the women's responsibility.[80] A salesclerk told Habberton that "she thought

75. Sonnichsen to Whitin, November 27, 1913, pp. 5–6, file 5, C14DSI.

76. Habberton, September 26, 1913, p. 11, file 3, C14DSI. See also MacLean, "Two Weeks in Department Stores," 724.

77. Sonnichsen, November 2, 1913, pp. 4–5, file 5, C14DSI.

78. "Committee of Fourteen," p. 8, file 2; Sonnichsen, November 2, 1913, p. 6, file 5, both C14DSI. See also Berebitsky, *Sex and the Office*, 36–37.

79. Sonnichsen, November 2, 1913, p. 6, file 5, C14DSI. Men in shipping departments were notoriously intimidating toward women; see Vapnek, *Breadwinners*, 95–96.

80. Remus, *Shopper's Paradise*, 163.

a girl was awfully silly to act fresh and then complain of the way a man treated her. It was generally the girl's fault and if it wasn't there was always *something* to be done."[81] Yet women salesclerks concurrently advised the investigators to ignore the "fresh fellows."[82] As they said, "Youll [*sic*] get used to it—theyre [*sic*] all that way."[83] Women workers at Macy's knew the danger of reporting what they called indecent talk. After one clerk went to the assistant superintendent, the buyer in the photo supply department removed all the chairs in retaliation. After that, no one dared make a complaint.[84] Worse, women feared that men would damage their reputation if they complained. "One girl said, 'You don't dare stop bad talk. If you do they think you're stuck up and then they get mad and give you a bad name all over the place. You can be sure if one of these fellers can't talk nasty *with* you they'll talk nasty *about* you.'"[85] She based this generalization on experience. "Miss King called the fellers down for the way they talk and they've made everyone think she's a bad one—just for spite."[86] Despite evidence that women tried to alter the tone of different departments, salesclerks insisted that women brought such treatment on themselves.[87] The Committee of Fourteen concluded that "the girls take the vulgar and suggestive remarks of the men in the different departments nonchalantly and as typical of the class."[88] While they tolerated ribald repartee, and sometimes even participated in it, saleswomen also knew the limits of their power to change workplace culture.

If Macy's employees were ambivalent about "smutty talk," they were more accepting of the men who casually touched women coworkers.[89] Sonnichsen observed that "there is a certain amount of familiarity in that the men touch the girls and handle them a little," but she concluded that such physical contact did not indicate sexual relationships on site, assuming that "if there is anything going on it is when they are outside."[90] Sidney reported that "I had occasion today to speak to one of the other floorwalkers on my floor. He took hold of my arm while speaking to me and was very friendly, but I think only as he would probably do to any of the girls."[91] Habber-

81. Habberton, September 26, 1913, p. 10, file 3, C14DSI, emphasis in original.

82. Sonnichsen, November 2, 1913, p. 6, file 5, C14DSI.

83. Sonnichsen, November 2, 1913, p. 6, file 5, C14DSI.

84. Habberton, [August 1913], p. 2, file 3, C14DSI.

85. Habberton, July 24, 1913, p. 4, file 3, C14DSI. See also Berebitsky, *Sex and the Office*, 55–56, emphasis in original.

86. Habberton, July 24, 1913, p. 4, file 3, C14DSI.

87. Sidney, November 1–8, 1913, p. 5, file 4; "Miss Habberton's Summary," p. 5, n.d., file 3, both C14DSI.

88. "Committee of Fourteen," p. 8. Sonnichsen phrased this conclusion differently: "There is a tendency on the part of some of the tracers and of all the men working in the different departments to make vulgar and suggestive remarks at every opportunity. Of course this is typical of that class of man, and the girls take this nonchalantly." Sonnichsen, November 19, 1913, p. 4, file 5, C14DSI.

89. For more about this "himpathy," as feminist philosopher Kate Manne calls the disproportionate empathy extended to sexual harassers, see Manne, *Entitled*, 36–37.

90. Sonnichsen, November 2, 1913, p. 11, file 5, C14DSI.

91. Sidney, October 13–15, 1913, p. 8, file 4, C14DSI.

ton seemed less sympathetic to Charlie, "a shapeless slouching youth," who touched every woman with whom he spoke. She even documented how, as a salesman, he challenged Miss Schwab, the department's floorwalker. "When Miss Schwab yells to him to 'git out,' [he] offers to kiss her."[92] Habberton shrugged off his behavior by infantilizing him. "He seems to have the little boy notion that he's not receiving enough attention." Yet at twenty-five, Charlie was likely older than most women in the department.[93] Other women excused him because he amused them. "Suddenly [he] comes upon 'Fattie,' a saleswoman, and announces she's so sweet he's going to kiss her. The other girls titter while he does it, but Fattie is too lazy to protest or respond, and the little wrapper explains that no one cares what Charlie does because he's so funny."[94] Humor gave men's harassment a gloss of acceptability.

Humor did not, however, protect women. When Burns, a delivery clerk, showed Rose Kaiser a raunchy rewrite of a popular song, she was delighted by both the sexual language and the clever recasting of the lyrics.[95] Kaiser showed it to other women and one of the men in the department. She had "one of the typewriters copy it to make four carbon copies" to give to her friends. Shapiro liked the poem so much that she wrote it in her commonplace book.[96] Sonnichsen questioned the girls about why they found the poem funny, but no one talked directly to Burns, even though he reputedly had a whole collection of sexual books, poetry, and pictures. Once again, the concern about women's morality meant management scrutinizing them while overlooking men's actions.[97] Sonnichsen called out this hypocrisy. "It seems to me that the person after whom Mr. Straus should get after is Burns, and not the girls. It is he who has a permanent collection of that sort of literature with appropriate pictures, one of which he showed Rose."[98] We do not know how the case was resolved, but it shows how a workplace culture in which both men and women participated blew back against women. To the Committee of Fourteen and Macy's upper management, raunchy humor was the purview of men.

Working-class women faced an impossible conundrum regarding workplace culture. Managers and middle-class consumers, and indeed the clerks themselves, expected women to act as moral gatekeepers who set and protected the workplace tone. But they had limited power. If men directed smutty talk toward them, they must be immoral. If they participated in the teasing, they got the conversation they deserved. If they were "straight," men would not feel emboldened to disrespect them.

92. Habberton, July 2, 1913, p. 11, file 3, C14DSI.

93. Habberton, July 14, 1913, p. 3, file 3, C14DSI. In Chicago in 1911, shopgirls averaged nineteen years old; see Bowen, *Department Store Girl*. In 1910, across the nation, approximately 15 percent of women retail workers were over twenty-five years old; see Tentler, *Wage-Earning Women*, 59.

94. Habberton, July 2, 1913, p. 12, file 3, C14DSI.

95. Sonnichsen to Whitin, January 7, [1913]; Sonnichsen, November 19, 1913, p. 1, both file 5, C14DSI.

96. Sonnichsen, November 19, 1913, p. 1, file 5, C14DSI.

97. Johnson discusses this phenomenon in "'The Rest Can Go to the Devil,'" 39.

98. Sonnichsen to Whitin, January 7, [1913], file 5. Whitin reported the incident to Percy Straus; see Frederick H. Whitin to Percy S. Straus, January 3, [1913], file 1, both C14DSI.

If they reported, they suffered retaliation from their immediate managers and from their coworkers. If they did not report, they were accused of not having any "real desire to promote the efficiency of the organization."[99] In the end, Macy's corporate reputation and its bottom line mattered more than daily microaggressions women experienced on the shop floor. As long as the Straus brothers could show that Macy's did not push women into prostitution, they could write off the smutty talk as harmlessly comparable to the "obscene talk in Chaucer and Shakespeare—primitive and vulgar."[100]

Promiscuous Flattery

The second case study considers the actions of Leon Dringer, the most talked-about man in Macy's.[101] Throughout the investigation, he worked as a floorwalker, first in Men's Underwear and later in Carpets and Rugs. Dringer had a reputation as a "fast man" who flirted with all the women in the store. Like many other employees, he engaged in "smutty talk," but he took it further: he teased both Sidney and Sonnichsen, saying that if it were not against the rules, he would take them out on a date. To more than one woman, Dringer mentioned the proximity of his apartment to the store. The repetition of sexualized conversations with all three investigators suggested that they were routine, which further investigation confirmed. Significantly, most of the men with whom the investigators talked made excuses for his behavior. A successful salesman, Dringer was well-liked by his male coworkers and managers. As with Schonfeld, numerous complaints were filed against him, and like Schonfeld, he kept his job. Although they alluded to him in the published report, the Committee of Fourteen emphasized Macy's commitment to good morals, arguing that they believed that Dringer "was more given to promiscuous flattery than anything of a serious nature."[102] Once again, the Fourteen affirmed workplace hierarchies. This section evaluates Dringer's reputation, why women considered his actions more burdensome than benign, and the way some of his coworkers covered for him.

Before she even started working at Macy's, Habberton had heard about Dringer's reputation as a "lady killer," but she dismissed the rumors because "the speakers were the kind of girls who make love to every presentable man and loathe him as 'no sport' if he fails to respond.'"[103] When she started working in the department next to his, she heard that he "had a 'dirty mouth' and 'talked filthy talk' to everyone." She doubted "these statements because I know that the girls who complain of this sort of thing are often the one who most clearly invite it."[104] When she met him, however, he made a "suggestive remark" and then proceeded to tell the

99. Habberton, July 2, 1913, p. 11, file 3, C14DSI.

100. *Department Store Investigation*, 10.

101. Sonnichsen, November 14, 1913, p. 1, file 5, C14DSI.

102. *Department Store Investigation*, 10; "Committee of Fourteen," 4.

103. "Committee of Fourteen," 4; Habberton to Whitin, February 27, 1914, file 1, C14DSI.

104. Habberton, July 17, 1913, pp. 1–4, file 3, C14DSI.

assembled salesclerks "how he lost his innocence as frankly and lightly as I would in describing the loss of an umbrella."[105] Her coworkers confirmed "that he constantly talks in the same tone to the little girls and also to the older clerks whose business ability he must respect."[106] When Dringer worked as a floorwalker in Men's Underwear, he relentlessly harassed the woman who ran the neighboring drug department. "He tried to annoy this woman in every possible way. He tried to flirt with her and was always getting in her way. She just hated him and would take no notice of him."[107] Dringer's conversations went beyond teasing, and he did not limit his attentions to those who might appreciate them.

Contributing to his reputation as a fast man, Dringer sounded out many of the saleswomen as to whether they would date him. Celia Shapiro told Sonnichsen that he "approaches every girl he meets with a plain proposal." He invited her to his apartment on Thirty-Fourth Street. "After that she was terse with him and showed him plainly that she did not approve of him, but that did not discourage him."[108] When Sidney started assisting him as a floorwalker, she commented that "he carried his talk to a considerable extreme and yet never attempted in any way to follow it up." Instead, he mentioned the rule forbidding employees to date, saying that otherwise he would have invited her to a special New Year's party he had arranged.[109] Dringer also said "if he had money he would marry me and take me to Los Angeles and we would have a wonderful time."[110] Dringer acted similarly with Sonnichsen. When she asked him about dating, he told her about two people who had dated and were instantly dismissed. "He added that I might have known some such rule existed or he would have been calling on me every night." Dringer told Sonnichsen "that I am going to marry him eventually. He decided where we are to live, how many children we are to have, etc., and does not hesitate to tell me or anyone else about his arrangements."[111] Spinning tales of fantasy futures allowed Dringer to playact respectable courtship rituals even as he imposed his vision on reluctant listeners. His behavior resembled what people now call grooming. While neither Shapiro, Sidney, nor Sonnichsen went out with Dringer, Shapiro suggested that others had, including Gladys, a special clerk.[112] Margaret, who worked in the china packers room, commented that Dringer "will not hesitate to invite a girl who is willing if she is fresh and pretty. He's fast and no good."[113] Shapiro further elaborated on Dringer's reputation: "'He demands a return

105. Habberton, July 17, 1913, pp. 1–4, file 3, C14DSI.

106. Habberton, July 17, 1913, p. 2, file 3, C14DSI.

107. Sonnichsen, November 6, 1913, pp. 3–4, file 5, C14DSI.

108. Sonnichsen, November 14, 1913, p. 1, file 5, C14DSI; Sidney confirmed that he had a room on Thirty-Fourth between Seventh and Eighth, Sidney, December 3–9, 1913, p. 7, file 4, C14DSI. It was located at the edge of the Tenderloin, New York City's most concentrated vice district; see Gilfoyle, *City of Eros*, 201–3.

109. "Committee of Fourteen," 4–5. See also Sidney, December 10–16, 1913, p. 4, file 4, both C14DSI.

110. Sidney, December 10–16, 1913, p. 3, file 4, C14DSI.

111. Sonnichsen, "As Regards Mr. Dringer," p. 1, file 5, C14DSI.

112. Sonnichsen, November 18, 1913, p. 4, file 5, C14DSI.

113. Sonnichsen, November 14, 1913, p. 1, file 5, C14DSI.

and he always gets it,' she added grimly."[114] Dringer's persistence and the repetition of tactics suggests an established pattern of harassment.

Dringer's notoriety affected store culture. When Sydney was transferring to Dringer's department, women warned her that he was "very much of a lady killer," while a number of men "came to her smiling ear to ear, telling her to be careful because of Dringer's reputation, but added confidentially that he was all right. The buyer in the department considers him valuable."[115] These exchanges served two purposes: they prepared Sydney to expect sexualized overtures and warned her that Dringer had the support of management. Celia Shapiro had previously reported him, but "he was told to mind what he said and nothing more was done to discipline him."[116] Miss Miller, a clerk in the framing department, told Habberton that numerous women had complained about Dringer, and that they had moved him to Carpets and Rugs because no women worked in the department. That move did not stop him from bothering women in adjacent departments. Miller wondered if the management realized that Dringer's actions affected the boys too. One of the boys in Dringer's department, "a salesman still in his teens," had started copying Dringer and the way he talked to women.[117] Dringer's continued employment gave tacit approval to his conduct.

In July, after first reporting Dringer, Habberton, who had great faith in management, was surprised when Mr. Byrnes, the general superintendent, did not fire Dringer after receiving her reports. Byrnes questioned her statement that Dringer used "indecent language" and said that he had made inquiries and that "he certainly had the best of reasons for believing that I had been misinformed." Habberton challenged Byrnes, saying that she had heard him make "indecent remarks in my hearing." Byrnes backed off and promised to discharge him.[118] Without the support of the Committee of Fourteen, and the knowledge that Habberton had the ear of the Straus brothers, Byrnes would probably have never placated her. Yet Byrnes did not deliver on his promise. Dringer remained an employee of the store through the end of December and maybe beyond, despite sexualizing workplace interactions.

Dringer kept his job for multiple reasons, not least of which was his reputation as a good salesman. His buyer considered him valuable, while an assistant floor manager considered him "a good boy and knows his business well."[119] Habberton

114. Sonnichsen, November 14, 1913, p. 1, file 5, C14DSI.

115. Sidney, December 3–9, 1913, p. 1, file 4; "Committee of Fourteen," p. 4, file 2, both C14DSI.

116. Sonnichsen, November 14, 1913, p. 2, file 5, C14DSI. This complaint may have been why he stopped directly asking women out and moved to a more subtle approach, framing his desire to date a woman in the conditional.

117. Habberton, July 17, 1913, p. 4, file 3, C14DSI.

118. Habberton, July 29, 1913, pp. 3–4, file 3, C14DSI. Byrnes is likely Sylvester Byrnes, who the Strauses hired as general manager in 1908. Hower, *History of Macy's*, 366–67.

119. "Committee of Fourteen," p. 4, file 2, C14DSI. Dringer was likely in his late twenties or early thirties when employed at Macy's. He had previously worked as a cabin boy on the Atlantic Transport Line, served in the navy, and worked for seven years as a floorwalker at department stores throughout New York City. See Sidney, December 3–9, 1913, p. 4, file 4, C14DSI.

similarly commented on "his popularity and good management."[120] Unlike Schonfeld, who also retained his job, Dringer was well liked by the men and had "a cordial greeting for many of the women customers as well as employees."[121] In this way, Dringer did not match the stereotypes of a man who ruined women. He was cheerful, handsome, and efficient, which gave him latitude with the management and led the women investigators to doubt their antipathy toward him.[122] Sydney, who worked the closest with him, commented that "he has not the earmarks of a man accustomed to late hours or dissipation." Moreover, "she reported he had his department thoroughly in hand; a situation which she believed to be impossible if his relations to his subordinates were not entirely proper."[123] Even though multiple women reported that Dringer's actions damaged morale, Macy's management and the Committee of Fourteen dismissed their distress because he ran an efficient department and did not force salesclerks into prostitution.

Dringer's case shows the limits of the white slavery scare as an interpretive framework for understanding how sexualized workplaces could harm women. In a world in which everyone from the lowliest wrapper to the head of the city's premier anti-vice commission believed that women invited men's amorous attentions, the fact that all three investigators accused Dringer of inappropriate persistence toward unwilling women stands out quite starkly. Dringer created what feminist lawyers since the 1970s have called a hostile work environment for women. He encouraged a sexualized atmosphere that made men "part of the club" and alienated women who refused to act as "good fellows." Yet because he apparently did not date the women he importuned, the Committee of Fourteen concluded that "the indecency of conversation" did not correlate with "improper relations."[124] Based on this rationale, the men of the Committee of Fourteen and Macy's management ignored their own investigators' reports of men who bullied women and imposed on them sexually. As long as women clerks were not having extramarital sex with male coworkers, Macy's management believed it could safely assert that department store work did not lead girls into prostitution.

Conclusion

Over a hundred years later, Macy's work environment seems eminently recognizable. Harassment existed on a continuum from teasing and casual touches to bullying and sexual aggression. The jokes, flirtation, and anger are only notable for their banality. It was not "different back then," but our understanding of how sexual harassment works has crystallized since 1913. As a result of the analytical insights of second-wave feminists and the revelations of #MeToo, present-day observers can better categorize

120. Habberton to Whitin, February 27, 1914, file 1, C14DSI.

121. "Committee of Fourteen," p. 4, file 2, C14DSI.

122. Sonnichsen, November 14, 1913, p. 1; Sonnichsen, November 27, 1913, p. 1, both file 5, C14DSI.

123. "Committee of Fourteen," p. 4, file 2, C14DSI.

124. *Department Store Investigation*, 10.

harassing actions. Although early twentieth-century reformers could see the work-place as a place of sexual danger, without conceptualizing sexualized interactions as damaging in and of themselves they dismissed women worker's concerns, reaffirmed gendered hierarchies, and legitimized oppressive management practices.

The focus on women's vulnerability obscured men's actions.[125] Trying to determine why women "go wrong," investigators scrutinized what women did. The Fourteen hired women investigators to get close to women clerks. They hired no men, despite having a cadre of male investigators on staff. They never sounded out what men thought about the women with whom they worked.[126] No one buddied up to Dringer, encouraging him to talk about his conquests. Nor did anyone ask the male tracers about either Schonfeld or their female coworkers. Meanwhile, Burns, the owner of the raunchy poem, escaped both investigators' questions and manage-ment's discipline. Instead, the Fourteen considered having Sonnichsen trail Rose Kaiser, the clerk with whom Burns shared the poem, to see how she behaved after hours.[127] When discussing store morality, no one suggested investigating how men spent their free time, but both Habberton and Sidney advised that Macy's should expand the welfare department to include an ongoing moral investigation of wom-en's "home life."[128] Habberton did, however, recommend that Macy's check men's references before hiring them. She had heard rumors that an unnamed floorwalker had lost his previous job "because his conduct with young girls was improper."[129] Her suggestion received no traction, highlighting the differential standard to which man-agement held men and women.

The organization of department stores—and the rise of middle management, a feature that distinguishes corporations with over three thousand workers—also increased women's vulnerability. Owners could not and often did not want to see the interactions within departments. Efficiency and profits mattered. "System" served as the watchword and the ultimate goal of managers. When Sonnichsen accused Schon-feld to his face of "a lack of system," the insult carried both personal and professional connotations.[130] Yet Sonnichsen, like other workers, had little recourse to change how her department worked. Men held most positions of power. A few women worked as floorwalkers and some even rose to buyer, but men comprised the general manag-ers, superintendents, and advisory board members. The bureaucratic opacity of such a large venture, combined with managerial reliance on department heads, meant women not only had to understand the store's structure to make a complaint about

125. Johnson, "'The Rest Can Go to the Devil,'" 39.

126. Men talk to each other differently than they talk to women when discussing sex; see Keire, "Swearing Allegiance."

127. Sonnichsen to Whitin, n.d., p. 1, file 5, C14DSI.

128. "Miss Habberton's Summary," n.d., pp. 11–12, file 3, C14DSI. Sidney, November 10–18, 1913, p. 1, file 4, both C14DSI.

129. Habberton, July 31, 1913, pp. 2–3, file 3, C14DSI.

130. Sonnichsen, November 18, 1913, p. 3, file 5, C14DSI. On "System," see Benson, *Counter Cultures*, 54–55.

a buyer or floorwalker, but they also had to contravene the rigorously enforced organizational hierarchies. Bypassing their managers, and flouting the directionality of decision making, turned women who complained into troublemakers.[131] Meanwhile, male floorwalkers and sections heads who harassed shopgirls did not challenge the way department stores functioned. They observed managerial hierarchies and stayed within their organizational lane. Their tone and treatment of workers held significance only if customers complained. Corporate reputation mattered more than women's structural inequality. ◪

MARA KEIRE is a Senior Research Fellow at the Rothermere American Institute, University of Oxford. She is the author of *For Business and Pleasure: Red-Light Districts and the Regulation of Vice in the United States, 1890–1933* (2010).

References

Addams, Jane. *A New Conscience and an Ancient Evil*. New York: Macmillan, 1912.

Ahmed, Sara. *What's the Use? On the Uses of Use*. Durham, NC: Duke University Press, 2019.

Baker, Carrie N. *The Women's Movement against Sexual Harassment*. Cambridge: Cambridge University Press, 2008.

Benson, Susan Porter. *Counter Cultures: Saleswomen, Managers, and Customers in American Department Stores, 1890–1940*. Urbana: University of Illinois Press, 1986.

Berebitsky, Julie. *Sex and the Office: A History of Gender, Power, and Desire*. New Haven, CT: Yale University Press, 2012.

Bowen, Louise De Koven. *The Department Store Girl; Based upon Interviews with 200 Girls*. [Chicago]: Juvenile Protective Association of Chicago, 1911.

Dreiser, Theodore. *Sister Carrie*. With a new introduction by Thomas P. Riggio. Philadelphia: University of Pennsylvania Press, 1981.

Gilfoyle, Timothy J. *City of Eros: New York City, Prostitution and the Commercialization of Sex, 1790–1920*. New York: Norton, 1992.

Grippo, Robert M. *Macy's: The Store. The Star. The Story. An Illustrated History of America's Most Celebrated Retail Emporium*. Garden City Park, NY: Square One, 2009.

Hirshman, Linda. *Reckoning: The Epic Battle against Sexual Abuse and Harassment*. New York: Houghton Mifflin Harcourt, 2019.

Howard, Vicki. *From Main Street to Mall: The Rise and Fall of the American Department Store*. Philadelphia: University of Pennsylvania Press, 2015.

Hower, Ralph M. *History of Macy's of New York, 1858–1919*. Cambridge, MA: Harvard University Press, 1943.

Johnson, Val Marie. "'The Rest Can Go to the Devil': Macy's Workers Negotiate Gender, Sex, and Class in the Progressive Era." *Journal of Women's History* 19, no. 1 (2007): 32–57.

Keire, Mara. "Swearing Allegiance: Street Language, US War Propaganda, and the Declining Status of Women in Northeastern Nightlife, 1900–1920." *Journal of the History of Sexuality* 25, no. 2 (2016): 246–66.

131. Ahmed, *What's the Use?*, 179–86.

Kessler-Harris, Alice. *Out to Work: A History of Wage-Earning Women in the United States*. Oxford: Oxford University Press, 1982.

Leach, William. *Land of Desire: Merchants, Power, and the Rise of a New American Culture*. New York: Pantheon Books, 1993.

MacKinnon, Catharine A. *Sexual Harassment of Working Women: A Case of Sex Discrimination*. New Haven, CT: Yale University Press, 1979.

MacLean, Annie Marion. "Two Weeks in Department Stores." *American Journal of Sociology* 4, no. 6 (1899): 721–41.

Malino, Sarah Smith. "Faces across the Counter: A Social History of Female Department Store Employees, 1870–1920." PhD diss., Columbia University, 1982.

Manne, Kate. *Down Girl: The Logic of Misogyny*. Oxford: Oxford University Press, 2018.

Manne, Kate. *Entitled: How Male Privilege Hurts Women*. London: Allen Lane, 2020.

Peiss, Kathy. *Cheap Amusements: Working Women and Leisure in Turn-of-the-Century New York*. Philadelphia: Temple University Press, 1986.

Remus, Emily. *A Shopper's Paradise: How the Ladies of Chicago Claimed Power and Pleasure in the New Downtown*. Cambridge, MA: Harvard University Press, 2019.

Tentler, Leslie. *Wage-Earning Women: Industrial Work and Family Life in the United States, 1900–1930*. Oxford: Oxford University Press, 1979.

Thomas, Gillian. *Because of Sex: One Law, Ten Cases, and Fifty Years That Changed American Women's Lives at Work*. New York: Picador, 2016.

US Congress. *Wage-Earning Women in Stores and Factories*, vol. 5 of *Report on Condition of Woman and Child Wage-Earners in the United States, 1910*. 61st Congress, 2nd sess., Sen. Doc. 645. Washington, 1910.

Vapnek, Lara. *Breadwinners: Working Women and Economic Independence, 1865–1920*. Urbana: University of Illinois Press, 2009.

"There Is Not a Factory Today Where This Same Immoral Condition Does Not Exist": Strikes against Sexual Harassment, 1912–2019

Annelise Orleck

"Rose dear. You know as well as I that there is not a factory today where the same immoral condition does not exist . . . [in] the cloak factories and all other shops in the city of New York and Chicago, every one of the men will talk to the girls, take advantage of them if the girls will let them. The foremen and the superintendent will flirt with the girls. . . . It is nothing new for those who know it exists everywhere."
—Pauline Newman to Rose Schneiderman, June 1912

"The time has passed when an employer can expect to hold girl employees who are subjected to indignities."
—Josephine Casey, 1912

"McDonald's monitors everything we do, from how fast the drive-through is moving to how we fold our customers' bags. Yet when I filed a complaint against my shift manager for regularly harassing me . . . McDonald's had no response. . . . I really needed that job and the money and I considered remaining silent."
—Cortez Clark, Flint, Michigan McDonald's worker, 2018

My thanks to Maya L. Khanna for her assistance. Epigraphs: Pauline Newman to Rose Schneiderman, July 11, 1912, Papers of the New York Women's Trade Union League and Its Principal Leaders, University Microfilms, quoted in Annelise Orleck, *Common Sense and a Little Fire: Women and Working-Class Politics in the United States, 1900–1965* (1995; anniv. ed., 2017); Josephine Casey, "Letter from Prison," *Detroit Times*, May 4, 1912; Annelise Orleck, "Me Too and McDonald's," *Jacobin*, September 20, 2018; Eve Cervantes quotation: Andrew Chang, "The MeToo McDonald's Movement Is Marching On," *Ms. Magazine*, December 11, 2019.

Labor: Studies in Working-Class History, Volume 19, Issue 1
DOI 10.1215/15476715-9475730   © 2022 by Labor and Working-Class History Association

Battling Sexual Harassment and Violence in the Workplace: The Long View

Women workers in the United States have organized against sexual harassment, unwanted touching, and full-on sexual violence in the workplace from the nineteenth century to the present. The odds have mostly been against them, resulting in long periods when little was done. But there have also been moments when the issue has attracted broad attention and sparked hope that progress was being made. These moments when change seemed possible have come at times when nationwide women's movements were actively exerting pressure on corporations, unions, and courts—when poor and working women had support from the educated and affluent.

Women workers have long understood that unions were troubled vehicles for pursuing charges of sexual harassment in the workplace. Union leaders were (and for the most part still are) half-hearted about investigating charges of harassment in their own organizations. Because many sexual misconduct suits brought by women workers have highlighted harassment of union members by other union members, labor leaders have often been reluctant to investigate sexual misconduct and even more squeamish about punishing their own.[1]

While campaigns in individual workplaces have been successful, and while some power brokers—from Hollywood mogul Harvey Weinstein to McDonald's CEO Steve Easterbrook—have recently lost their jobs as a result of their predatory behavior, the climate for women workers remains fraught. As recently as 2015, one in four women workers reported experiencing sexual harassment on the job. And that percentage is much higher among the more than 13 million women, mostly women of color, who perform low-wage jobs.[2]

In part, as a result of the #MeToo movement, by 2021 there was growing momentum behind the idea that sexual harassment and violence in the workplace is not only illegal (in many cases) but also morally unacceptable. Still, low-wage women workers and their allies remain divided about how best to challenge this behavior. This article looks at two moments—in the second decades of the twentieth and twenty-first centuries, when groups of women workers decided to deploy the most fraught and most powerful expression of workers' discontent: the strike. In the 1910s and then again in the 2010s, groups of low-wage women workers used the tactic of strikes to exert pressure on employers who actively engaged in, or did little to stop, sexual harassment and sexual violence in the workplace.

There are clear differences between the two eras and the two strikes. The early twentieth century was a time of rapid and militant expansion of trade unionism in the garment industry. The 1912 Kalamazoo corset makers' strike described below came in the middle of a decade of women's strikes involving hundreds of thousands

1. Lerner, "Women's Rights and American Feminism," 244.

2. "Testimony of Fatima Goss Graves, Vice President of the National Women's Law Center," US Equal Employment Opportunity Commission hearing on *Preventing and Addressing Workplace Harassment,* January 14, 2015, www.eeoc.gov/meetings/meeting-january-14-2015-workplace-harassment/graves.

of garment workers. The era was also a time when sexual harassment and coercion in the shops was widely viewed as an issue that was not appropriate to address via strikes or labor-management negotiations. Similarly, the grassroots of the immigrant women's labor movement had not yet begun to embrace African American workers or racial justice issues. Immigrant leaders such as Leonora O'Reilly (a founder of the NAACP) were already speaking out about commonalities between ethnic, religious, and national oppression facing immigrant workers and the ravages of white supremacy and racism in the United States. However, the 1909–19 women's strike wave involved a largely white immigrant workforce. Interactions and collaborations between immigrant women on the shop floor and African American women workers would not really begin for another decade.

The strike, as a tactic, changed significantly from the 1910s to the 2010s. In the 1910s, strikes were used as a direct pressure tactic intended to bring employers to the bargaining table by making them feel financial pain resulting from long-term halts in manufacturing. But precisely because such strikes could drag on for weeks or months, they also brought pain and food insecurity to workers and their families, sometimes resulting in long-term unemployment.

By the twenty-first century, service work had supplanted manufacturing as the primary growth sector in the United States, and the labor movement was on life support. Union membership had been dropping for at least three decades. After 2010, antiunion "right to work" laws were passing state legislatures even in former union strongholds like Michigan and Wisconsin. Old-line male-dominated trade unions still existed, but the energy of the labor movement had shifted to public sector unions, many of them comprising primarily women of color.

The 2010s were also the #MeToo era, a decade when millions of women had begun anew to express disgust and anger at the sexual harassment and violence so many were subjected to—in schools, on public transportation, and in the workplace. The 2018–19 strike wave against sexual harassment described below was launched by fast-food workers, hotel housekeepers, and janitors—a workforce that was and is majority women of color. Unlike the first strike wave, these labor actions (and the Fight for $15 movement which nurtured them) were inextricable from the Black Lives Matter movement—conceived and driven by Black women activists and taken up by young people across the United States in 2020.

Their choice to use the strike in 2018 to highlight endemic sexual harassment in their workplaces was supported not only by the Service Employees International Union (SEIU) but also by the Time's Up Legal Defense Fund, established by Hollywood actresses whose own experiences with sexual violence in the workplace had moved them to speak out and to provide legal support to working-class women facing the same kinds of harassment. And unlike the earlier strikes, which could drag on for weeks or even months, these were a new kind of strike—the "flash strike" taking place in many cities at once, part of a series of successive actions, not dependent on professional media coverage but self-publicized via cell phone videos and social media posts, and usually lasting just one day at a time. This was often enough to make the points that workers wanted made and to tarnish expensively publicized corporate brands without costing workers their jobs or paychecks.

There were, of course, some fundamental similarities between these two strike waves a century apart. In both eras, the lowest-paid, most disfranchised women workers, members of ethnic and racial minority groups, facing desperation, rose up in ways that sometimes cost them jobs that were all that stood between their families and dire poverty, homelessness, and hunger. In each era, they summoned up more than they or their employers knew they had in them. And in each era they helped to change the national conversation about a very thorny issue—that there is not a workplace where, as Pauline Newman put it, the same immoral condition does not exist. This was as true in 2018 as in 1912.

Sexual Harassment and Women's Labor in the Progressive Era

By spring 1912, the eight hundred workers at Michigan's Kalamazoo Corset Company were growing restless. A year earlier, after the owner announced sudden wage cuts, speedups, and more, Kalamazoo's corset makers had made up their minds to unionize. Most of them were young women, infuriated by the roving hands and eyes of company foremen. So to everyone's surprise, both in the International Ladies' Garment Workers' Union (ILGWU) and in company executive suites, the corset makers painstakingly organized a union, ILGWU Local 82. It was no small feat for this very young, female workforce. Homer Waterman, a resident of Kalamazoo and General Secretary of the Michigan Federation of Labor was impressed by the militance of these new trade unionists. But he was also shocked by their youth. He would report incredulously to ILGWU Secretary John Dyche that one of the corset makers arrived on roller skates to pay her union dues.[3]

Like so many strikes in the 1910s, a decade of "girls' uprisings" in the US garment industry, the Kalamazoo corset makers were definitely little Davidas rising up against an industrial Goliath. The Kalamazoo Corset Company (KCC) was the world's biggest corset maker. It was also Kalamazoo's largest employer, the economic engine of a midwestern industrial town of about forty-three thousand.[4] KCC was known for its Madame Grace and American Beauty corsets. Instead of using whalebone to cinch in women's waists, these fashionable corsets were lined by very light "featherbones," made from turkey feathers. This innovative technology made the company a global success and probably extended the life of the hated corset for a few decades by making new corsets that were infinitely more comfortable than the older whalebone variety. Because Kalamazoo was so small and KCC so relatively large, its owner, James Hatfield, was connected to every level of Kalamazoo's elite, making it difficult for the union corset makers to find a sympathetic ear anywhere in town.[5]

3. Mason, "Feeling the Pinch."

4. US Department of Commerce, Bureau of the Census, *Estimates of Population 1910, 1911, 1912, 1913, 1914.*

5. Scott, "Kalamazoo Corset Company."

On March 2, 1912, the corset makers, over the vociferous objection of everyone older and wiser in the union, voted to strike. (Such expressions of concern by male labor leaders and middle-class women allies was also the norm in that era of "girls' strikes.") The Kalamazoo corset makers were moved to take this serious action when the contract they had negotiated a year earlier, on forming their union, came up for renewal. The company fired the twelve workers most active in organizing the union. Management then rejected the proposed contract, which was very similar to the one they had agreed to one year earlier. And the owner threatened to close up shop and move the factory to Dearborn, which would have cost hundreds of women their jobs and forced the union to organize from the ground up—all over again. Plus, the threat made the union look bad in a town where the corset company, directly or indirectly, kept food on the tables of thousands.[6]

When the workers walked out on March 2, both the union and the press referred to the strike as "spontaneous." Anyone reviewing contemporaneous press coverage of the many mass women's strikes from 1909–19 will find that word often: *spontaneous*. The 1909–10 general strike of dress- and waist-makers, the so-called "Uprising of the 20,000" in New York City, was described by the socialist newspaper the *New York Call* as a "spontaneous overflow of abuse and exhaustion." Similar language was used to describe the Philadelphia dressmakers' uprising in 1910, as well as women garment workers' strikes in Boston and Cleveland in 1910 and 1911, and now Kalamazoo. Six hundred workers joined the Kalamazoo strike within two days of the strike vote. Like the allegedly spontaneous 1955 Montgomery Bus Boycott, in which thousands of leaflets were delivered to prospective boycotters by the next morning, everything about this strike indicated careful planning over an extended period of time. Rosa Parks did not suddenly decide to sit down on the bus. Nor did the corset makers walk out spontaneously. Still, no one besides the corset makers and Homer Waterman, self-described "father and mother" of the corset union, seemed able to imagine that anything but an emotional girls' outburst had started the strike.[7]

But this strike, like so many other "girls' strikes" of that era, was a slow burn, with a careful plan. It was not only about sexual harassment—not at all. Wage cuts. Dangerous conditions. Being forced to endure filth at a level that even the very poor—who lived in conditions that were difficult, even crushing—could not abide. It wasn't just that the washrooms were "filthy." It was that they had to share towels in the washrooms with men sporting "loathsome sores" that eroded their sense of dignity and self-possession. And all of that was crystallized, summed up, by a day-to-day environment in which bosses asked workers to trade sex for subsistence. And in some ways even worse, they were asked to trade sex for hope, for ambition, for the desire to have a measure of success.

The young corset makers understood that the best jobs were reserved for those workers who submitted to sexual advances. They knew that foremen offered

6. Mason, "Feeling the Pinch"; Scott, "Kalamazoo Corset Company."
7. Mason, "Feeling the Pinch"; Orleck, *Common Sense*, 53–87.

to forget the fees that workers were charged for the thread they used in making the corsets—if a worker gave something to the foreman, or to the boss. Fees for thread? This was the forerunner of the gig economy that we have now. Garment workers had to pay for everything they needed to make a garment. They were paid for piece-work, which meant that garment workers had to pay for the thread they used to sew, the electricity they used to run their machines. They had to bring their own sewing machines—to the largest corset manufacturer in the world.

Would it make life easier if you had sex with the foreman? Sure it would. If you had a promotion, if you just didn't have to pay for thread and electricity, you just might make it on one job. It might be a little less grinding to earn a living. A woman doctor hired by the cross-class women's progressive labor organization, the National Women's Trade Union League (WTUL), found that many of the workers at Kalamazoo had sexually transmitted diseases. Their work, and the pressure to have sex with foremen and bosses, was literally making them sick. So that's why they struck. Because that felt so wrong, so soul corrupting.

Only a union might change their conditions. But KCC was threatening to leave town if the union kept pushing. Leaving was worth it to Hatfield, the owner, if it would break the union, if he could leave union workers behind. The ILGWU played the issue lightly. They didn't talk about transactional sex. They highlighted degraded "moral conditions."

The Boston Women's Trade Union League (WTUL) activist and former organizer of streetcar conductors, Josephine Casey, was sent to Kalamazoo by the ILGWU. She had been living and working in New York City at that time, but she still carried the air of a "native" American. Raised in Tennessee, though her parents were Irish immigrants, she almost fit in, because the Irish by this time were American enough, white enough. The ILGWU sent Casey to Kalamazoo, some speculated, because the corset company strike was being waged by "an entirely American element." Those were the words of the first woman organizer for the ILGWU, the Lithuanian Jewish immigrant Pauline Newman. Later, toward the end of the battle, she would be sent in to handle the strike negotiations. But at first the union thought someone softer, more Christian, more "American" would work better.[8]

Casey came, and she was impressed by the spirit and militance of the strikers. "This is a strike for our rights and I'm going to stand by you to the end," she assured the strikers. And she did until she was jailed. Then the union sent Gertrude Barnum, and then Newman to negotiate a settlement.

Casey ended up jailed because Hatfield obtained several court injunctions against picketing. Seeking ways around the court order, Casey urged the picketers not to be "disorderly" but instead to engage in prayer and silent meditation. It was a novel mode of labor unrest, and it earned the strikers nationwide headlines. They sang hymns and knelt in a line when strikebreakers tried to enter the factory. The strik-

---

8. Pauline M. Newman to Rose Schneiderman, February 22, March 5, April 14, July 11, 1912, Papers of the NYWTUL; see also Mason, "Kalamazoo Corset Company."

ers did everything they could think of to protest while not violating the injunction. They held dances to raise money for the strike fund. They held a parade, attended by masons and bricklayers and other union men who wanted to show their support for the striking corset makers. On March 30, 2012, fifteen hundred union workers marched in this parade through the center of town.[9]

The court mandate that the Kalamazoo corset makers must not be "disorderly" evokes the reflections of Jacqueline Dowd Hall in her field-changing 1986 article about the Elizabethton, Tennessee, textile mill strike of 1929, seventeen years after Kalamazoo. As Hall put it: "Instances of female militancy were seen and not seen. Because they contradicted conventional wisdom they were easily dismissed." Hall insisted that we understand the "venerable tradition of disorderly women, women who in times of political upheaval, embody tensions that are half conscious or only dimly understood." Hall urged us to go beyond easy categorizations, to take a closer look "at women's distinctive forms of collective action, using language and gesture as points of entry to a culture." The Kalamazoo strike demands that of us.[10]

At first glance, Josephine Casey wasn't the obvious "disorderly woman." One Kalamazoo reporter described her as "cultured, broadminded and refined . . . a type distinctly different from the anarchic strike leading individual so often pictured as a trades union leader." Her parents were Irish immigrants but, because she grew up in Tennessee, she had an accent that the reporter found "charming." She was legible, as the Jewish male union leaders in the ILGWU knew she would be, and as the tie-wearing, gender-ambiguous Pauline Newman, the other female ILGWU organizer at that moment, just would not be. Could not be.[11]

Casey would, unlike Newman a decade hence, support an Equal Rights Amendment to the Constitution, arguing that laws aimed only at women or at male workers were inherently wrong. In that last decade before the Nineteenth Amendment gave women across the United States the right to vote, Casey both thought in terms of "women's issues" and believed that laws must be gender neutral, that any law, for example laws mandating a minimum wage for women workers but not for men, must be eliminated in favor of gender-neutral laws that conferred rights based on citizenship—on citizenship alone, regardless of sex or gender.[12]

Casey wrote about the Kalamazoo strike in a 1912 letter to the *Detroit Times*: "We are fighting to purify the factory, to bring about the dismissal of the foreman and those male employees who have been continually insulting the girl employees, and who have been dragging not a few of them down to ruin. The time has passed when an employer can expect to hold girl employees who are subjected to indignities."[13]

9. Mason, "Feeling the Pinch."
10. Hall, "Disorderly Women."
11. Mason, "Feeling the Pinch," 143.
12. Tash, "Biographical Sketch of Josephine Casey, 1876–1950."
13. Casey, "Letter from Prison."

Casey hoped that by making appeals to feminine injury and moral decline, the corset makers would win the sympathy of the middle-class clubwomen of Kalamazoo. But that is not what happened. Part of the problem for middle-class Kalamazoo clubwomen may have been that in such a basically small town, "respectable" women and the corset factory owner and his family traveled in the same social circles. Spreading "dirt" about the company managers did not go over well with the Kalamazoo "smart set."

The ILGWU newspaper, the *Ladies' Garment Worker*, understood that. In a May 1912 article titled "12 Jailed for Exposing Kalamazoo Firm's Sins" the union journal argued that when Casey and eleven other strike organizers were jailed for violating the court injunction against picketing even though the pickets were silent, or hymn singing, or sitting and meditating rather than chanting, marching, and carrying signs, the judge's decision was not based on actual law. No, said the union. They were jailed not for violating the injunction against picketing but for "unearthing a vicious system by which capitalist enterprise escaped the payment of just wages by subjecting the girls in their employ to shame and dishonor." That was, the union argued, "just too much for the city and state to admit." It was "not so much the picketing for which the brave strikers were sentenced as for the manner in which they brought a scandalous and shameful situation of shame and filth and syphilitic disease before the public, for which managers and superintendents of the Kalamazoo corset company were directly responsible."[14]

Was the *Ladies' Garment Worker* correct? Had it been shocking that Casey and the corset makers decided to expose sexual harassment as endemic in their factory labors? Were most people not aware of just how widespread this sort of exploitation of low-wage women workers was? Not according to Pauline Newman, who would be sent in later that spring by the ILGWU to take over for Casey. "[In] the cloak factories and all other shops in the city of New York and Chicago, every one of the men will talk to the girls, take advantage of them if the girls will let them. The foremen and the superintendent will flirt with the girls. . . . It is nothing new for those who know it exists everywhere." From what I've seen, different kinds of literature examining women in the workplace during that era openly discussed sexual harassment in industrial shops, as well as the power dynamics involved: in other words, the younger, poorer, less-skilled workers were most likely to face and bear such mistreatment.

Male employees, bosses, and supervisors thought "factory girls" were fair game because they were "low class," because they were cast out of the realm of respectable womanhood by their poverty and their need to venture into the public sphere to engage in paid industrial labor. One cigar maker told a state investigating committee in those years that "many men who would not under any circumstances offer the slightest insult or disrespectful remark or glance to a female in the streets . . .

---

14. *Ladies' Garment Worker*, "12 Jailed for Exposing Kalamazoo Firm's Sins."

in the shop will whoop and give . . . cat calls and a peculiar noise made with their lips which is supposed to be an endearing salutation."[15]

By the time that Casey and eleven strikers were jailed, they had shifted strike strategy several times. As strike energy waned in the face of injunctions, Casey sent some of the better speakers among the corset makers to travel through the Midwest to tell their stories, to detail the kinds of harassment they experienced, to try to win the hearts and minds of clubwomen in Chicago, Detroit, and other regional cities. The goal was to move them to pressure the company to settle.

"This is a fight for the womanhood of Kalamazoo" is how Casey framed the strike. But at least in Kalamazoo, few elite women were buying. One woman physician with a practice in Kalamazoo thought the strategy too transparent, yet at the same time too brazen. She wondered aloud why the issue of sexual harassment had not been emphasized from the beginning, which was why, to her it seemed more of a ploy than realistic. Then there was the question of airing dirty laundry, saying things not normally said in polite society. "If they had taken a more tactful stand," she wrote, "every mother in town would have been with them." And, unlike upper-class suffragists in larger cities who fought to win strikers for the woman suffrage cause, this Kalamazoo doctor thought it "pathetic" that the corset makers did not seem to "realize how much they need the right to vote."[16]

When Pauline Newman was sent in to lead the strike on June 4, she brought a mixed strategy. On the one hand, she came in ready for a fight. She bristled at the descriptions of the strike by one local journalist as becoming "more pinkteaish every day," a not-so-subtle sexist belittling of the quiet, religious picketing style adopted by the corset strikers to get around court injunctions. When Casey and other strikers were arrested in late April, ILGWU Secretary Dyche had bailed out the men and left the women in prison because he thought it would evoke both outrage and sympathy to know that such young women were languishing behind bars for asserting their rights. When the ILGWU sent in Gertrude Barnum on May 7 to take over for the jailed Casey, she urged the strikers to return to the picket lines but to "avoid disorder or threats of violence" to ensure that there would be no more arrests and to keep public opinion on their side. This play for support based on images of company, police, and courts abusing peaceable young women did not work, and the tough-talking Newman wanted no part of it.[17]

She arrived on June 4 and was given full control. Casey and Barnum headed back to New York. Newman promised that she would "make Kalamazoo lively." She began immediately. Handed a copy of the injunction against picketing by police

---

15. Peiss, *Cheap Amusements*, 50–51. Peiss is quoting a woman cigar-maker testifying at a hearing of the New York State Bureau of Labor Statistics in 1895. She also cites other literature from that time alluding to the issue of men harassing women industrial workers.

16. Casey, "Letter from Prison"; Mason, "Feeling the Pinch," 150–51.

17. Mason, "Feeling the Pinch," 152; Letter, Pauline M. Newman to Rose Schneiderman, April 4, June 9, July 11, 1912, Rose Schneiderman Collection, Papers of the NYWTUL and Its Principal Leaders, Tamiment Library, New York University.

as she stepped from her train, she ripped it up and handed it back. "I'm supposed to play the part of the diplomat when I'd rather be the fighter," she said, warning that no great fight was ever won "without some martyrs." She pulled the strikers back to the picket lines and, to their surprise and amusement, urged them to be as loud and militant as they wanted. Arrest orders for Newman were issued, but because she was new to town, no one knew what she looked like, and police were flummoxed in their attempts to haul her to jail.[18]

Newman's friend and colleague in the New York WTUL, Irish immigrant dressmaker Leonora O'Reilly, supported the idea of highlighting sexual harassment as a driving motivation for the strike. The workers were paid so little, and there were so few other options for jobs in Kalamazoo, she worried that the "wages of sin . . . are alluring." Newman echoed the ILGWU newspaper, arguing that making an issue of sexual harassment would make the company and town feel attacked, that KCC would refuse to negotiate.[19]

Interestingly, she never suggested that sexual harassment was not a problem for women workers. Writing Rose Schneiderman, her close friend, New York Women's Trade Union League leader and organizer for the hat and cap maker's union, Newman asserted that the very ubiquity of such harassment made it hard to see and hard to fight using conventional union strategies. "[In] the cloak factories and all other shops in the city of New York and Chicago, every one of the men will talk to the girls, take advantage of the girls if they will let them." The problem, she wrote Schneiderman, can be best handled by "educating the girls."

Why would the tough socialist Jewish immigrant from Lithuania shy away from incorporating the issue of sexual harassment into her union work? She was the woman organizer who famously wore ties, slicked back her hair, and became one of the boys, always ready—in the words of her younger colleague Leon Stein—to "smoke a cigar with the best of them." Precisely because it made her feel vulnerable, and because it highlighted the difference between Newman and male organizers, between women in the labor struggle and their male colleagues. And Newman always wanted to highlight strength.

Perhaps it was an attempt to erase her own vulnerability. At the time of the Kalamazoo strike, Newman was only twenty-one years old and had already become the first woman hired to organize for the ILGWU. Single, lonely, she had been sent to wander the country for several years, organizing and supporting strikes. She herself had been sexually harassed by one of the most powerful men in her own union, John Dyche, and had chosen not to make a public issue of it. In 1911, after the Triangle Shirtwaist Factory fire, she sank into a deep depression, unable for a time to work or travel. Homesickness and cheap hotels full of predatory men overwhelmed the young organizer. When she returned to the struggle in Kalamazoo, she was more

18. Letter, Newman to Schneiderman; Mason, "Feeling the Pinch," 154; Orleck, *Common Sense*, 72–73.
19. O'Reilly, "The Story of Kalamazoo," 228.

determined than ever to present an image of strength. She did not want to muddy the morally clear battleground of class struggle with images of helpless women, prey to sexual predators. Newman presented herself as bulletproof, invulnerable—likely covering her own insecurities with bravado—but unshakeable in her belief that presenting strength and courage was the only way for women to succeed in the labor movement. And she portrayed them that way in all of her writings in those years—for the socialist and labor press.[20]

In the end, neither Casey's nor Newman's strategies really worked in Kalamazoo. Three and a half months after the strike began, corset company officials offered a contract that the union had already rejected. They promised to hire union workers back but individually, not as a group, and not necessarily to their old jobs. They promised a minimum wage of $5 weekly after twelve weeks on the job, a slight, insignificant wage increase. And KCC offered to create a "joint board" of manufacturer's representatives, union appointees and health officials to investigate dangerous conditions. The workers did not want to accept the contract, but Michigan labor leaders and John Dyche pushed them to vote yes. When they did, just barely, approve the contract, Leonora O'Reilly mourned that "the corset manufacturer has succeeded in getting everything and the worker takes all the humiliation." When the company did not abide even by this unsatisfactory agreement, the strikers returned to a traditional woman's strategy, launching a boycott of KCC corsets. After two years, they won a pyrrhic victory, driving the company out of business and costing hundreds of women their jobs. "There is no peace," O'Reilly concluded. And there would not be another strike against sexual harassment for more than a century.

#MeToo McDonald's: Battling #McSexualViolence and #McShame in the Twenty-First Century

> "Employees should not have to endure violation of their humanity and bodily autonomy as the price of earning a paycheck."
> —Eve Cervantes, 2019

A full century after Kalamazoo, women workers at McDonald's walked off their jobs in ten cities, during the lunchtime rush to create maximum disruption of the burger giant's business. Hungry consumers hoping for a Big Mac and fries instead found women workers picketing in front of McDonald's stores across San Francisco, Los Angeles, Miami, New Orleans, Orlando, Chicago, Detroit, St. Louis, Durham, and Kansas City. Some chanted "End McShame" or "End McSexual Violence." Some carried signs that said: "McDonald's, Hands Off My Buns." But many of the picketers— like those so long ago in Kalamazoo—made no sound at all. Instead they covered their mouths with blue masking tape emblazoned with the words *#MeToo*. The tape,

20. Letter, Newman to Schneiderman, February 22, 1912, NYWTUL Papers; Orleck, *Common Sense*, 72–73.

the women told me later, signified attempts by their shift managers, store managers, and the McDonald's Corporation to silence them after they tried to come forward with complaints of sexual harassment on the job.[21]

From 2016 to 2019, McDonald's workers had filed fifty suits against the company with the Equal Employment Opportunity Commission (EEOC), alleging that sexual harassment, sexual violence, and verbal abuse were everyday occurrences on the job. And when workers complained, they said they were silenced by managers who cut their hours, verbally abused them in front of customers and colleagues, or gave them work schedules that were so obviously inconvenient (especially employing split shifts) that the workers had little choice but to "put up and shut up" or quit.[22]

What these twenty-first-century women workers experienced was no more anomalous than the sexual harassment that Pauline Newman found so common in 1912. Restaurant workers file more claims of sexual harassment than workers in any other profession. One study publicized by *BuzzFeed* found that 90 percent of women and 70 percent of men working in restaurants across the United States had been sexually harassed—by shift supervisors, restaurant owners, other workers, and customers.[23] Still, says attorney Eve Cervantez, who has represented McDonald's workers in sexual harassment suits since 2015: "McDonald's is among fast food's worst offenders when it comes to protecting the workers who make the company's success possible."[24]

One of the lead organizers in Michigan, a McDonald's worker from Flint named Cortez Clerk, came to feel that she could no longer accept corporate silencing. That decision cost her the job she desperately needed. Her supervisor liked to trap her in the narrow space between the cash register and the grill, touch her all over, and shove pictures of his genitals in front of her eyes. Other workers talked about being trapped in similar spots by harassing supervisors—or being followed into the bathrooms and assaulted. "McDonald's monitors everything we do, from how fast the drive-through is moving to how we fold our customers' bags," she said, when she joined an EEOC suit in May 2018. "Yet when I filed a complaint against my shift manager for regularly harassing me . . . McDonald's had no response." In the end, says Clerk, she had no option but to quit. "I really needed that job and the money and I considered remaining silent." But the stress was too much. She was actually surprised to find that McDonald's corporate did not "have my back," she said. She had thought that problem was with her franchise. She believed that McDonald's was serious about its corporate policy of "zero tolerance for sexual harassment." She soon realized that the problem of sexual harassment and unwanted touching at McDonald's was systemic, that it was about the power imbalance between workers and supervisors in McDonald's stores across the country.[25]

21. Orleck, "Me Too and McDonald's."
22. Orleck, "Me Too and McDonald's."
23. Garza, "Restaurant Workers File More Sexual Harassment Claims."
24. Chang, "MeToo McDonald's Movement Is Marching On."
25. Orleck, "Me Too and McDonald's."

Folsom, California, worker Kristi Maisenbach also joined the EEOC complaint that brought twenty-five charges of sexual harassment against McDonald's and then helped organize the September 2018 strike. Maisenbach too experienced unwanted touching. Her manager grabbed her breasts and rubbed his genitals against her—again trapping her in the small space where most front-of-the-house McDonald's workers spend all of their work time, between the cash registers, the grill, and the fryers. When Maisenbach complained to the store manager, her hours were cut so severely that she had no choice but to quit and find another job. It was a question of keeping a roof over her family's heads.[26]

The one-day, multicity strike against sexual harassment at McDonald's was in keeping with the strategy of one-day "flash strikes" that has been employed by the Fight for $15 movement since 2012. Because most fast-food workers in the United States live very close to the margins, many of them forced to hold two or even three jobs to pay their bills, the living wage movement among fast-food and retail workers has stayed away from long, drawn-out strikes that can do more harm to workers than to management.

This is especially true when the employers that workers are seeking concessions from are global giants like McDonald's, the second-largest private employer in the world, and Walmart, the largest. Both companies have majority women-of-color workforces and majority male (often white male) managers. According to workers like Walmart former assistant managers Venanzi Luna and Denise Barlage, Walmart builds sexual harassment and physical intimidation into their disciplinary procedures. "They call you into the manager's office and have a big guy stand over a small woman." The managers use loud voices, intimidating tones, belittling language like *little girl*, or *honey*, or *sweetheart*, and often put their hands on the worker being "coached"—Walmart terminology for discipline. Once the Organization United for Respect at Walmart began its campaign in 2012, workers began demanding that another woman come into the office with them, which is their right. The Walmart strikers received international coverage for hosting the first strike against a North American Walmart in 2012 and again in intervening years. But most of those counseling other women to demand this right have been fired since the movement began.[27]

The historic nature of the 2018 McDonald's strike against sexual harassment drew extensive press coverage—even from foreign press. Workers demanded that the burger giant strengthen and enforce its stated zero-tolerance policy for sexual harassment, begin mandatory training for both managers and employees, create a streamlined system for receiving and responding to complaints with a clear timeline for action, and protect workers from retaliation. Workers also demanded the creation of a modern-day "joint board" of workers, corporate executives, and representatives

26. Orleck, "Me Too and McDonald's."

27. Author's interview with Venanzi Luna, Pico, Rivera, CA, September 9, 2015; author's phone interviews with Denise Barlage, September 9, 2015, January 18, 2017, cited in Orleck, *We Are All Fast-Food Workers Now.*

of feminist organizations and franchise reps to design and implement policies to keep women workers safe.[28]

The lead organizers of the September 2018 strike and subsequent strikes and suits were the same ten women (from ten different cities) who were lead plaintiffs in a series of EEOC complaints and lawsuits. They had met in the spring of 2018 at a McDonald's shareholder meeting where they had gone to tell their stories. Talking to each other led them to understand that this was a systemic rather than an individual issue, and they began gathering stories from their ten cities and launching committees of women workers in each city who became the backbone of the strike.

They began to conduct sexual harassment trainings at stores across their cities. They also began a database of sexual harassment and violence stories. They convened online gatherings to enlist women consumers to support the strikers, produced *Know Your Rights* pamphlets, and set up a worker sexual abuse hotline. McDonald's initially hired the firm Seyfarth Shaw, which represented Harvey Weinstein and Kay Jewelers in their sexual harassment/assault cases. Strikers successfully pressured them to cut ties with that firm. McDonald's announced that they would instead hire the Rape, Abuse and Incest National Network (RAINN), a highly respected consortium of experts on sexual violence and sexual harassment. Certainly the idea of hiring them was more credible than using Harvey Weinstein's firm, but it is not clear that anything came of that plan. In any case, the problem continued to worsen across the country.[29]

In May 2019, the ACLU and Fight for $15 filed twenty-three charges of sexual harassment against McDonald's: twenty EEOC complaints and three civil rights lawsuits. Some were paid for by the Time's Up Legal Defense Fund, which was created after the Harvey Weinstein story broke and is housed at the National Women's Law Center. The fund, created by Hollywood actresses to support working-class people seeking to forward sexual harassment cases, received just under five thousand requests for legal assistance from low-wage women workers. The largest share were McDonald's workers. McDonald's corporate executives responded as they long had regarding worker complaints about workplace safety, wage theft, and inconsistent scheduling. Like so many corporations in the age when so many workers are purposely misclassified as "independent contractors," McDonald's tried to shield itself by saying that the corporation dealt with franchise owners and these owners were the actual employers of frontline McDonald's workers. So the responsibility fell on them to combat sexual harassment in their shops. The workers brought the case before the National Labor Relations Board, and in 2016 the Obama administration's National Labor Relations Board (NLRB) ruled that McDonald's corporate and local franchise

28. Orleck, "Me Too and McDonald's"; Whitten, "McDonald's Employees Stage First #MeToo Strike"; Colyar, "Sexual Harassment Strikes against McDonald's"; Silva, "McDonald's Workers Go on Strike"; Elsesser, "McDonald's Are Striking over Sexual Harassment."

29. Orleck, "Me Too and McDonald's"; Shaban, "McDonald's Employees Say 'Time's Up'"; Ryczik, "In Test of Their Power, #MeToo's Legal Forces Take on McDonald's."

owners were in fact joint employers. The first attempt by the Trump administration's NLRB to overturn this ruling failed because Trump's appointee to the board had to recuse himself, as he was one of the lawyers who argued on the McDonald's Corporation's side in the 2016 case.[30]

In November 2019, McDonald's CEO Steve Easterbrook, who had made all sorts of promises to strengthen the burger giant's sexual harassment and unwanted touching policies, was fired by the company's board of directors for lying to the board about his own coercive physical relationships with three of his employees and for sending nude photos of his employees to his personal accounts.

That same month, the ACLU filed a class-action lawsuit against McDonald's for "a systemic problem" of sexual harassment in its restaurants across the country. Jennie Ries, a former employee, was one of the lead plaintiffs. "I lived in constant fear of losing my job because I didn't want to be treated like trash and because I didn't give in to my harasser's disgusting behavior," she explained. She and other plaintiffs took a photo of themselves wearing blue tape over their mouths emblazoned with the words *#MeToo*.

Eve Cervantez, who has represented McDonald's workers in their suits, echoes a sentiment that many expressed in the Progressive Era, in years after the 1911 Triangle fire: "Employees should not have to endure a violation of their humanity and bodily autonomy as the price of earning a paycheck." Plaintiffs in the suit are, in the words of Sanford, Florida, McDonald's worker and sexual harassment survivor Jamelia Farley, "demanding McDonald's new CEO sit down with worker survivors and hear our stories. McDonald's needs to let survivors and our advocates drive the solution. Nothing is going to change for us without us."[31]

In December 2019, a newly constituted, Trump-dominant NLRB ruled that McDonald's corporation is not responsible for wages, hours, conditions, or sexual harassment in individual franchise restaurants. What will happen to the cases currently before the NLRB now rests in the hands of a Biden NLRB which, while friendlier to labor than the Trump NLRB, in October 2021 failed to acknowledge McDonald's as a "joint employer." Meanwhile, the cases and the activism move forward, continuing a historic struggle that began in Kalamazoo 107 years earlier.[32]

That same month, #MeTooMcDonald's activists disrupted an Executives' Club of Chicago Best Practices Roundtable on Talent Retention, led by the company's vice president, Melanie Steinbach. The putative purpose of the roundtable was to help executives better understand how to keep employees content and productive. One worker survivor spoke out at the event: "While McDonald's is telling people how to 'manage culture' to keep their workers happy on the job, cooks and cashiers are being sexually harassed in your stores on a regular basis. And, more often than not,

30. Elejalde-Ruiz, "Why Should McDonald's Be a Joint Employer?"; Iafolla and Wiessner, "NLRB Judge Breaks Up McDonald's Joint Employment Cases."

31. Chang, "#MeToo McDonald's Movement Is Marching On."

32. Selyukh, "NLRB Says McDonald's Not Responsible for Franchisees."

when we report the harassment, we're dismissed, made fun of, our hours are cut, or we're forced to quit."

Her words echoed a statement that was part of an op-ed that had appeared one day earlier in *USA Today* on #MeToo and "Managing Culture." In the op-ed, endorsed by the ACLU, Color of Change, and the National Women's Law Center, workers argued that "McDonald's has repeatedly failed to keep its workers, many of them women of color, safe from groping, lewd comments and worse." Sixty members of the US Congress and 115 local and state officials also signed a letter to McDonald's leadership urging them to finally live up to its stated goal of "zero tolerance for sexual harassment."[33]

In the responses of McDonald's, Walmart, and other major employers facing charges of allowing and even encouraging sexual harassment of low-wage workers as a means of instilling fear and submissiveness, we have seen echoes of Pauline Newman's short-sighted comment that the problem can be solved "by educating the girls." The workers of #MeTooMcDonald's and United for Respect at Walmart have educated themselves about corporate responsibility codes and their legal rights. Sadly, Josephine Casey's assertion that the time is past when employers can hold on to employees who are subject to harassment still does not ring true a century later.

Still, sexual harassment has become an issue integral to labor organizing in the twenty-first century. Indeed, when I conducted interviews for my 2018 book, *We Are All Fast-Food Workers Now: The Global Uprising against Poverty Wages,* I heard again and again from workers that women's issues, and first and foremost sexual harassment and violence in the workplace, have been the driving force in sparking and sustaining the new global campaign for living wages, safety, and respect. Beyond McDonald's, the 2010s saw sustained and often successful organizing against sexual harassment and violence on the job in a range of low-wage workplaces.

One of the hallmarks of the twenty-first-century "gig economy" has been a fundamental transformation in what constitutes the working class. The erosion of the status of full-time employee and the rise of "independent contractors" has generated new kinds of working-class solidarity. So has the corporatization of academe. The 2010s saw highly educated workers such as adjunct professors and graduate students organizing for living wages and medical benefits and against sexual harassment alongside workers from low-wage service sector jobs such as fast food, home health care, and hotel housekeeping. In 2015, a history graduate student named Keegan Shepard explained why he had taken up organizing alongside fast-food and home health care workers. "We are all fast-food workers now," he said, outlining the many hours of free labor graduate students are told to perform weekly as part of their "education" requirements. Most of them, he said, earned little enough that they qualified for various forms of public assistance. In addition to the free labor graduate organizers call "wage theft," sexual harassment has been as big an issue for graduate students as

---

33. *USA Today,* "Managing Culture."

it has been for the McDonald's workers alongside whom they have been organizing over the past few years.[34]

In a 2017 hunger strike by the Yale Graduate Student Organization, student activists asserted that more than 58 percent of women graduate students at Yale had been subject to sexual harassment by professors, lab supervisors, and other students while attempting to fulfill teaching, research, and lab responsibilities. They wanted protections built into their union contracts. Yale, like NYU and other academic institutions, continues to resist recognizing the graduate student union and attempted to take advantage of the composition of the Trump NLRB to overturn an Obama-era NLRB decision recognizing graduate students as workers. The battle continues. Yale tried to shame the graduate students by publishing an editorial in the *Chronicle of Higher Education* calling the students spoiled and suggesting that they did not have the need or moral standing to adopt tactics employed by worker leaders such as Cesar Chavez and Dolores Huerta. Huerta quickly rejected such divide-and-conquer tactics and asserted her strong support for the graduate student union drive and for their anti-sexual-harassment campaign. (Women farm workers have been staging hunger strikes against sexual harassment in the fields for twenty years; in 2018 they struck in front of the offices of Wendy's board chair, in Manhattan.)[35]

Chicago's unionized hotel housekeepers launched a different kind of campaign resulting in a citywide ordinance, passed in 2017, named for their slogan "Hands Off, Pants On," mandating a range of measures to protect workers in an industry where between 40 percent and 75 percent (housekeepers), say they have been subject to unwanted touching and worse. When the bill went into effect in summer 2018, Karen Kent, president of UNITE-HERE Local 1 in Chicago, heralded "a new day for women working in Chicago hotels." California hotel workers have tried to get a similar bill passed statewide, so far without success, but local ordinances have been passed in Long Beach and Sacramento. A similar ordinance was passed in Miami Beach. And between 2012 and 2020, hotel union locals in New York City, Washington, DC, and Las Vegas built anti-sexual-harassment policies into their contracts. Increasingly the issue is becoming standard for hotel union negotiators as contracts come up for renewal.[36]

Domestic workers who labor in private homes—another workplace in which sexual harassment has long been endemic—have also had some success organizing to fight sexual harassment. They have succeeded in passing statewide Domestic Workers' Bills of Rights in New York, Hawaii, California, Massachusetts, Oregon, Con-

34. Author's interview with Keegan Shepard, Tampa, FL, March 25, 2015.

35. Milian, "Student Teachers at Yale on 'Indefinite' Hunger Strike"; Anderson, "23 Graduate Students Arrested as Yale Hunger Strike Continues"; Mack, "Yale Graduate Students Hold Peaceful Protest and End Hunger Strike"; Hungerford, "Why the Yale Hunger Strike Is Misguided"; Saha, "Too Privileged to Protest?"; Orleck, *We Are All Fast-Food Workers Now*, 90–91; Coalition of Immokalee Workers, "National Faith Leaders Announce Major Wendy's Boycott, Fast and Action."

36. Mullin, "Panic Button Laws Make Their Way across the U.S."; Boesch and Frye, "Driving Change in States."

Figure 1. Protesters outside McDonald's restaurant near Times Square, New York City, October 6, 2016. Spencer Platt / Getty Images.

necticut, Illinois, and Nevada. These bills have mandated "special cause of action" rules for workers facing sexual harassment or racial discrimination from employers, as well as overtime pay and a day of rest each week.[37]

Workers at Big Tech firms—including Uber, Lyft, Google, Microsoft, Facebook, and Airbnb—have forced management to enact changes in how they deal with charges of sexual harassment. Most important among these has been an end to forced arbitration contracts limiting what workers can say publicly about their experiences with sexual harassment. As at McDonald's, the issue of sexual harassment caused Uber's former CEO, Travis Kalanick, to step down. A number of these firms have agreed to worker demands to release annual reports on the number of sexual harassment charges they've faced and how they have handled these cases. And Uber, a company with one of the worst rates of sexual harassment charges—of customers by employees, and of employees by managers—has committed $5 million over five years to developing programs to improve their workplace culture.[38]

The movement against sexual harassment and violence on the job is not limited to the United States. In Bangladesh, Cambodia, and the Philippines, women garment, fast-food, and hotel workers have taken courageous stands against shop owners and government officials to protest sexual violence on the job. In Manila, women activists in the progressive union confederation SENTRO have staged repeated street demonstrations in which they have named names of offenders seeking to embarrass them and build momentum for legislation that streamlines reporting and disciplinary procedures. This has continued even under the violent authoritarian regime of Rodrigo Duterte and even as labor activists are being assassinated by police and government-affiliated paramilitaries. In Dhaka, Bangladesh, and Phnom Penh, Cambodia, garment workers are engaging in "consciousness-raising groups" that run for weeks and slowly build workers' confidence and courage to name names of bosses

37. Boesch and Frye, "Driving Change in States."
38. Boesch and Frye, "Driving Change in States."

who are assaulting or harassing them on the shop floor. And in the Western Cape wine country of South Africa, the 2010s saw similar organizing. One major goal for the global movement is an International Labor Organization convention mandating zero tolerance for sexual violence or harassment in the workplace, which workers then try to get their national governments to ratify.[39]

Across the UK, strikes by thousands of McStrikers and university lecturers have highlighted sexual harassment, along with uncertain scheduling, low pay, and hours of unpaid labor each week, as primary issues. Melissa Evans, a leader of the November 2019 McStrike that rocked London, Bristol, Manchester, Plymouth, Brighton, Cardiff, Southampton, and Glasgow, argued that respect and decent treatment were as important to her as higher pay. "I had a breakdown from all the stress of the job," she said. "I had to take a leave for my mental health."

All of the stresses, the hours, fast turnaround, and injuries from hot grills were all part of her reason for leaving. But the verbal abuse and sexual harassment were the final factors. She believes that austerity politics has been "a war on poor people, a war on our families." Respect is as big an issue as money. And the right to work free from fear of sexual assault or harassment seems basic. "We get shouted at. We get disrespected. I don't go to work to be spoken to like a child," she said, or like a sexual plaything. In the course of her work, Melissa was visited by Labour MP Dawn Butler Brent, who argued: "It's about time we incorporate respect for women and our bodies into workplace policies."[40]

On a raw, wet, windy London November day, Jo Grady, president of the UCU, the UK union of college and university lecturers, told a group of McStrikers demanding an end to McSexualViolence and McShame, and mistreatment of women workers of color, that solidarity across professions and across classes was the only way to bring change in this intractable and ancient problem. "We are with you," she said, promising that university adjuncts and lecturers and even some tenure-line professors were in for the long haul on this issue. "When you walk a wet picket line, we walk a wet picket line." As the rain continued to fall on us all, I could almost feel the Kalamazoo strikers murmur in assent as they silently raised their fists.

. . . .

The McDonald's workers' campaign in 2018–19, like the Kalamazoo corset uprising in 1912, raises questions about the use of strikes as a weapon to fight sexual harassment and violence in the workplace. The strike was less controversial as a tactic in the early twentieth century than it has become in the twenty-first. Conversely, the Kalamazoo strikers were condemned by many in the labor movement for muddy-

39. Interviews by author, of Kalpona Akter (president of the Bangladesh Center for Worker Solidarity, Montreal, Canada, and Burlington, VT, 2016–18.); Em Atienza (SENTRO, Quezon City, Philippines, November 2015); and Vun Em (United Sisterhood Alliance, Phnom Penh, Cambodia, November 2015), December 2015–March 2018.
40. Orleck, "McStrike Comes to 10 Downing Street."

ing the clear waters of class struggle by introducing as a point of negotiation a work-place issue that everyone acknowledged was endemic but that most trade unionists at the time thought should only be discussed behind closed doors. By 2018, women in fast food angered by sexual harassment on the job had big unions such as SEIU and UNITE-HERE behind them, as well as a range of women's organizations.

In some ways, the strikes were successful in both eras. But the workers' victories were nominal. The final contract won by Kalamazoo corset makers was far less than they had demanded when the strike began. And because the company went out of business, they were soon without jobs at all. The McDonald's campaigns, and his own sexual misconduct, brought down CEO Steve Easterbrook and shamed the burger giant into hiring a widely respected consortium of sexual violence advocates to develop strategies for strengthening and enforcing its corporate code of conduct around sexual harassment.

Still, more than a century after the first US strikes against sexual harassment, the behavior remains normalized in myriad workplaces. Hitting the problem on all fronts, workers have amplified the power of strikes with legal lawsuits. The law certainly is more on workers' side than it was in 1912. Still, sexual harassment cases remain difficult to litigate and win. So in the end, the strike remains an important option for bringing the issue of sexual harassment and violence in the workplace from the shadows into the light, and into the realm of public discourse. As one McDonald's organizer told me in 2018, "If we get in between a customer and her Egg McMuffin, you're going to have a conversation." There are undoubtedly many more such conversations on the horizon. ◩

ANNELISE ORLECK is professor of history at Dartmouth College and founding copresident of Dartmouth's AAUP chapter. She is the author of five books and has published numerous articles on women's, poor people's, and labor movements in the United States. Among these are *Common Sense and a Little Fire: Women and Working-Class Politics in the United States* (1995); *Storming Caesars' Palace: How Black Mothers Fought Their Own War on Poverty* (2005); *Rethinking American Women's Activism* (2014) and *We Are All Fast-Food Workers Now: The Global Uprising against Poverty Wages* (2018). She is also coeditor of two books, including *The War on Poverty, 1964–1980: A New Grassroots History* (2011).

References

Anderson, Theo. "23 Graduate Students Arrested as Yale Hunger Strike Continues." *Salon,* May 21, 2017.

Boesch, Diana, and Jocelyn Frye. "Driving Change in States to Combat Sexual Harassment." *Center for American Progress,* January 15, 2019. www.americanprogress.org/issues /women/reports/2019/01/15/465100/driving-change-states-combat-sexual-harassment/.

Casey, Josephine. "Letter from Prison." *Detroit Times,* May 4, 1912.

Chang, Jonathan. "The MeToo McDonald's Movement Is Marching On." *Ms. Magazine,* December 11, 2019.

Coalition of Immokalee Workers. "National Faith Leaders Announce Major Wendy's Boycott, Fast and Action." *Coalition of Immokalee Workers* (blog), November 8, 2017. https://ciw-online.org/blog/2017/11/jan-18-faith-leader-fast/.

Colyar, Brock. "The Sexual Harassment Strikes against McDonald's Were Only the Beginning." *Ms. Magazine*, July 25, 2019.

Elejalde-Ruiz, Alexia. "Why Should McDonald's Be a Joint Employer? NLRB Starts to Provide Answers." *Chicago Tribune*, March 10, 2016. www.chicagotribune.com/business/ct-McDonald's-labor-case-0311-biz-20160310-story.html.

Elsesser, Kim. "McDonald's Are Striking over Sexual Harassment." *Forbes*, September 17, 2018.

Garza, Daniela. "Restaurant Workers File More Sexual Harassment Claims Than Employees of Any Other Industry." *Eater*, December 7, 2017.

Hall, Jacquelyn Dowd. "Disorderly Women: Gender and Labor Militancy in the Appalachian South." *Journal of American History* 73, no. 2 (1986): 354–82.

Hungerford, Amy. "Why the Yale Hunger Strike Is Misguided." *Chronicle of Higher Education*, May 9, 2017.

Iafolla, Robert, and Daniel Wiessner. "NLRB Judge Breaks Up McDonald's Joint Employment Cases." *Reuters Legal*, October 14, 2016. www.reuters.com/article/labor-McDonald's-idUSL1N1CK0AA.

Ladies' Garment Worker. "12 Jailed for Exposing Kalamazoo Firm's Sins." In *ILGWU New History: The Protocol Years, 1912–1915*, June 1912. www.marxists.org/subject/jewish/ilgwu-history/ilg-5.pdf, 1–3.

Lerner, Gerda. "Women's Rights and American Feminism." *American Scholar* 40, no. 2 (1971): 244.

Mack, Lori. "Yale Graduate Students Hold Peaceful Protest and End Hunger Strike." *WNPR*, May 22, 2017. www.wnpr.org/post/yale-graduate-students-hold-peaceful-protest-and-end-hunger-strike.

Mason, Karen M. "Feeling the Pinch: The Kalamazoo Corset Makers' Strike of 1912." In *To Toil the Livelong Day: America's Women at Work*, edited by Carol Groneman and Mary Beth Norton, 141–60. Ithaca, NY: Cornell University Press, 1987.

Milian, Gabriela. "Student Teachers at Yale on 'Indefinite' Hunger Strike." *ABC News*, May 1, 2017.

Mullin, Sheppard. "Panic Button Laws Make Their Way across the U.S." *Labor and Employment Law* (blog), May 9, 2019. www.jdsupra.com/legalnews/panic-button-laws-make-their-way-across-49238/.

Newman, Pauline. Letter to Rose Schneiderman. Papers of the New York Women's Trade Union League and Its Principal Leaders. February 22, March 5, April 4, April 14, June 9, July 11, 1912, University Microfilms.

O'Reilly, Leonora. "The Story of Kalamazoo." *Life and Labor* 2, no. 8 (1912): 228–30.

Orleck, Annelise. *Common Sense and a Little Fire: Women and Working-Class Politics in the United States, 1900–1965.* 1995; anniv. ed., Chapel Hill: University of North Carolina Press, 2017.

Orleck, Annelise. "McStrike Comes to 10 Downing Street." *Jacobin*, November 15, 2019.

Orleck, Annelise. "Me Too and McDonald's." *Jacobin*, September 20, 2018.

Orleck, Annelise. *We Are All Fast-Food Workers Now: The Global Uprising against Poverty Wages.* Boston: Beacon, 2018.

Peiss, Kathy. *Cheap Amusements: Working Women and Leisure in Turn-of-the-Century New York*. Philadelphia: Temple University Press, 1985.

Ryczik, Melena. "In Test of Their Power, #MeToo's Legal Forces Take on McDonald's." *New York Times*, May 21, 2019.

Saha, Poulomi. "Too Privileged to Protest?" *Chronicle of Higher Education*, May 21, 2017.

Scott, Beth. "Kalamazoo Corset Company." Kalamazoo Public Library, 1997, updated 2017. www.kpl.gov/local-history/kalamazoo-history/women/kalamazoo-corset-company-2/.

Selyukh, Alina. "NLRB Says McDonald's Not Responsible for Franchisees." *National Public Radio*, December 12, 2019. www.npr.org/2019/12/12/787126119/McDonald's-not-responsible-for-how-franchisees-treat-workers-u-s-agency-rules.

Shaban, Hamza. "McDonald's Employees Say 'Time's Up' in New Round of Sexual Harassment Complaints." *Washington Post*, May 21, 2019.

Silva, Daniela. "McDonald's Workers Go on Strike over Sexual Harassment." *NBC News*, September 18, 2018. www.nbcnews.com/news/us-news/mcdonald-s-workers-go-strike-over-sexual-harassment-n910656.

Tash, Delia. "Biographical Sketch of Josephine Casey, 1876–1950." *Biographical Dictionary of Militant Woman Suffragists, 1913–1920, Women and Social Movements Documents*. https://documents.alexanderstreet.com/d/1009995320 (accessed August 31, 2020).

USA Today. "Managing Culture." December 10, 2019.

US Department of Commerce, Bureau of the Census. *Estimates of Population 1910, 1911, 1912, 1913, 1914*. Washington: Government Printing Office, 1914.

Whitten, Sarah. "McDonald's Employees Stage First #MeToo Strike." *USA Today*, September 18, 2018.

Before #MeToo:
The History of the 9to5 Job Survival Hotline

Emily E. LB. Twarog

When Sharon Kinsella arrived at her office in Cleveland, Ohio, she pressed play on the blinking answering machine. It was her job to transcribe the messages from the machine, research the problems, and return the calls. Overnight, a woman who worked in a factory had called and left a message. The message told a disturbing story. The soap dispenser in women's bathroom at her workplace was not filled with soap, as she and her female colleagues had logically assumed. Instead it was filled with semen. According to the message, her male colleagues had been ejaculating into the soap dispenser for some time and the women had been none the wiser, until now. It was reports from the field such as this one that led to the establishment of a national hotline called the 9to5 Job Survival Hotline. This article examines how the hotline was used as an organizing tool by 9to5, National Association of Working Women to help pave the way for the rise of the MeToo movement.

Karen Nussbaum and Ellen Cassedy were best friends and both working as clerical typists at Harvard University when they came together with eight other Boston area office workers to establish 9to5. Inspired by years of protesting against the Vietnam War and in support of civil rights, Nussbaum began to realize that she could organize in her own workplace. Nussbaum recalls, "We met for a year. We met once a week for a year and we told each other our stories about how we got to be where we were and what we thought and what were our values and we went through this whole experience and then we talked about what kind of an organization we wanted to create."[1] Initially the group began publishing a newsletter called *9to5: Newsletter for*

This research was supported by a generous grant from the University of Illinois Campus Research Board, an American Council for Learned Societies Frederick Burkhardt Residential Fellowship, and the Newberry Library, Chicago. I received helpful feedback from Margot Canaday, Leon Fink, Christopher Phelps, and the participants of the Newberry Library Colloquium Series.

1. Karen Nussbaum, interview by Kathleen Banks Nutter, Voice of Feminism Oral History Project, Sophia Smith Collection, Smith College, December 18–19, 2003, 20. See also Windham, *Knocking on Labor's Door*, chap. 7, for more on 9to5.

Labor: Studies in Working-Class History, Volume 19, Issue 1
DOI 10.1215/15476715-9475744   © 2022 by Labor and Working-Class History Association

Boston Area Office Workers with the intention of sharing what it was like to work in the clerical industry. They handed out the newsletter around town to women heading into work, and soon women began to respond. They held their first meeting at the YWCA in November 1973 and over 150 women turned out.[2] Over the next few years, the organization "continually [had] actions" with "achievable goals so we could have victories and to have our membership be the activists, the spokespeople, the leadership of all of our activities," according to Nussbaum. "We defined our goals as being understandable. . . . It wasn't about radical analysis. . . . It was more: you've got a problem on the job. It's probably related to the fact that you're a woman, and it's not any accident."[3] This was an ideology that resonated with the increasing number of women entering the workforce in the 1970s.

On the other side of town, another group of women were talking with a more radical voice. For the Alliance against Sexual Coercion (AASC) gender violence such as sexual harassment in the workplace was "a highly effective tool of social control."[4] They argued, "Sexist attitudes, along with racist and classist beliefs, are vital parts of the U.S. economic system. Not until an egalitarian and democratic work structure is established will sexual harassment be eradicated."[5] AASC was founded by a group of women who came together through their work at a Cambridge rape crisis center. During their work at the rape crisis center, they met women who experienced sexual harassment in the workplace and realized that the services offered at the rape crisis center were inadequate to address the specific needs of women experiencing sexual harassment at work. As women were becoming increasingly financially independent by entering the workforce in larger numbers, the logic would follow that women would gain more confidence and independence. Yet, AASC argued, "the reality of violence inhibits more women from acting independently." AASC was an explicitly feminist organization that sought the "transformation of society" through the systematic elimination of sexual harassment.[6]

In the 1970s and 1980s, the tension between achievable goals and systemic change defined the work of the women's movement. For Nussbaum and her colleagues in 9to5, their organizing efforts stemmed from the antiwar movement and their time working as clerical workers. For the many working-class women who joined 9to5 in the early days, winning small victories that would have an immediate impact on their day-to-day work lives was critical.[7] Women workers by and large did not have any workplace system or organization to respond to their experiences of sexual harassment. As one 9to5 organizer in Baltimore recalled, "I'd meet women for

2. Nussbaum interview, 20–22.

3. Nussbaum interview, 23.

4. AASC, *Sexual Harassment at the Workplace*, 5. For more on AASC, see Baker, "Emergence of Organized Feminist Resistance to Sexual Harassment"; Backhouse and Cohen, *Secret Oppression*, chap. 6.

5. AASC, *Sexual Harassment at the Workplace*, 11.

6. AASC, *Sexual Harassment at the Workplace*, 24.

7. Turk, *Equality on Trial*.

lunch to talk about 9to5 and would hear, over and over, women expressing a sense of relief that finally there was a group hearing and action on their unspoken concerns and aspirations."[8] In short, working women needed to create their own effective means of response, hence the early success of 9to5. It would be many years before 9to5 embraced a more radical and transformative approach to combating gender discrimination as well as a public hearing that made the nation utter the term *sexual harassment*.

The Office and Sexual Politics

While women's employment in offices skyrocketed in the 1980s, women working in the office setting was not new. In fact, women began working in offices at the apex of the Industrial Revolution. In 1891, seventy-five thousand women worked in clerical work making up 20 percent of all clerical workers.[9] But during the first three decades of the twentieth century, office work grew into an increasingly complicated web of hierarchies and gendered divisions of labor. As industrialization expanded, so did the need for more discrete office jobs. There was an overall increase in middle-management occupations that went beyond bookkeeping and typing. As historian Sharon Hartman Strom notes, this created

> a series of administrative units or departments that had only existed in primitive
> forms in most businesses before 1890. These units required new kinds of office
> employees and records. . . . To keep the now far more detailed records that
> were required, new office staffs of clerks were essential. The coordination and
> management of these administrative systems was dependent upon the manufacture
> of paperwork, paperwork not required under the old order.[10]

As this new office structure evolved, women clerical workers found themselves relegated to the most low-skilled and menial tasks with no career ladders. But for working-class women, the opportunity to work in a clean and well-lighted office was often far more appealing than factory work, with its drudgery and toxic work environments. Trade publications such as *The Office Economist* fed into the desire for cleaner and more respectable work as they wove narratives of office work accompanied by images of women with coiffed hair and glamorous clothing.[11] The social and cultural status of office work appealed to working women despite the low and stagnant wages. In the 1950s, Addie Wyatt, a young African American woman, went to Armour and Company, a Chicago meatpacking company, to apply for a job in the front office. She was denied the clerical job because of her race and offered a job on the factory floor in the canning department. However, when the opportunity later arose to work in the front office, she realized that her wages were much better on the

8. Cameron, "Noon at 9 to 5," 105.
9. Berebitsky, *Sex and the Office*, 2.
10. Strom, *Beyond the Typewriter*, 26.
11. Strom, *Beyond the Typewriter*, 1–2.

factory floor because her job was covered by the Amalgamated Meat Cutters union contract, unlike those of the office clerks. So she stayed on the factory floor. Over time she became a national leader within the labor movement as well as the civil rights and women's movements, and she was eventually named *Time* magazine's Woman of the Year.[12]

By the 1980s, the primary occupation for women was office work, resulting in 7 million women working in an office setting. To put this in perspective, the number of women working as elementary school teachers at the same time was a mere 1.7 million. Furthermore, over 55 percent of adult women were now working outside the home as compared to a generation earlier when only 34 percent were working outside the home. The 7 million women working in office jobs represent a drastic shift away from jobs such as manufacturing, domestic labor, and other service labor jobs.[13]

In 1977, a Yale spokesman held that sexual harassment is "not a new thing, but it is also a major problem."[14] The spokesman was correct—sexual harassment was not a new thing, but it most certainly was (and remains) a problem of epidemic proportions. Secretaries in particular had long been sexualized. Between 1975 and 1977, there were several surveys conducted to measure women workers' experiences of sexual harassment. Overwhelmingly, women reported that they had experienced sexual harassment in the workplace. In 1976 *Redbook*, a national women's magazine, conducted one of these surveys. Of the nine thousand readers who returned the survey, 88 percent reported that they had experienced some form of sexual harassment, while 92 percent considered sexual harassment a serious issue. In other studies conducted by sociologists, professional women's organizations, and a naval officer, the results were the same—a large majority of women surveyed had experienced some form of sexual harassment in her job, and very few had ever reported the issue. Sociologist Sandra Harley Carey wrote, "A woman is socialized to be the victim and not to fight," and as a result, women chose not to report their harassment for many reasons—fear of economic instability, embarrassment, shame, guilt, and physical ailments, just to name a few. Despite the sexual harassment epidemic women workers were confronting, management persisted in their belief that this was not a workplace issue. A *Harvard Business Review* poll of fifteen hundred male managers reported that most "did not feel their organizations had any responsibility to alter their employees' attitudes towards women."[15]

The term *sexual harassment* was coined in the 1970s and finally gave a name to the gender violence women have faced in the workplace. By naming the violence, women's organizations began to craft a universal definition of sexual harassment. The AASC focused their definition on how sexual harassment endangered a woman's economic livelihood. The New York–based Working Women United Institute

12. For more on Addie Wyatt see Walker-McWilliams, *Reverend Addie Wyatt.*

13. Bui, "Fifty Years of Shrinking Union Membership."

14. Quoted in Backhouse and Cohen, *Secret Oppression,* 46.

15. Backhouse and Cohen, *Secret Oppression,* 39–41.

Figure 1. Sexual harassment speak-out poster, Working Women United, Ithaca, New York, May 1975. The phrase *sexual harassment* was coined by the same group that year. Courtesy of K. C. Wagner.

highlighted the repetitive nature "of unwanted sexual comments, looks, suggestions or physical contact that you find objectionable or offensive and causes you discomfort on the job." The National Organization for Women pointed out that sexual harassment was "an issue which is been shrouded in silence because its occurrence is seen as both humiliating and trivial."[16]

Gender, Telephones, and Organizing

This was the social and cultural climate in which 9to5 launched their first telephone hotline for women workers needing advice and support. The telephone has been a critical organizing tool that has continued to evolve over time. The evolution of the telephone has allowed women to engage in private conversations—"an important social process, serving . . . to renew networks and communities."[17] Although it would be the 1960s and 1970s before telephones were nearly universal in the United States, the telephone served such a significant role in the early twentieth century that in the 1920s more households had a telephone than an indoor toilet. General Federation of Women's Clubs president Mary Sherman commented, "Before toilets are installed or washbasins put into homes . . . telephones are connected . . . because the housewife for generations has sought to escape the monotony rather than the drudgery of her lot."[18]

16. Quoted in Backhouse and Cohen, *Secret Oppression*, 38.
17. Fischer, "Gender and the Residential Telephone, 1890–1940," 212.

Organizations realized that the telephone was an important new tool in their organizing arsenal. It created what sociologist Sidney H. Aronson calls a "psychological
network." This network expanded a person's reach, allowing them to "develop intimate social networks based on . . . shared interests that transcended the boundaries"
beyond their home, their community, and their workplace.[19] Historian Barbara Keys
goes on to argue that the telephone provided "immediate personal contact [and] an
opportunity for genuine exchange." Phone calls helped to provide "motivation: the
sense of being part of a larger movement, the sense of value, the sense of making an
important contribution."[20]

The use of the phone as an organizing tool also linked to gender roles: women
felt more comfortable talking on the phone. By appropriating "a supposedly mas-
culine technology," sociologist Claude Fischer argues, women took over the phone
for "distinctly feminine needs." Fischer argues that conversation, even gossip, "is an
important social process serving among other ends to redo networks and communities."[21] Over time, society began to view talking on the telephone as a female practice. During the 1948 meat boycotts Texas housewives ingenuously created a phone
tree or "chain" using their social networks as well as the phonebook to broaden and
diversify the scope of their boycott.[22] During the 1968 meat boycotts, Mickey DeLo-
renzo, a Long Island housewife, was so inundated with telephone calls from housewives around the country requesting advice on how to organize their own local boycotts that she installed a second phone line in her home. When the technician arrived
to install the new telephone line, he commented that he did not understand why a
single-family home needed an additional line. But the phone began ringing as soon
as it was installed.[23]

The 9to5 Hotline

The hotline launched by 9to5 in 1980 allowed the organization to "survey workers, distribute informational leaflets and to organize an employee committee."[24] The
organization was strategic about where it established these hotlines, which were not
national but local. As Karen Nussbaum told the *Chicago Tribune*, "We're [9to5] not a
union but in some of the right-to-work states, clerical workers are uncertain they have

18. Quoted in Fischer, "Gender and the Residential Telephone, 1890–1940," 216.

19. Aronson, "Sociology of the Telephone," 162.

20. Barbara Keys's work focuses on the Central American solidarity movement in the United States
during the 1970s and 1980s and how the telephone played a pivotal role in that organizing. Despite the difference activist focus, her theories are applicable to the work of 9to5. Keys, "Telephone and Its Uses in 1980s
Activism," 488.

21. Fischer, "Gender and the Residential Telephone, 1890–1940," 212.

22. For more on the 1948 Texas meat boycotts, see Robbins, "'It's a Texas Custom to Show Fight.'" See
also Rakow, *Gender on the Line*, on the relationship between gender and phone use; and Jacquet, *Injustices
of Rape*, chap. 3, for a discussion of the establishment of rape crisis hotlines.

23. Twarog, *Politics of the Pantry*, chap. 5.

24. Kleiman, "From Hot Tips to Cold Facts."

any rights at all."[25] The regional hotlines in Georgia, Tennessee, North Carolina, and South Carolina were primarily staffed by volunteers. Volunteers were trained to listen and direct callers to the proper resource. They sifted through an enormous binder of resources organized by topic area—pregnancy discrimination, wage discrimination, health and safety, sexual harassment, and so on. The hotline benefited the organization in multiple ways. First, it provided much-needed information for women who had nowhere else to turn for information. Second, the connection with the helpline volunteer offered the caller crucial emotional support. 9to5 was using the hotlines to build their membership base.

9to5 soon became a thorn in management's side. They published an "Office Workers' Bill of Rights" and used street actions and theater to pressure employers to improve working conditions. The slogan "Raises, Rights, and Respect" harkened back to the 1912 Bread and Roses strikes of New England factory workers, and 9to5 used this messaging as they appeared on "the doorstep of a company to dramatize conditions of unfair treatment."[26] However, 9to5's organizing tactics quickly drew the attention of management. Chambers of commerce and management consultants began to offer trainings on "how to control or 'manage' white-collar workers and 'militant feminists' like 9to5."[27]

In 1988, 9to5 launched a national toll-free number based in Cleveland, Ohio, called the Job Survival Hotline, hoping that it would help to "develop a vision of a much larger organization" and "learn more about the problems facing working women and to help millions of women who work in offices around the country."[28] Using grant money, 9to5 was able to hire one full-time position to staff the Job Survival Hotline during business hours; in the evening, callers could leave a message on the answering machine. They hired Sharon Kinsella as the hotline staffer.

Kinsella had what communications scholars call a "telephone personality."[29] She was described as a "brash, quick-witted, mother of three" who evolved into what some call "a radical feminist and strident working-class flag waver" who staffed the hotline six hours a day. She was one of those people "you could never knock down" who had experienced many of the things that women were reporting to the hotline. "I think that came through in how she counseled women," recalled Barbara Otto, a former 9to5 staff member who worked closely with Kinsella in Cleveland.[30] Kinsella was a working-class midwestern white woman who did not grow up marching with Gloria Steinem and reading *Ms.* magazine. Her feminist consciousness was born out of workplace discrimination. Having grown up in northern Ohio, a region that was shifting from prosperous manufacturing towns to shuttered factories and high unemployment, Kinsella was all too aware of the financial reality women faced. Kinsella

25. Kleiman, "From Hot Tips to Cold Facts."

26 .Cameron, "Noon at 9 to 5," 107.

27. Cameron, "Noon at 9 to 5," 107.

28. 9to5, *Business as Usual*, 2.

29. Keys, "Telephone and Its Uses in 1980s Activism," 499–500.

30. Barbara Otto, interview with the author, March 3, 2020, Oak Park, IL.

told an *LA Times* reporter, "Bottom line is, they want cheap people they can spit out after they chew 'em up." When she wasn't answering the hotline, Kinsella ran a singing telegram service called Red-Hot Mama of the Big Belly Telly, "where she belt[ed] out Sophie Tucker songs or parodies of Beatles songs. . . . The songs she [wrote were] often about the labor movement."[31]

The Job Survival Hotline was a huge success. Over the course of one year, 1989–90, "the hotline received over 60,000 phone calls from every state in the country." 9to5 engaged in public campaigns such as National Boss Context to highlight employers who fell into three categories—"the good, the bad, and the ugly." Barbara Otto was in her twenties when she left a comfortable job in corporate America to work as 9to5's Director of Programs and Public Affairs. As a first-generation college student, it was a bold move to leave the consistency of a corporate job to work for a small women's organization, but she realized that "all of the secretaries [at her job], some of which had more education that [she did], were making less money than I was because of their role as a secretary or executive assistant."[32] Otto was recruited by Ellen Bravo, an organizer with the Milwaukee 9to5 chapter. She moved to Cleveland to work in the national 9to5 office.

The National Boss Contest became her project. Working with a public relations firm, the contest had three goals. First, 9to5 wanted to raise awareness about what women were experiencing in the workplace beyond conversations about the proverbial glass ceiling. Second, the organization wanted to highlight health and safety issues along with the lack of family and medical leave. Finally, it sought to engage in a national conversation about the workplace more generally. 9to5 gathered submissions from around the country, often through the Job Survival Hotline. "We heard from a lot of women," Otto recalls, "and frankly we got some entries from men, who were in really unsafe workplaces, usually in the South. But also that was the beginning of the wave of video display terminals and . . . repetitive stress injuries." Otto enlisted celebrity judges who could not believe that "people still worked like this."[33] The media attention garnered by the contest further promoted the Job Survival Hotline as a critical resource for women workers. The widespread national press in magazines such as *Mademoiselle*, *Ladies Home Journal*, and *Money* resulted in jammed-up phone lines.

9to5 took a very broad approach to getting the word out about the hotline, including traditional forms such as newspapers, radio and news programming, and magazines. But they also managed to get the hotline number listed in company newsletters and bulletin boards and in employee washrooms. In some cases, they succeeded in getting it inserted into company paychecks. They used events like International Women's Day in March and International Workers Day on May First to draw

31. Bob Baker, "Workplace Horror Stories," *Los Angeles Times*, April 30, 1990, E1.

32. Otto interview.

33. Otto interview.

attention to the Job Survival Hotline.[34] This often resulted in significant surges in calls. For example, in March 1990 the hotline had more than 13,000 calls—an average of 420 calls a day.[35] About one-third of the calls were related to pregnancy discrimination and concerns; another third were made up of discrimination and sexual harassment–related issues.[36] Some excerpts from the calls include these two women's experiences:

> Margaret is a credit manager for a food distribution company. The general manager is harassing her, telling her, "If you let me pull off your clothes, wash your face and brush out your hair, then we can talk." The first step in the company's grievance procedure is to file a complaint with the general manager.

> Sharon worked as the administrative assistant to the vice president of a small firm. The owner's son constantly propositioned her and she turned him down. He called her at home late at night many times; he would also call her into his office and scream at her because she wouldn't go out with him. While she was on vacation, the company left a message on her answering machine saying she was fired.[37]

The majority of the callers worked in offices in the private sector. Despite 9to5's early efforts to connect to women workers in the southern states, by 1990 the top ten states included only two southern states—Florida and Texas—along with California, New York, Pennsylvania, Illinois, Ohio, Massachusetts, New Jersey, and Michigan. However, women did call from all fifty states and Puerto Rico.[38]

After arriving in the office, Kinsella would spend the first part of the morning taking all the calls off the hotline that were received overnight. "She would spend the day calling people back, sometimes having to research things, sometimes getting in touch with chapters, or she come in and [say] you would not believe what I just heard . . . "[39] Kinsella had a massive binder that was divided into various workplace concerns—pregnancy, racial discrimination, firings, sexual harassment, and so on. Callers were given the option to become associate members of the Service Employee International Union District 925 for a small fee. Associate membership provided access to reduced-fee legal advice, but not union benefits.[40]

34. Otto interview.

35. 9to5, *Business as Usual*, 2.

36. 9to5, *Business as Usual*, 2.

37. 9to5, *Business as Usual*, 7.

38. 9to5, *Business as Usual*, 16.

39. Otto interview.

40. See Windham for more on the formation of the office workers union, SEIU Local 925 and the subsequent SEIU District 925, that came out of the national association, 9to5. They were two separate organizations, but they maintained close ties, including leadership: for example, Karen Nussbaum worked for both 9to5 and the SEIU Local 925 for a number of years before leaving to work in the Clinton administration.

The Thomas-Hill Hearings and 9to5's Shift from Hotline to Training

In 1991, President George H. W. Bush nominated Clarence Thomas to the Supreme Court. Anita Hill came forward during the confirmation hearing committee and told her story of sexual harassment by Justice Thomas while she worked for him at the Department of Education and the Equal Employment Opportunity Commission. Hill's testimony transformed women's relationship to their experiences of sexual harassment. As journalist Nina Totenberg recalled, "The hearings ripped open the subject of sexual harassment like some sort of long-festering sore. It oozed over every workplace, creating everything from heated discussions to an avalanche of lawsuits."[41] In two weeks, the hotline received over two thousand phone calls "mostly from people who had never told anybody about what happened to them." One woman called the hotline to share her story of sexual harassment. Whenever her family was having economic trouble, her husband would complain that she left the job. As she and her husband watched the news coverage of the Hill testimony, she pointed to the TV: "She said that's why I'm not at that job. And he said I'm so sorry. I will never say that again."[42] She had never told her own husband that she experienced sexual harassment at work. Hill's testimony changed women's lives.

After Hill's nationally televised testimony, sexual harassment entered the popular vernacular. It had taken almost two decades for the term to gain traction. Sexual violence in the workplace was not a new phenomenon. In fact, women workers had come to expect it. The term *sexual harassment* made its public debut in 1975 when journalist Lin Farley testified before the Commission on Human Rights of New York City. A few years later, the term entered the legal lexicon in 1979 with legal scholar Catherine MacKinnon's *Sexual Harassment of Working Women*.[43] But it was the Thomas-Hill fracas that truly cracked open the silence, and the Job Survival Hotline was there to field the calls.

In the post–Anita Hill era, 9to5 worked to use the Job Survival Hotline as an organizing mechanism to engage more callers. "The word is out about sexual harassment because of Anita Hill, and what's most important is that, for the first time, it is being recognized not as a sexual issue but as an issue of power," said 9to5's Otto. "It's not about sex or sexuality, it's about power."[44] This shift in discussion to one of power was critical for 9to5 to encourage callers to join 9to5 but also to become "reps." 9to5 published an effective report, *Business as Usual*, on the work of the hotline to generate publicity, but their membership renewals were low. The 9to5 leadership wanted to involve callers by asking them to be trained as "reps" for hotline callers. This would allow Sharon Kinsella to focus on training and fielding calls, while volunteer reps would be able to follow up with hotline callers on their issues. The hotline staff helped develop a packet to access callers' interest. Kinsella worked with both

41. Miller, *Complete Transcripts of the Clarence Thomas–Anita Hill Hearings*, 7.
42. Ellen Bravo, interview by the author, November 26, 2019.
43. MacKinnon, *Sexual Harassment of Working Women*.
44. Kleiman, "Then and Now, Sexual Harassment Widespread."

hotline volunteers as well as members from the union, District 925, to train them in following up on hotline callers.[45] By the mid-1990s, the hotline was receiving thousands of calls with regional callers to the 800 line being routed automatically to local chapters in Boston, New York, Milwaukee, Atlanta, and Cincinnati. Over time, the volunteer reps grew into a more stable Response Team, so by 1995 the total number of Response Team members was more than sixty.[46]

Ultimately, the effectiveness of the Response Team was underwhelming. The organization found themselves shifting their focus to training. In 1991, Ellen Bravo was the national director of 9to5, which was now based in Milwaukee, Wisconsin. During the late 1980s she had developed a sexual harassment training curriculum when a friend who worked as a bus driver was being harassed by her dispatcher asked her to come to her union and conduct a training. "I just created a training and the union liked it so much that they got the company to get me to come back and do it for management and then do it for all the bus drivers," recalled Bravo.[47] In the wake of the public Thomas-Hill clash, Bravo found herself conducting more trainings and ultimately a book on how to prevent sexual harassment. Bravo and her 9to5 colleague Ellen wrote for two months, shipping drafts back and forth. A year later, Wiley released *The 9to5 Guide to Combatting Sexual Harassment: Candid Advice from 9to5. The National Association of Working Women.*[48]

The publication of the book and their national sexual harassment trainings placed 9to5 in the center of the movement to end sexual harassment. They continued to embrace a pragmatic approach to organizational strategies. Using their reputation as a well-regarded national training organization meant that they were called on by businesses and the government alike to conduct trainings. For example, in 1996, a former deputy sheriff, Connie Harmon sued the sheriff's department of Stark County, Ohio, for sexual harassment. The court ruled in Harmon's favor and mandated an "unprecedented provision for mandatory sexual harassment training." The sheriff's department hired 9to5 to conduct the "sensitivity training." Connie Harmon's attorney noted, "Without hiring 9to5, a premier women's rights organization, Connie would not settle this case."[49] The Harmon case was one of many legal proceedings that engaged the assistance of 9to5. In the wake of the Thomas-Hill hearings, 9to5 helped to build a pathway to the MeToo movement. The hotline was a transitional form of organizing enabling the kind of reciprocal interaction and political communication that is now carried out more often through social media, but its history pro-

45. Ellen Bravo, "1990–91 Program/Organizing Report," Papers of 9to5 WI, box 5, folder Reports Programming Org, 1989–95, Schlesinger Library, Radcliffe Institute, Cambridge, MA (hereafter Schlesinger Library).

46. "1994/95 Program and Organizing Report," Papers of 9to5 WI, box 5, folder Reports Programming Org, 1989–95, Schlesinger Library.

47. Bravo interview.

48. Bravo and Cassedy, *9to5 Guide to Combatting Sexual Harassment.* 9to5 published a second edition in 1999.

49. 9to5, "Press Release, March 7, 1996," Papers of 9to5, WI, box 12, folder 12, Schlesinger Library.

vides still-useful organizing strategies for ending sexual violence in the workplace by a worker-focused approach that fosters opportunities for collaboration across gender, race, class, and occupational distinctions. ◢

EMILY E. LB. TWAROG is associate professor in the School of Labor and Employment Relations at the University of Illinois at Urbana-Champaign. She is the author of *Politics of the Pantry: Food, Housewives, and Consumer Protest in Twentieth-Century America* (2017) and several articles on women's union leadership in the United States. She is currently working on a book manuscript about the history of sexual harassment resistance in the service sector.

References

9to5, National Association of Working Women. *Business as Usual: Stories from the 9to5 Job Survival Hotline.* Cleveland, OH: 9to5, National Association of Working Women, 1991.

AASC (Alliance against Sexual Coercion). *Sexual Harassment at the Workplace.* Cambridge, MA: AASC, 1977. https://documents.alexanderstreet.com/d/1000689709.

Aronson, Sidney H. "The Sociology of the Telephone." *International Journal of Comparative Sociology* 12, no. 2 (1971): 153–69.

Backhouse, Constance, and Leah Cohen. *The Secret Oppression: Sexual Harassment of Working Women.* Toronto: Macmillan, 1978.

Baker, Carrie N. "The Emergence of Organized Feminist Resistance to Sexual Harassment in the United States in the 1970s." In *Study of Women and Gender: Faculty Publications* (Smith College, Northampton, MA), Fall 2007. https://scholarworks.smith.edu/swg_facpubs/12.

Berebitsky, Julie. *Sex and the Office: A History of Gender, Power, and Desire.* New Haven, CT: Yale University Press, 2012.

Bravo, Ellen, and Ellen Cassedy. *The 9to5 Guide to Combatting Sexual Harassment: Candid Advice from 9to5, the National Association of Working Women.* New York: Wiley, 1991.

Bui, Quoctrung. "Fifty Years of Shrinking Union Membership, in One Map." *Planet Money,* NPR, February 23, 2015. www.npr.org/sections/money/2015/02/23/385843576/50-years-of-shrinking-union-membership-in-one-map.

Cameron, Cindia. "Noon at 9 to 5: Reflections on a Decade of Organizing." *Labor Research Review* 1, no. 8 (1986): 103–9.

Fischer, Claude S. "Gender and the Residential Telephone, 1890–1940: Technologies of Sociability." *Sociological Forum* 3, no. 2 (1988): 211–33.

Jacquet, Catherine O. *The Injustices of Rape: How Activists Responded to Sexual Violence, 1950–1980.* Chapel Hill: University of North Carolina Press, 2019.

Keys, Barbara. "The Telephone and Its Uses in 1980s Activism." *Journal of Interdisciplinary History* 48, no. 4 (2018): 485–509.

Kleiman, Carol. "From Hot Tips to Cold Facts, Dial Up 9to5 Hotlines." *Chicago Tribune,* November 27, 1989.

Kleiman, Carol. "Then and Now, Sexual Harassment Widespread." *Chicago Tribune,* December 9, 1991.

MacKinnon, Catherine. *Sexual Harassment of Working Women: A Case of Sex Discrimination.* New Haven, CT: Yale University Press, 1979.

Miller, Anita ed. *The Complete Transcripts of the Clarence Thomas–Anita Hill Hearings, October 11, 12, 13, 1991.* Chicago: Academy Chicago, 1994.

Nussbaum, Karen. Interview by Kathleen Banks Nutter. Voice of Feminism Oral History Project, Sophia Smith Collection, Smith College, December 18–19, 2003.

Rakow, Lana F. *Gender on the Line: Women, the Telephone, and Community Life.* Urbana: University of Illinois Press, 1992.

Robbins, Mark. "'It's a Texas Custom to Show Fight': The Cultural Politics of Meat Boycotts in Mid-Twentieth Century Texas." *Southwestern Historical Quarterly* (forthcoming).

Strom, Sharon Hartman. *Beyond the Typewriter: Gender, Class, and the Origins of Modern American Office Work, 1900–1930.* Urbana: University of Illinois Press, 1992.

Turk, Katherine. *Equality on Trial: Gender and Rights in the Modern American Workplace.* Philadelphia: University of Pennsylvania Press, 2016.

Twarog, Emily E. LB. *Politics of the Pantry: Food, Housewives, and Consumer Protest in Twentieth-Century America.* New York: Oxford University Press, 2017.

Walker-McWilliams, Marcia. *Reverend Addie Wyatt: Faith and the Fight for Labor, Gender, and Racial Equality.* Urbana: University of Illinois Press, 2016.

Windham, Lane. *Knocking on Labor's Door: Union Organizing in the 1970s and the Roots of a New Economic Divide.* Chapel Hill: University of North Carolina Press, 2017.

From Sexual Harassment to Gender Violence at Work: The ILO's Road to Convention #190

Eileen Boris

"The definition of Domestic Violence must be challenged . . . , widened in order to include violence at the hands of the employer to the domestic worker." In 2001, at the beginning of an international domestic worker movement for a new century, the Rights, Equality, Solidarity, Power, Europe, Co-operation, Today network (RESPECT) understood what became a mantra among organizers within twenty years: your home is my workplace. The concept of relationship—between perpetrator and the woman survivor—required stretching beyond intimate partners to cover migrant domestic workers.[1] These activists led by Kalayaan! in London and SOLIDAR in Brussels conducted focus groups throughout the continent with migrants from Asia and Latin America, both those with work permits and the undocumented. They would make visible physical, psychological, and sexual abuse behind the closed doors of households. They would define lack of proper nutrition and overwork as forms of violence. In demanding that providers of services for victims of domestic violence expand their purview to address the precarious position of workers dependent on their employers for housing as well as livelihood, RESPECT spoke not in terms of workplace sexual harassment but in the powerful language of domestic violence. They linked worker rights to embodied dignity.

Decades before the hashtag #MeToo galvanized women worldwide to denounce workplace sexual abuse, the concept of violence against women provided numerous feminists with a weapon to wage campaigns for redress in national, regional, and international forums. The concept had become an integral plank of United Nations (UN) declarations since the 1975 Mexico City World Conference on Women, where activists asserted that "rape, immolation, forced sterilization, indecent

---

1. RESPECT, *Accessibility of Services for Migrant Domestic Workers Survivors of Domestic Violence*, 21, 6; Schwenken, "RESPECT for All."

Labor: Studies in Working-Class History, Volume 19, Issue 1
DOI 10.1215/15476715-9475758   © 2022 by Labor and Working-Class History Association

assault, infibulation, unwanted pregnancy, clitorectomy, unnecessary surgery and wife beating and shackling" kept women down and enhanced discrimination in all facets of social life.[2] The follow-up Copenhagen World Conference on Women in 1980 advised governments to enact and enforce legislation "to prevent domestic and sexual violence against women," cast in terms of women's health and relationships between men and women in the family. But it also called for protection of migrant women, like those championed by RESPECT, from "violence, exploitation and ill-treatment."[3]

Missing from these initial resolutions was a direct statement on workplace sexual harassment, already a subject of agitation and litigation in the United States and the European Union.[4] The 1985 Nairobi Forward-Looking Strategies for the Advancement of Women rectified this omission, speaking of "sexual harassment on the job and sexual exploitation in specific jobs."[5] Nairobi singled out domestic work as a particularly vulnerable form of employment.[6] More than three decades later, the International Labour Organization (ILO) passed "Violence and Harassment Convention, 2019 (No. 190)," subsuming sexual harassment under gender violence in the world of work for men and women. Convention No. 190 couldn't have come at a better time: though consideration had begun before the new focus on sexual harassment, the presence of the global #MeToo movement cemented ILO consideration and amplified its import.

Why did it take over three decades to win a global labor convention against workplace violence? What political and social forces lay behind the move away from sexual harassment to the language of violence, the concept that earlier framed international declarations and that RESPECT deployed in its quest for justice for migrant domestic workers? A confluence of labor activism and bureaucratic jockeying came together with the passage of Convention No. 190, but this outcome was hardly predetermined. Creating a global standard flexible enough to accommodate national and regional gendered political economies was no easy task. It took concerted efforts of women in the global labor unions and the international labor secretariats, along with feminist staff within the ILO and key delegates to its International Labour Conference (ILC), to push the process along. The plight of domestic workers, whose organization labor feminists and NGOs helped to birth, dramatized the need for such redress. Women unionists, including domestic workers, and ILO staff together built on "Decent Work for Domestics Convention, 2011 (No. 189)," the pathbreak-

2. Quoted in Olcott, *International Women's Year*, 123; *Report of the World Conference of the International Women's Year*, 78, 93, 124, 133. For a critique of UN interventions, see Kang, *Traffic in Asian Women*.

3. *Report of the World Conference of the United Nations Decade for Women*, 20, 65.

4. Baker, *Women's Movement against Sexual Harassment*; MacKinnon, *Sexual Harassment of Working Women*; Husbands, "Sexual Harassment Law in Employment." Undoubtedly women elsewhere also fought workplace assault but were less visible in UN documents.

5. Husbands, "Sexual Harassment Law in Employment," 545; "Combating Sexual Harassment at Work," 24–25, 26–43.

6. UN, *Report of the World Conference to Review and Appraise the Achievements of the United Nations Decade for Women*, 35.

ing instrument that seemed to make the ILO relevant again for a world of nonstandard work.[7] In tracing the competing terms by which workplace violence emerged as a proper subject for international convention making, this article argues that change depends on the power of transnational labor movements to demand redress and break through systems of international governance—but requires insider partners. By the mid-2010s, enough of a worldwide consensus had emerged for action on an issue that women unionists and feminist staff refused to eliminate from the ILO's agenda despite employers' hindrance.

Founded in the aftermath of World War I with the League of Nations, the ILO has served as a norm-setting body, charged with researching and formulating rules for workplaces. Its tripartite structure—consisting of representatives from governments, organized workers, and employer associations—dilutes workers' power but also, uniquely among UN agencies, allows for their input. Governments have more say, however, because they send two delegates and select the single worker and single employer representative, usually from the main national organizations (in the US case, the AFL-CIO and the US Chamber of Commerce, both of which recommend their delegate and advisers). It has brought together delegates to pass treaty-like conventions, aspirational counterweights to the vicissitudes of the market, that member states are to ratify and then implement. Over the last century, it has maintained a basic structure—the International Labour Office (the Office) under an elected Director-General, the Governing Body, an annual ILC, and tripartite sectoral committees of experts (assembled by the Office in conjunction with governments, unions, and employer organizations). Influence within shifted from the European nations, still colonial powers in 1919, to the United States after World War II and then to regional blocs since the 1970s. By the 1990s, employers obstructed formulation of new standards.

Though international bureaucracies appear as relics from an earlier world order, they remain meaningful for countries that depend on their services, funding, and guidance. Since the 1970s, the ILO has offered technical assistance to less developed and developing nations, with a staff increasingly from such areas. For much of the world, ILO conventions have provided templates and expressed norms. Latin American nations, for example, long have ratified conventions, more so than the United States has. Certainly trade unions proposed national legislation in light of such instruments and, with more limited success, attempted to mitigate against multinational undercutting of national standards and collective bargaining. Moreover, the ILO's bureaucracy of researchers and civil servants have generated the very facts available to policymakers and scholars alike, setting the terms for analysis—which makes the ILO a useful arena for writing conceptual history.[8]

7. Boris and Fish, "'Slaves No More.'"

8. Rodgers et al., *International Labour Organization*; Linden, "International Labor Organization, 1919–2019"; on conceptual history, Berrebi-Hoffmann et al., *Categories in Context*.

Internal disagreement among its staff illuminates the terms woven into debates over sexual harassment. Arguments among labor standards specialists reflected disjunctures within mainstream Western feminism between women-only protection and male-normed equality. Haunting these discussions was another dichotomy: the persistent tension between universality and particularity within the ILO and global policymaking at large. Staff had to overcome the institutional history of classifying the women worker as the particular to the universal norm, outside general labor standards and in need of special treatment. She deserved equality but required protection. Despite the reality that any woman could experience sexual harassment, some women were more likely to do so because of their identities—such as race, ethnicity, sexuality, and citizenship—and the location and type of their labor, often overdetermined by occupational segregation by those very factors of race and gender.[9]

Charges of particularity encompassed other legacies of global inequality. Staff responsible for monitoring both antidiscrimination and working conditions of women confronted pushback by other staff who viewed harassment as a Western problem rather than a proper subject for universal standard making in a world of uneven and unequal economic development. To maneuver around entrenched notions of appropriate topics, supporters turned to occupational health and safety as a vehicle for improving conditions that otherwise would remain outside the ILO's purview. Some deployed equality discourse; still others spoke of dignity and respect. That violence emerged as the frame with the most resonance reflected not only the move from woman to gender in public life but also a perception of violence as an acceptable umbrella term for global action.

Staff could impede but not pass conventions. Obtaining an international instrument depended on satisfying a majority out of government, employer, and worker delegates, many of whom were subject to pressure from various constituencies. Standards making existed along with, if not always in a direct relation to, social movements.[10] The influence that global trade unions and their international secretariats had in formulating the ILO's agenda provided an opening for a new generation of feminists to fight sexual harassment not only within their unions but also on this international stage. Competing labor agendas, uneven power of women's committees within unions, and the ILO's bureaucratic procedures slowed the process until momentum grew in the 2010s, when a critical mass of union federations sought to rectify gender inequality within their organizations and enough governments already had adopted means for redress. Prodded by key staff, supported by unions, with the approach of its centennial in 2019, the ILO then passed a convention against gender violence to advance decent work for a new century.

9. Boris, *Making the Woman Worker*.
10. Keck and Sikkink, *Activists beyond Borders*; Brysk, *Struggle for Freedom from Fear*.

Neither a Vanguard nor a Laggard

ILO thought on sexual harassment evolved along with its position on the woman worker. From the start, it claimed that all of its instruments applied to women but that special women-only ones would address perceived social and biological difference. After World War II, it increasingly emphasized equal over special treatment except when it came to maternity. "Equal" did not necessarily mean "identical," as with equal remuneration for comparable worth and targeted training programs. During the UN Decade for Women, 1975–85, the Geneva organization formulated a future agenda to enhance "equal opportunities and equal treatment for men and women in employment." Its laborite standpoint was liberal: it believed that removing barriers to equal rights to work would eliminate discrimination and thus enhance "the promotion of full, productive and freely chosen employment."[11] Though such a stance appeared compatible with a growing neoliberal feminism that emphasized individual striving in a market economy, it was tempered by adherence to collective rights and state regulation.[12]

ILO framing of the issue in terms of equality and nondiscrimination represented a structural rather than personalistic or individual understanding of harm. For the 1985 Nairobi conference, it promulgated a "Resolution on Equal Opportunity and Equal Treatment" that specified sexual harassment as a condition impeding equality. Rather than a subset of violence against women, sexual harassment belonged to the category of "working conditions and environment," a practice "detrimental to . . . employment and promotion prospects." The practice hampered "the advancement of equality."[13] This framing probably came from the efforts of the influential Canadian government representative Lucille Caron, who served on the ILO's Governing Body. A fierce advocate for gender equality, Caron headed the International Affairs section of the Canadian Department of Labor. Canadian feminists were well aware of sexual harassment; the Canadian Human Rights Commission had flagged unwanted sexual attention as impacting men as well as women.[14] These activists had taken the lead in alerting the world to violence against Indigenous women. Caron pushed for the full implementation of the Nairobi recommendations.[15] Three years later, the key committee reviewing adherence to conventions defined sexual harassment as a form of sex discrimination. Surveying the operation of "Discrimination (Employment and Occupation) Convention, 1958 (No. 111)," it reaffirmed the practice as a byproduct of inequality rather than as an initiator, to be remedied by implementing equality policies.[16]

11. Mrs. Smirnova's Report on Mission to Vienna, ESC 77-16-1001 Jacket 1, International Labour Organization (ILO) Archives, Geneva. All archival materials come from the ILO Archives unless noted.

12. Rottenberg, *Rise of Neoliberal Feminism.*

13. ILC, *Record of Proceedings*, Seventy-First Session, 36/16.

14. ILC, *Record of Proceedings*, Seventy-Fifth Session, 43, 168.

15. Lee Swepston, email to Eileen Boris, January 20, 2020. On Caron, see Carol Riegelman Lubin and Anne Winslow, *Social Justice for Women*, 185, 224.

16. Lubin and Winslow, *Social Justice for Women*, 43–44, 168; ILC, *Record of Proceedings*, Seventy-Fifth Session, 28/16.

The problem of sexual harassment gained further notice when the ILO began a decade-long process that would lead to gender inclusive revisions of earlier protective measures on night work and hazardous substances. Its experts wrestled with improving health and safety on the job and during the journey to work without precipitating employer discrimination against hiring women if they had to be treated the same as men. The major impediment to equality, then, was not women-only standards "but the attitudes and behavior of both employers and fellow workers." To replace protection with equality of opportunity required creating "a working environment which was equally safe for men and women workers."[17] That goal necessitated health and safety protections to ensure "personal security of workers (notably [from] sexual harassment and violence arising from work)."[18] This 1989 recommendation first linked sexual harassment with violence at work, a conceptualization that would reappear in Convention No. 190. A belief in special treatment persisted, however, with ILO experts arguing that women-dominated occupations and women's entry into male-dominated nontraditional ones generated "special exposure to risk of violence" and thus required distinct attention.[19]

The first convention mentioning sexual harassment was the "Indigenous and Tribal Peoples Convention, 1989 (No. 169)," a revision of a 1957 instrument. The previous emphasis on ending discrimination shifted to the goal of promoting equal opportunity for the Indigenous within nation-states, even as Convention No. 169 sought to exchange an assimilationist approach for recognition of the social, cultural, and economic rights of such peoples. Worker members presented an amendment to what became article 20, "Recruitment and Conditions of Employment," which included "equal opportunities and equal treatment in employment for men and women, and protection from sexual harassment."[20] Caron again played a key role, blocking further action until acceptance of this language. Employers countered that the proposed article already included equality "and that there was no need to specifically mention sexual harassment, in view of the wide-spread legislation against it." They actually were wrong about "widespread legislation."[21] With enough governments supporting the amendment, the employers retreated.[22] Though Indigenous members of Government and Worker delegations, as well as from NGOs, rebuked compromises on land rights and other vexing issues, the article on sexual harassment passed without commentary.[23]

---

17. Governing Body, *Minutes of the Governing Body*, 244th Session, 8, 12, 14.

18. "Combating Sexual Harassment at Work," 44.

19. Governing Body, *Minutes of the Governing Body*, 244th Session, 17.

20. C169—Indigenous and Tribal Peoples Convention, 1989.

21. Husbands, "Sexual Harassment Law in Employment."

22. Swepston, *Foundations*, 159–60; Swepston to Boris; ILO, *Partial Revision of the Indigenous and Tribal Populations Convention*, Report 6, 64–68, compared to ILO, *Partial Revision of the Indigenous and Tribal Populations Convention*, Report 4, no. 2A, 51–53.

23. ILC, *Record of Proceedings*, Seventy-Fifth Session, 3/19–20; Swepston, *Foundations*, 163.

At subsequent meetings, both workers and employers continued to clash over practical measures against sexual harassment.[24] During a 1990 symposium on equality of opportunity and treatment, for example, the workers proposed using Convention No. 111 to adopt supplementary standards for reviewing sexual harassment policies. Employers objected, claiming that many states outside the industrialized West considered the topic "taboo." This symposium only could agree that the ILO should compile best practices on "curbing" harassment. Employers should develop and institute preventive and zero tolerance policies, trade unions should bargain on the issue and create internal practices, and governments should conduct general awareness and educational campaigns through codes of conduct and guidelines.[25] Over the years, sectorial committees on health and medical services, hotels and tourism, arts, and financial services more equanimously discussed the issue. In 2003 the Governing Body adopted a nonbinding Code of Practice for workplace violence in the service sector; a safety and health in agriculture code in 2011 also encompassed sexual harassment.[26]

Pushing union advocacy was the Women's Committee of the International Confederation of Free Trade Unions (ICFTU; after 2006, ITUF). It lobbied the ILO and then used ILO pronouncements for further mobilization. This group of women pressured the Workers group within the ILO to support the 1985 resolution that included sexual harassment. Belgian Marcelle Dehareng, head of the ICFTU Women's Bureau, served as secretary to the Workers group during those original discussions.[27] Before Nairobi, the ICFTU Women's Committee underscored the fight against sexual harassment, advising that "unions should encourage women to report instances of sexual harassment and negotiate sexual harassment clauses in collective environments." It raised the issue at its regional meetings and recommended that unions treat the problem like all others by establishing clear policies.[28] Responding to the 1985 ILO resolution on equal treatment, the ICFTU Women's Bureau widely distributed a guide based on the practices of affiliates. Within months, it issued reprints in English, French, and German editions and produced additional translations in Thai, Portuguese, and Japanese. In reaching unions, political parties, governments, universities, journalists, lawyers, and the ILO itself, it sought to build a constituency to press for action.[29] Shortly afterward came a special issue of *Women at Work*, the

24. ILO, Tripartite Symposium on Equality of Opportunity and Treatment for Men and Women in Employment in Industrialised Countries, *Report*, 1–3; ILC, *Gender Equality at the Heart of Decent Work*, Table I, 2.

25. "Tripartite Symposium on Equality," 3–15, 12, 17, 21, 24–26.

26. *Gender Equality at the Heart of Decent Work*, 34–35; draft "Sexual Harassment," CWL 1-6-6 Jacket 3; Pillinger, *Violence and Harassment*, 5.

27. ICFTU, Sixtieth Meeting of the Women's Committee, Agenda Item 6, Folder: ICFTU Women's Committee Brussels, ICFTU Records, International Institute of Social History (IISA), Amsterdam.

28. OCFTU/COTU Pan-African Seminar/Conference for Trade Union Women, Nairobi, Kenya, 5, folder Women's Committee 50th Meeting; "ICFTU/CCL Regional Women's Seminar—BWU Labour College, Barbados," 1–2, folder 52th Meeting, ICFTU Records.

29. ICFTU, 53rd Meeting of the Woman's Committee, Brussels, 4, folder 53rd Meeting; ICFTU, Executive Board, "Agenda Item 12," 4–6, folder 55th Meeting; ICFTU, Executive Board, "Agenda Item

Bulletin of the Women's Committee of the International Union of Food, Agricultural, Hotel, Restaurant, Catering, Tobacco and Allied Workers' Associations (IUF), a major ICFTU affiliate; this special issue was titled "When I *Say* No, I *Mean* No." This progressive union had addressed gender equity both internally through union representation and leadership and externally through collective bargaining and legislation since the 1970s and would spearhead sectorial initiatives leading up to the ILO convention.[30]

By the early 1990s, other UN entities were tackling sexual harassment. The Committee on the Elimination of Discrimination against Women (CEDAW) included "sexual harassment at the workplace" as one example of "violence in everyday life."[31] It joined the language of gender violence to that of sexual harassment in chiding nations for inadequate action on women's human rights, including the trafficking of domestic workers from developing to industrialized locales. The 1993 World Conference on Human Rights requested that the ILO create guidelines on employer responsibility for "a safe place and system of work," especially in export-processing zones and other areas impacted by the neoliberal reorganization of the world economy.[32] Two years later, the Beijing Platform solidified these discussions when exhorting employers and trade unions to move against sexual harassment as a harm jeopardizing health, safety, and other working conditions while interfering with recruitment and promotion.[33] Protection at the workplace became a measure that states could instigate to advance equal rights. No longer seen as opposite strategies, protection and rights could reinforce each other.

Insider Deliberations

Whether the ILO would develop these pronouncements depended on convincing key staff in the Office and the Governing Body. Director-General Michel Hansenne, a former minister of employment and labor in Belgium, came to the ILO in 1989 at a time when women's labor force participation had gained saliency amid intensified global economic uncertainties—and the World Bank and other organizations were subsuming the ILO's portfolio. Hansenne launched the Interdepartmental Project on Equality for Women in Employment with the goal to strengthen existing standards and develop new ones. The budget included funds for regional seminars and

---

15," 4–5; ICFTU, 56th Meeting of the Women's Committee, "Agenda Item 8," 3, both in folder 56th Meeting; ICFTU, 57th Meeting of the Women's Committee, "Agenda Item 3," 5, folder 57th Meeting, ICFTU Records.

30. Pillinger, *Violence and Harassment*, 69–72; Barbro Budin, retired IUF Equality official, to Eileen Boris, emails, December 18–19, 2020.

31. CEDAW, General Recommendation No. 12: Violence against Women, Eighth Session, and General Recommendation No. 19: Violence against Women, Eleventh Session.

32. Report of Committee on Experts and Draft Declaration for the 1993 UN World Conference on Human Rights, 11, CWL 7-1-1-9 Jacket 3.

33. "Platform for Action," United Nations Fourth World Conference on Women, Beijing, China, September 1995, www.un.org/womenwatch/daw/beijing/platform/violence.htm (accessed February 24, 2020).

a monograph on sexual harassment under the leadership of the Working Conditions and Environment (CONDI/T) section of the Office.[34] This funding—some $2.5 million out of a budget of $330 million—marked this initiative as a low priority, which was further reduced due to financial shortfalls.[35]

Despite a paucity of women staff and lack of internal personnel policies against sexual harassment, Hansenne advanced a milieu in which research and technical cooperation on women's equality could flourish.[36] He brought together feminists scattered throughout the Office. ILO women equality experts formed a network of researchers, government and union officials, and advocates seeking redress. Staff included Marie-Claire Séguret, chief of the Work, Gender, and Family section of CONDI/T; Linda Wirth of the same branch; and lawyers Constance Thomas and Jane Hodges of the Equality of Rights section (EQUALITE). These ILO feminists understood sexual harassment "in the context of the struggles for women's rights and recognition and promotion of substantive gender equality," Thomas explained.[37]

The ILO classified these initiatives "as part of its programme to promote workers' privacy, dignity and equality."[38] A 1992 *Conditions of Work Digest* summarized sexual harassment practices of twenty-three industrialized countries; catalogued responses by international organizations, employers, unions, women's groups, and other NGOs; and surveyed nation-based legal approaches.[39] For the Beijing Women's Conference, the Office commissioned research on laws and practices in developing countries (including Uruguay, Jamaica, Malaysia, and Tanzania).[40] Staff members placed the subject into various information packets, as well as added trainings during trips to regional events.[41] They attended workshops organized by the UN, union federations, and governments, such as the 1991 Conference of European Ministers on Physical and Sexual Violence against Women.[42] They intervened to place

34. ILO, *Budget for the Biennium 1992–93*, 5, 11, 15, 140/6, 140/11.

35. ILO, *Budget for the Biennium 1992–93*, 30; Minute Sheet from E. Date-Bah to Mr. Martin, Mr. Inoue, and Mr. Sorensen, May 11, 1993, CWL 7-1-12-9-100-84 Jacket 1; Minute, Date-Bah to CONDI/T et al., February 11, 1992, CWL 7-1-12-9 Jacket 1.

36. Marieke Louis, "Women's Representation at the ILO," 207, 219; ILO, "Women's Empowerment."

37. Constance Thomas and Conny Wedda, "Mission Report," March 1997, 6, CWL 1-6-6 Jacket 3.

38. "Sexual Harassment in Judicial and Administrative Decisions," 3, 2, 8, 95, in CWL 7-1-12-9 Jacket 1.

39. "Combating Sexual Harassment at Work."

40. ILO, "Protection against Sexual Harassment at Work in the Developing Countries: Avenues of Action," typescript, CWL 7-1-12-9 Jacket 1; Note for the File, Meeting of Section on Work, Gender and Family, February 10, 1993; Andrea M. Singh on ILO Study, both in CWL 7-1-12-9 Jacket 2.

41. F. Josefina Dy to J. Decker Mathews, September 1, 1994, CWL 7-1-12-9 Jacket 4; "4. Safety, Health and Working Conditions: Sexual Harassment," draft attached to F. J. Dy to P. Brannen, January 30, 1995, CWL 7-1-12-9 Jacket 1; Constance Thomas to Josefina Dy, November 24, 1995, CWL 1-6-8 Jacket 2.

42. Memo to Mme. Perret-Nguyan from Marcel Bourlard, 1991; Linda Wirth, "Mission Report, European Trade Union Conference Seminar on Sexual Harassment," December 1991; Constance Thomas, "Mission Report: Conference on Sexual Harassment" and "Workshop on Sexual Harassment, Implementing Policies and Procedures," June 1992; Thomas, "Critical Mission Report: Intersessional Working Group of the Commission on the Status of Women on Violence against Women," September 1992, CWL 7-1-12-9 Jacket 1.

workplace sexual harassment into UN statements about gendered violence.[43] They also supported initiatives at ILO regional branches.[44] Meanwhile, the World Bank consulted ILO women experts on policies for its staff.[45]

The Philippines was one place where the feminist experts prepared for new legislation by organizing a successful Tripartite Regional Seminar.[46] A significant launching pad for ILO initiatives in Asia, the Philippines stood as a major "exporter" of domestic workers, whose remittances underwrote higher household standards.[47] Present in November 1993 were Wirth and Séguret from Geneva and Senior Specialist on Women and Gender Questions Lin Lean Lim from the Asia and Pacific Region.[48] These connections proved invaluable in generating an equal-opportunity and anti-violence agenda and in facilitating workshops.

The terms of discussion at the Manila seminar reverberated with those at UN meetings and the halls of the ILO itself. Speakers admitted that cultural restraints and traditional attitudes toward women inhibited discussion, while conditions in the informal sector and among the unorganized exacerbated harms. In this respect, Asian countries were like African ones, where "the question of sexual harassment is often downplayed and labelled a 'Western concept.'"[49] But in underscoring the analysis of "our comrade women activists in the feminist movement," one labor leader attributed the "culture of violence that breeds and tolerates sexual harassment" not only to gender relations under patriarchy but also to the exploitation of workers. All workers, he argued, needed to fight sexual harassment. Government representatives also spoke in terms of "human rights and dignity . . . unequal gender relations and sex discrimination," but they stressed the impact of harassment on "productivity, industrial relations, worker morale, working conditions and corporate and even national image."[50] Employers agreed that sexual harassment hampered workplace efficiency, but stressed the difficulty of monitoring the many small businesses, while feelings of shame would inhibit reports of abuse. Labor and government participants only could recommend more education of informal sector workers and "gender-sensitization programmes" for policymakers, businesses, and unions.[51]

The question of how to move the ILO forward generated controversy. Filipina Fe Josefina Dy (later, Dy-Hammar), the chief of CONDI/T, created obstacles

43. Thomas, "Critical Mission Report."

44. Minute, Alice Ouédraogo to C. Dumont, February 23, 1993, CWL 7-1-12-9 Jacket 2.

45. Minute, Marit Wiig visit to Séguret and Thomas, July 6, 1993, CWL 7-1-12-9 Jacket 2.

46. Reeta Bandopadhyay, "Brief Report on Tripartite Regional Seminar on Combating Sexual Harassment at Work," 1993, in CWL 7-1-12-9-100-84 Jacket 1.

47. Francisco-Menchavez, *Labor of Care.*

48. Bandopadhyay, "Brief Report on Tripartite Regional Seminar," 3–4.

49. Memorandum to A. Ouédraogo from B. Essenberg, February 15, 1993, CWL 7-1-12-9 Jacket 2.

50. Bandopadhyay, "Brief Report on Tripartite Regional Seminar," 2–3.

51. M.-C. Séguret and L. Wirth, "Mission Report," December 15, 1993, CWL 7-1-12-9-100-84 Jacket 1; Claudia Coenjaerts, "Mission Report: Tripartite Regional Seminar on Combating Sexual Harassment at the Workplace, 19–21, CWL 7-1-12-9 Jacket 4.

to developing a standard on sexual harassment. Resistance also came from Cornelie Hak, a Dutch Employer delegate and Governing Body member noted for opposition to organized feminism.[52] In 1995, Séguret recommended that the Office draft a code of practice to be submitted to a meeting of experts, which then could be forwarded to the Governing Body. Under the umbrella of providing "*broadly acceptable guidance* on policies, procedures, guidelines and programmes," Dy decided to present draft guidelines to a powerless symposium rather than to formal experts.[53] Since information was lacking for much of the global South and former state socialist economies, "sufficient universal relevance is questionable," she would explain to the Committee on Standards (NORMES), which sent proposals for standard setting to the Governing Body.[54] She would not recommend sexual harassment as a topic for general consideration.

The discussion on sexual harassment as a topic for convention-making underscores the pulls of gender equity, global relevance, and competing topics for protection and rights within the ILO. It further illustrates the hurdles of moving an issue through this bureaucracy. While Dy could obstruct, she could not control the internal debate within NORMES. In the late 1990s, the Office on Women (FEMMES) and EQUALITE advocated for sexual harassment as a topic for ILC deliberation.[55] This debate occurred while the Office was having difficulty abiding by consistent procedures for selection of issues that would strategically gain success in the Governing Body.

With support from ILO feminists, Kari Tapiola, the Finnish Worker delegate who had become an Assistant Director-General, proposed action in 1997. He suggested bringing to the Governing Body the issue of sexual harassment by itself or as part of a plank on the dignity of workers. Hodges, who had updated legal trends for the ILO's own journal, emphasized that preparatory work already existed and many nations already had specific legislation.[56] FEMMES encouraged a convention as a response to the Beijing Conference on Women, which had highlighted sexual violence.[57] Other units wondered whether a sexual harassment convention could be ratified or enforced. The legal division questioned whether it was even appropriate, since the subject failed the criteria of universality; they suggested that it might be bet-

52. Constance Thomas, interview with author, January 24, 2020; Manuela Tomei, interview with author, July 2, 2020; Lubin and Winslow, *Social Justice for* Women, 188–89.

53. M.-C. Séguret to Dy, "Draft Guidelines on the Prevention of Sexual Harassment at Work," October 12, 1995; Wirth to Dy and Séguret, October 31, 1995, F. J. Dy to Séguret, October 16, 1995, CWL 1-6-8 Jacket 1.

54. Minute Sheet from F. J. Dy to Mr. Bequele, "Proposed Standards for 2000 ILC and Beyond," 5.11.96, CWL 1-6-8 Jacket 1.

55. Minute, from Hector Bartolomei to K. Tapiola and others, Committee Report of Meeting, 8.5.98, CWL 1-6-8 Jacket 4.

56. Aeberhard-Hodges, "Sexual Harassment in Employment."

57. Notes on Standards Committee, July 10, 1997, Standards Committee Report of Meeting 1.9.97, CWL 1-6-6 Jacket 3.

ter to wait for reactions to forthcoming nonbinding principles for prevention. But the lawyer heading NORMES countered, "If we always used the criteria of universality, standards on fundamental human rights never would have been adopted. It is universal because [it is] also found in developing countries." The Employers section of the Office thought that since there was already a code of practice, it was not necessary to have another instrument.[58]

Tapiola mediated the conflicting positions. Lee Swepston, EQUALITE's champion of Indigenous rights, noted the need to formulate future action through a formal "Meeting of Experts," while Dy remained skeptical about standard setting, wanting a background paper, not the usual "law and practice" report developed for proposed conventions. She felt that the question related closely to Convention No. 111, the instrument under Swepston's section that addressed workplace sexual harassment as a form of sex discrimination.[59] Into the new millennium, the Employers group, and not only skeptics among the staff, would deploy this understanding to argue against a separate instrument.[60] In 1998, NORMES called for taking up sexual harassment on the basis of growing numbers of countries adopting legislation and regulations, which made the topic ripe for convention consideration.[61]

The Governing Body choose ILC topics over a number of sessions and initially retained workplace sexual harassment as a possibility. The Office continuously argued that "even when the phenomenon in a particular society is denied by some, its existence is equally positively asserted by those who suffer from it, indicating that lack of awareness of its existence does not necessarily mean that it is not present."[62] It garnered support from the Workers group and a few governments. Employers were strongly opposed, but their objections varied. In 1998, for example, the Employers group Vice-Chair, Rolf Thüsing from the Confederation of German Employers' Associations, argued for the item's removal because "the subject was too serious to be considered in the present heated climate when lucrative lawsuits were eagerly sought by unscrupulous lawyers. Moreover, the subject concerned society as a whole, not only the workplace." National legislation was enough.[63] The following year, he contended that it was "unreasonable to place responsibility on employers for something that they would like to prevent but could not always influence." However, a Meeting of Experts "could be of use" before any other action.[64] Into the next century, the Employers Vice-

58. Notes on Standards Committee, July 10, 1997.

59. Comment, C. Thomas to Swepston et al., September 22, 1993, CWL 7-1-12-9 Jacket 2; Standards Committee Report of Meeting, September 9, 1997; Minute from Dy to Bequele, Taqi, and Bartolomei, February 5, 1998, CWL 1-6-6 Jacket 3.

60. Constance Thomas and Conny Wedda Mission Report, March 4–7, 1997.

61. Minute Sheet, Edits from Dy to Bequele and Laviec, September 29, 1998, CWL 1-6-8 Jacket 4.

62. Proposals for the Agenda of the 88th Session (2000) of the ILC, Draft Portfolio, Second Item on the Agenda, Governing Body, November 1997, 38, CWL 1-6-6 Jacket 3.

63. Governing Body, *Minutes of the 271st Session*, 1/5.

64. Governing Body, *Minutes of the 276th Session*, 1/2.

Chair rejected the topic both on the basis of its "cultural implications" and because it was already the "subject of several instruments, policies, and programmes." Despite connecting prevention of sexual harassment to gender equality, governments, including Canada and the United States, agreed that the topic came under Convention No. 111 and thus rejected separate action.[65]

Nonetheless, a framework emerged. What began as a feminist conceptualization traveled beyond women to include a variety of abuses. The European Commission recommendation "on the protection of the dignity of women and men at work" subsumed sexual harassment. This yoking of sexual harassment to dignity at work appeared as one origin of its later coupling with gender violence. Another section of the Office already explained that a general discussion of respect and dignity for workers would cover "physical constraints and violence at the place of work, physical damage, restrictive measures compared to certain fundamental liberties and improper exercise of power by those with authority, including sexual harassment."[66] Some members of the Governing Board agreed. During March 1998 discussions, the member from the Swedish government reported that her nation was for extending prevention of workplace sexual harassment "to other kinds of victimization at work," which justified further research and preparatory work. The Canadian government member also supported "possible inclusion of other forms of harassment."[67] Reinforcing the violence framework was the ILO's 1998 publication of *Violence at Work* that listed sexual harassment along with shootings, bullying, mobbing, and additional aggressive acts, psychological as well as physical.[68] Despite championship of the violence framework by Canada at the Governing Body, NORMES still recommended "that the scope of the proposal should be maintained and not extended to include other forms of violence at work."[69]

Formidable opposition remained at the beginning of a new century. Within the Office, CONDI/T still was reluctant, though it planned regional seminars and additional research. New procedures for selecting items for the ILC made it difficult to push for "complicated" topics, which seemed to include sexual harassment.[70] Competing measures on youth employment, investment and employment, and cooperatives had stronger support. Employment of women and gender equality won backing, which eventually bode well for addressing sexual harassment. In 2004, Canada linked the two items. Other nations expressed support, but the Employers group was

65. Governing Body, *Minutes of the 291st Session*, 1–5.

66. Governing Body, *Minutes of the 291st Session*, 1–5.

67. Governing Body, *Minutes of the 271st Session*, 1/9, 1/11.

68. Chappell and Martino, *Violence at Work*.

69. Governing Body, *276th Session*, 42. See also Portfolio of Proposals for the Agenda of the 89th Session (2001), Minute Sheet, September 24, 1998, 34, CWL 1-6-8 Jacket 4.

70. Memo, Lee Swepston to Zarka-Martres, October 13, 2000; email to Petra Ulshoefer from Monique Zarka-Martres, October 19, 2000; and Memo, Dy-Hammar to M. Zarka-Martres, September 28, 2001, CWL 1-6-8-2 Jacket 1.

unmoved.[71] Rather than revealing organizational disfunction, from another angle such stalling actually fulfilled an institutional imperative to wait for acceptance by a majority of member states.

Migrant Domestic Workers and Union Responses

Speaking for the Group of Latin American and Caribbean States, in 2008 Uruguay brought before the Governing Body a resolution to combat violence against migrant women workers.[72] Such workers were ahead of ILO delegates; for over a decade they had mobilized to fight against sexual harassment despite vulnerability from being temporary sojourners and noncitizens. They understood workplace sexual harassment as "a form of violence against women . . . a form of power and control violated by men and rooted in patriarchy."[73] Among migrants, domestic workers seemed uniquely vulnerable. Because their workplace and home were the same, if they escaped harassment through quitting they risked becoming unhoused, increasing the trauma associated with abuse.[74] Migrant domestic workers and their advocates thus developed strategies to combat sexual harassment that included self-care and social support groups. A global network protested sexual violence and other employment conditions. Filipinas notably pressured their own government and publicized death sentences given to overseas workers charged with murdering abusive employers.[75]

Worker centers in Canada, a preferred destination for overseas care workers, illuminate the feminist mobilization that ran from the local to the global and enhanced domestic worker organization. Such grassroots groups dared to hold international institutions accountable for stopping workplace harassment. In 1995, for example, INTERCEDE, the fifteen-year-old Toronto Organization for Domestic Workers' Rights, responded to a UN invitation to states to end violence against women migrant workers with its own call for continued pressure "for stronger and stronger measures from governments that benefit from the labour and hardship of women migrant workers."[76] Such groups worked with feminists inside and outside government, solidifying the kinds of coalitional politics between NGOs, feminists, and worker organizations that proved essential to wage campaigns in the international realm as well as in local and national arenas.[77] They recognized that pronouncements by international organizations were not enough.

Under coordinator Fely Villasin, INTERCEDE catered mostly to Filipina migrant caregivers, informing them of their rights, providing advice on a range of practical matters, and running a hotline for those facing sexual harassment. It sought

71. See Governing Body, *Minutes of the 282th Session*, November 2001; *288th Session*, November 2003; *291st Session*, November 2004.

72. Governing Body, *Minutes of the 303rd Session*, 63.

73. "Sexual Harassment in the Workplace."

74. "Landmark Decision on Sexual Harassment," 2.

75. Francisco-Menchavez, *Labor of Care*; for example, "Sarah Balagbagan's Life Spared," 4.

76. Carol Salmon, "Violence Stalks Migrant Women," *Domestics' Cross-Cultural News*, April 1996, 2, IISHA.

77. Marchetti, Cherubini, and Garofalo Geymonat, *Global Domestic Workers*.

to reach not only those legally in Canada as part of the Live-In Caregiver Program but also entrants on limited work permits, including "women who are prostituted by poverty and economic need." It lobbied against proposed immigration reform to argue for landed status rather than the employer-based system that enhanced dependency, encouraging abuse. Through participatory research, storytelling, and public gatherings, it publicized working conditions, such as the "inability to sleep in security," fear of deportation, passport confiscation, isolation, hunger, and overwork.[78] It reported on cases of abuse and shared examples of successful redress by human rights commissions and courts. Believing that "no employer should feel free to abuse a domestic worker without being made to account for it," INTERCEDE wielded exposure as a tool for change.[79]

Worker centers were not alone in fighting sexual harassment. At the forefront were unions, even though not all within were "fully at ease with the subject," noted the ILO in 1993.[80] Over a decade later, the Red Flag Women's Movement in Sri Lanka, as part of a campaign on domestic work, still chastised unions "to take up violence at the workplace [and sexual abuse] as worker related issues."[81] As early as 1990, however, some migrant members of Kalayaan! had joined Britain's venerable Transport and General Workers' Union, which for over fifty years had included domestic workers.[82] Unions in the Netherlands and Spain begun to combat sexual harassment. The Australian Council of Trade Unions sought elimination through collective bargaining. An internal zero tolerance policy meant that it would "*not* support any member found guilty of sexually harassing any other employee at the workplace." The Canadian Labour Congress issued numerous resolutions and policy statements, while the Equal Opportunities Department of the Canadian Union of Public Employees distributed a kit of educational materials as part of its national awareness campaign. The French Confederation of Democratic Trade Unions supported amending the labor code. Women's committees led the way, like the Coalition of Labor Union Women in the United States.[83] In 2002, Public Services International partnered with the ILO on guidelines for addressing violence among health workers and then the overall service sector; affiliates in Brazil, Korea, and elsewhere promoted stop the violence campaigns. The International Transport Workers' Federation simultaneously initiated proclamations and campaigns combating violence and sexual harassment of women within seafaring, railway, transit, and airline sectors. In 2007, it launched "Say No to Violence" with exemplary actions by affiliates in Bangkok and Bulgaria.[84]

78. "Focus on Abuse, Violence in the Live-In Caregiver Program," *Domestics' Cross-Cultural News*, August 2000, 1–2; "Delegates Validate INTERCEDED Research Findings," *Domestics' Cross-Cultural News*, December 2000/January 2001, 3–5, IISHA.

79. "5074 Contacts Made to Intercede Services," *Domestics' Cross-Cultural News*, July 2000, 1, IISHA; Geraldine Pratt, *Families Apart*.

80. "Combating Sexual Harassment at Work," 279, 229.

81. Red Flag Women's Movement, *Space to Speak*, 25.

82. Pillinger, *Violence and Harassment*, 43; Boris, *Making the Woman Worker*, 203.

83. "Combating Sexual Harassment at Work," 233, 241–42, 246, 272–73, 275–78.

84. Pillinger, *Violence and Harassment*, 74–75, 67–68.

Leading the way were the ICFTU and the IUF. These global formations legitimized action against sexual harassment as a form of discrimination, affront to worker dignity, and a necessary component to women's equality. The ICFTU promoted guidelines at its Fifteenth World Congress in Venezuela as part of a resolution on equality and would go on to advocate for ILO action in the 2000s. The IUF initiated regional programs. In 1995, its Asia-Pacific Women's Education Manual included a section titled "Dealing with Sexual Harassment" that proposed individual support, member education, steward training, contract provisions, legislation, and litigation.[85] An African regional women's project in 2007, aided by Swedish affiliates, promoted slogans like "Make My Workplace Safe—Dignity for Hotel Housekeepers." The union subsequently reached agreements with Chiquita, Unilever, Sodexo, and other international companies to "tackle" workplace sexual harassment.[86] Its Latin American region mobilized with women's NGOs.[87] Both ITUC and IUF staff would advise the international domestic worker movement in its campaign for ILO recognition and then ratification of Convention No. 189.[88]

The Road to Convention No. 190

"Nothing is possible without us," South African Myrtle Witbooi reminded a UN Women webinar in August 2020. Witbooi, the president of the International Domestic Worker Federation (IDWF), explained the importance of Convention No. 190 for domestic workers by emphasizing, "The employer is always in a position of power and is often prone to abuse this power."[89] Convention No. 189 had underscored this potential, and ILO Worker and Government groups highlighted domestic workers' vulnerability. "The fact that the workplace is a private home means that violence against women is an occupational safety issue," noted the AFL-CIO in a joint answer with the National Domestic Workers Alliance to an ILO questionnaire in 2010. The Chilean government similarly replied, "Special mention should be made of sexual harassment at the workplace, which is an unacceptable form of violence."[90] Such observations became Article 5 of the domestic work convention. The accompanying Recommendation (No. 201) spoke of the obligation by states, employers, and unions to establish protective mechanisms, such as compliance procedures and relocation/rehabilitation programs.[91] Domestic workers mobilized in Geneva for their convention and returned to lobby for action on sexual harassment.

---

85. IUF A/P Women's Education Manual, May 1995, in author's possession.

86. Adwoa Sakyi, speech at "Long-Term Global Perspectives on Preventing Sexual Harassment in the Workplace," 3, 5, in author's possession; Celia Mather, *From Lusaka to Accra*.

87. *HRCT Trade Group Conference*, November 10–11, 2016, 3, in author's possession.

88. Fish, *Domestic Workers of the World Unite!*; *Claiming Rights*.

89. IDWF e-Newsletter no. 38.

90. ILC, *Decent Work for Domestic Workers*, 171, 126.

91. ILO, "C189—Domestic Workers Convention, 2011 (No. 189)," www.ilo.org/dyn/normlex /en/f?p=NORMLEXPUB:12100:0::NO::P12100_ILO_CODE:C189 (accessed September 14, 2021); ILO, "R201 - Domestic Workers Recommendation, 2011 (No. 201)," www.ilo.org/dyn/normlex/en/f?p=NORM LEXPUB:12100:0::NO:12100:P12100_INSTRUMENT_ID:2551502:NO (accessed September 14, 2021).

From the mid-2000s, sentiment within the Governing Body grew for address-ing the issue, aided by strong support by members of the Workers group. In 2012, fol-lowing the successful domestic worker convention, the IUF turned to winning a mea-sure. So did the ICTU, spurred on by the same activists who had mobilized unions for the domestic workers.[92] In 2014 the Workers group listed as their top item "vio-lence in the workplace," which "cost the economy millions of dollars in health care, court cases, lost wages and sick pay," the Workers Vice-Chair argued; it was "central to the ILO's objective of promoting decent work."[93] The Employers group continued to delay, proposing more research, a tactic to postpone an issue that had garnered con-siderable momentum. Employers admitted "that it was extremely important," which became a reason for additional preparation "to analyse the need for a labour stan-dard."[94] Despite this reluctance, the Governing Body in November 2015 agreed to "violence against women and men in the world of work" for standard setting. This boarder conception won the support of enough governments to overcome the employ-ers.[95] Efforts by union women were paying off, although not necessarily on their pre-ferred terms. Among the challenges ahead, the IUF noted was "the widening of the scope from gender based violence to violence against men and women in the world of work which will considerably weaken the much needed focus on violence against women."[96]

Fault lines between the Employers and Workers groups persisted during the 2016 Tripartite Meeting on the subject, which would frame ILC deliberations. The Employers group still insisted, as their Vice-Chair explained, "that not all issues of violence could be solved through legislation." For them, violence was not primarily a workplace issue, thus they preferred voluntary measures like "prevention; risk man-agement; training; care and support to those affected; and monitoring and evalu-ation." They had come to view it as a question of health and safety rather than dis-crimination. Highlighting the vulnerability of workers in the informal sector and female dominated occupations, the Workers Vice-Chair, Catherine Passchier from the Netherlands Trade Union Confederation (FNV), saw the convention as an oppor-tunity to "help define violence, including gender-based." Praising the ILO for recog-nizing the home as a workplace, feminist experts noted the dangers from "unequal responsibility for care work" and the ways that "gender-based violence" served "to control women's labour and autonomy." In accepting Passchier's call to include "harassment" in the title of future deliberations, the meeting sought to respond to feminist concerns over sexual harassment being eclipsed by the violence framework.[97]

92. Pillinger, *Violence and Harassment*, 69–70; author notes at IDWF congresses October 2013 (Mon-tevideo) and November 2018 (Cape Town).

93. Governing Body, *Minutes of the 320th Session*, 4–5.

94. Governing Body, *Minutes of the 323rd Session*, 4–6.

95. Governing Body, *Minutes of the 325th Session*, 1; ILO, *Meeting of Experts on Violence against Women and Men in the World of Work*, 1–2.

96. *HRCT Trade Group Conference*, 4.

97. ILO, *Final Report: Meeting of Experts on Violence against Women and Men*, 4–7, 10, 29, 33; Budin to Boris.

Two years later, gender violence and harassment at work finally stood as an item for standard setting at the ILC. Workers and NGO allies, like Women in Informal Employment Globalizing and Organizing (WIEGO), campaigned for passage. Organized domestic workers returned to Geneva for lobbying. The IDWF offered a platform for inclusion of its members, whose workplace was still "not accepted as a 'workplace'" or subject to labor inspection or occupational health and safety regulations.[98] Support came from civil society stakeholders like CARE and sex worker rights groups. Eight-five governments, 179 worker organizations and 29 employer organizations submitted reactions.[99] The resulting convention, supplemented by a more detailed recommendation, covered not only the workplace but also the journey to work; not only employees but also interns and applicants; and not only the formal economy but also the informal. It recognized the spillover impact of domestic violence on employment.[100]

Multiple reasons determined the final timing. In the twenty-first century, the ILO increasingly focused on the informal sector and gender at work. Both of these areas illuminated how previous understandings of the workplace excluded vast numbers from social protection or any mechanism for redress. Then–Director General Juan Somavía, a Chilean diplomat, introduced the decent work agenda to meet the exergies of a new globalization, stressing principles and rights rather than convention setting.[101] In 2009, the ILO committed to "Gender Equity" as a key to "Decent Work," which included combating violence at work. The accompanying document nestled sexual harassment into violence; it suggested, for example, that various ILO tools on workplace sexual harassment could aid the UN's campaign to end violence against women and girls.[102] A subsequent 2012 survey, *Giving Globalization a Human Face*, highlighted the difficulty of applying Convention No. 111 to specific groups, especially domestic workers and others in the informal sector. By compiling nation-based legislative and legal measures, including human rights acts, the report offered an evidentiary basis for action.[103] Proponents also built on renewed attention to forced labor, the subject of a 2014 protocol. Other instruments also championed protective measures against violence: for seafarers, an occupation historically subject to bullying; for HIV/AIDS, the presence of which in the workplace had led to violence and harassment; for informal workers and women along the global supply chain; for displaced persons, refugees, and migrants; and for users of private employment agencies.[104]

98. IDWF, *Platform of Demands*, 4.

99. ILC, *Ending Violence and Harassment against Women and Men in the World of Work*, Report 5, no. 2, 1.

100. ILO, "C190 - Violence and Harassment Convention, 2019 (No. 190)," www.ilo.org/dyn/normlex/en/f?p=NORMLEXPUB:12100:0::NO::P12100_ILO_CODE:C190 (accessed September 14, 2021).

101. Tomei interview.

102. *Gender Equality at the Heart of Decent Work*, 33–35, 95–96, 143.

103. ILO, *Giving Globalization a Human Face*.

104. ILC, *Ending Violence and Harassment against Women and Men in the World of Work*, Report 5, no. 1, 34–37.

This time ILO feminists had gained more prominent positions. Guiding the effort were Manuela Tomei, who was the director of the newly named Conditions of Work and Equality Department and the staff person responsible for Convention No. 189, and Shauna Olney, director of the Gender Equality and Diversity branch.[105] Recognizing the necessity of a broad framework, including but not limited to gender equality, they brought before the Governing Body recent ILO statements on gender, sustainable development (including UN millennial goals), the informal sector, violence, and care work. They argued in terms of both human rights and economic efficiency and showed that the world was moving on the issue. By the penultimate 2015 Governing Board meeting, a wide range of governments, including Norway, Mexico, and the United States, pushed for action. The Director-General's representative tasked Olney's branch to clarify definitions, summarize preparatory work, and show the "added value" of a standard.[106] Efficiency and "added value" were flexible terms to capture neoliberal as well as social responsibility predilections.

"Violence and harassment" subsequently emerged as an area of inequality pinpointed by the Initiative on Women's Work, part of the centennial effort of Guy Ryder, a British unionist and former ICFTU official who at time was the Director-General.[107] He wanted to pass a convention to mark the centennial; one on harassment would make a splash, as had the 2011 convention on domestic work, because it showed the organization recognizing a major impediment to human rights and workplace equity. At the end, nearly all the delegates voted for adoption. But passage required removing the specificity of the first draft that included lists of those covered, including LGBTQ people who experienced myriad forms of workplace violence, a category to which some nations objected.[108]

Coming in the midst of #MeToo, it was inevitable that the ILO standard would be talked about in relation to a movement that exploded in the United States after the election of Donald J. Trump but had earlier origins in Black women's pain and anger.[109] During 2018 deliberations, the Workers Vice-Chair, Canadian M. Clarke Walker, stressed timeliness "following the emergence of social movements such as #MeToo, #YoTambién, #NiUnaMenos, and many others" that brought working-class women's voices to the world stage. Interviewed immediately after passage the following year, Director-General Ryder emphasized that "the momentum and the significance of this process has been accentuated by the #MeToo movement."[110] Indeed, the seeds of success had been planted decades before, watered by feminists within and outside the ILO, nurtured by women in the global trade unions

105. Interview with Tomei; Shauna Olney interview, July 13, 2020.

106. Governing Body, *Minutes of 325th Session*, 6, 16–19.

107. ILO, *Women at Work Initiative*.

108. Boris, *Making the Woman Worker*, 234–38.

109. Rothna Begum, "Two Years after #MeToo."

110. ILC, *Provisional Record*, 107th Session, 126; Stephanie Nebehay, "U.N. Labor Body Adopts #MeToo Pact against Violence at Work."

and embodied at the ILO by the presence of domestic workers themselves. By 2021, the minimum number of nations had ratified the convention for it to take effect—the latest, but not the last, step toward securing gender justice at work.[111] ◧

EILEEN BORIS, the Hull Professor and Distinguished Professor of Feminist Studies, University of California, Santa Barbara, specializes on home-based work and the racialized gendered state. Her books include the prize-winners *Home to Work: Motherhood and the Politics of Industrial Homework in the United States* (1994) and *Caring for America: Home Health Workers in the Shadow of the Welfare State*, with Jennifer Klein (2012, 2015). She is the coeditor, with Rachel Parreñas, of *Intimate Labors*. Her latest books are *Women's ILO: Transnational Networks, Global Labor Standards, and Gender Equity* (2018), coedited with Dorothea Hoehtker and Susan Zimmermann, and *Making the Woman Worker: Precarious Labor and the Fight for Global Standards, 1919–2019* (2019). She now is writing on the less-than-free labor of migrant domestic workers, legal regulation, and struggles against labor brokers since World War II.

References

Aeberhard-Hodges, Jane. "Sexual Harassment in Employment: Recent Judicial and Arbitral Trends." *International Labour Review* 135, no. 5 (1996): 499–533.

Baker, Carrie N. *The Women's Movement against Sexual Harassment*. New York: Cambridge University Press, 2008.

Begum, Rothna. "Two Years after #MeToo, New Treaty Anchors Workplace Protections." December 20, 2019. www.hrw.org/news/2019/12/20/two-years-after-metoo-new-treaty -anchors-workplace-protections#.

Berrebi-Hoffmann, Isabelle, Olivier Giraud, Léa Renard, and Theresa Wobbe, eds. *Categories in Context: Gender and Work in France and Germany, 1900–Present*. New York: Berghahn Books, 2019.

Boris, Eileen. *Making the Woman Worker: Precarious Labor and the Fight for Global Standards, 1919–2019*. New York: Oxford University Press, 2019.

Boris, Eileen, and Jennifer N. Fish. "'Slaves No More': Making Global Labor Standards for Domestic Workers." *Feminist Studies* 40, no. 3 (2014): 411–43.

Brysk, Allison. *The Struggle for Freedom from Fear: Contesting Violence against Women at the Frontiers of Globalization*. New York: Oxford University Press, 2018.

CEDAW. 1989. General Recommendation No. 12: Violence against Women, Eighth Session, at INT_CEDAW_GEC_5831_E.pd.

CEDAW. 1992. General Recommendation No. 19: Violence against Women, Eleventh Session, at INT_CEDAW_GEC_3731_E.pdf.

Chappell, Duncan, and Vittorio Di Martino. *Violence at Work*. Geneva: ILO, 1998.

Claiming Rights: Domestic Workers' Movements and Global Advances for Labor Reform. New York: Human Rights Watch, 2013.

Final Report: Meeting of Experts on Violence against Women and Men in the World of Work. Vols. 4–7, 10, 29. Geneva: ILO, 2016.

111. "Ratifications of C190."

Fish, Jennifer N. *Domestic Workers of the World Unite! A Global Movement for Dignity and Human Rights*. New York: New York University Press, 2017.

Francisco-Menchavez, Valerie. *The Labor of Care: Filipina Migrants and Transnational Families in the Digital Age*. Urbana: University of Illinois Press, 2018.

Husbands, Robert. "Sexual Harassment Law in Employment: An International Perspective." *International Labour Review* 31, no. 6 (1992): 535–59.

IDWF. E-Newsletter No. 38. 2020. https://mailchi.mp/aef05a0952d0/idwf-e-newsletter-38-20-august-2020?e=d187ad5750 (accessed April 11, 2021).

IDWF. *Platform of Demands: Violence and Harassment against Women and Men in the World of Work*. n.d. www.idwfed.org/en/resources/platform-of-demands-violence-and-harassment-against-women-and-men-in-the-world-of-work (accessed May 22, 2021).

ILC. *Decent Work for Domestic Workers*. Report 4, no. 2. Geneva: ILO, 2010.

ILC. "Ending Violence and Harassment against Women and Men in the World of Work." *Report* 5, no. 1 (2017): 34–37.

ILC. "Ending Violence and Harassment against Women and Men in the World of Work." *Report* 5, no. 1 (2018): 1.

ILC. *Gender Equality at the Heart of Decent Work*. Report 6. Geneva: ILO, 2009.

ILC. Provisional Record 8B (Rev. 1) 107th Session. Report of Standard Setting Committee. Summary of Proceedings. Geneva: ILO, 2018.

ILC. *Record of Proceedings*, Seventy-First Session. Geneva: ILO, 1985.

ILC. *Record of Proceedings*, Seventy-Fifth Session. Geneva: ILO, 1988.

ILO. *Budget for the Biennium 1992–93*. Geneva: ILO, 1991.

ILO. *C169—Indigenous and Tribal Peoples Convention*. 1989. www.ilo.org/dyn/normlex/en/f?p=NORMLEXPUB:12100:0::NO::P12100_ILO_CODE:C169.

ILO. "Combating Sexual Harassment at Work," *Conditions of Work Digest*, 11, no. 1 (1992): 1–300.

ILO. *Final Report: Meeting of Experts on Violence against Women and Men in the World of Work*. Geneva: ILO, 2016.

ILO. *Giving Globalization a Human Face*. Geneva: ILO, 2012.

ILO. *Meeting of Experts on Violence against Women and Men in the World of Work*. Geneva: ILO, 2016.

ILO. *Partial Revision of the Indigenous and Tribal Populations Convention*. Report 6, no. 2. Geneva: ILO, 1988.

ILO. *Partial Revision of the Indigenous and Tribal Populations Convention*. Report 4, no. 2A. Geneva: ILO, 1989.

ILO. *Tripartite Symposium on Equality of Opportunity and Treatment for Men and Women in Employment in Industrialised Countries, Report*. Geneva: ILO, 1990.

ILO. *The Women at Work Initiative: The Push for Equality*. Geneva: ILO, 2018.

ILO. *Women's Empowerment: 90 Years of ILO Action!* www.ilo.org/wcmsp5/groups/public/—dgreports/—gender/documents/publication/wcms_105088.pdf (accessed October 16, 2021).

ILO Governing Body. *Minutes of the 244th Session*. Geneva: ILO, 1998.

ILO Governing Body. *Minutes of the 271st Session*. Geneva: ILO, 1989.

ILO Governing Body. *Minutes of the 276th Session*. Geneva: ILO, 1999.

ILO Governing Body. *Minutes of the 282nd Session*. Geneva: ILO, 2001.

ILO Governing Body. *Minutes of the 288th Session*. Geneva: ILO, 2003.

ILO Governing Body. *Minutes of the 291st Session*. Geneva: ILO, 2004.

ILO Governing Body. *Minutes of the 303rd Session*. Geneva: ILO, 2008.

ILO Governing Body. *Minutes of the 320th Session*. Geneva: ILO, 2014.

ILO Governing Body. *Minutes of the 323rd Session*. Geneva: ILO, 2015.

ILO Governing Body. *Minutes of the 325th Session*. Geneva: ILO, 2015.

Kang, Laura Hyum Yi. *Traffic in Asian Women*. Durham, NC: Duke University Press, 2020.

Keck, Margaret E., and Kathryn Sikkink. *Activists beyond Borders: Advocacy Networks in International Politics*. Ithaca, NY: Cornell University Press, 1998.

"Landmark Decision on Sexual Harassment." *Nannies' Voice* 10, no. 2 (February 1997): 2.

Linden, Marcel van der. "The International Labor Organization, 1919–2019: An Appraisal." *Labor: Studies in Working-Class History* 16, no. 2 (2019): 11–41.

Louis, Marieke. "Women's Representation at the ILO: A Hundred Years of Marginalization." In *Women's ILO: Transnational Networks, Global Labour Standards and Gender Equity, 1919 to Present*, edited by Eileen Boris, Dorothea Hoehtker, and Susan Zimmermann, 202–26. Leiden: Brill, 2018.

Lubin, Carol Riegelman, and Anne Winslow. *Social Justice for Women: The International Labor Organization and Women*. Durham, NC: Duke University Press, 1990.

MacKinnon, Catherine A. *Sexual Harassment of Working Women*. New Haven, CT: Yale University Press, 1979.

Marchetti, Sabrina, Daniela Cherubini, and Giulia Garofalo Geymonat. *Global Domestic Workers: Intersectional Inequalities and Struggles for Rights*. Bristol: Bristol University Press, 2021.

Mather, Celia. *From Lusaka to Accra: More Women, Doing More, Building Our Unions: IUF Africa Regional Women's Project, 2007–2011*. n.d. https://iuf.org/ha/publications/lusaka-to-accra/ (accessed October 16, 2021).

Nebehay, Stephanie. "U.N. Labor Body Adopts #MeToo Pact against Violence at Work." *Reuters*, June 2019. www.reuters.com/article/us-un-labour-harassment-idUSKCN1TM1CM.

Olcott, Jocelyn. *International Women's Year: The Greatest Consciousness-Raising Event in History*. New York: Oxford University Press, 2017.

Pillinger, Jane. *Violence and Harassment against Women and Men in the World of Work: Trade Union Perspectives and Action*. Geneva: ILO, 2017.

Red Flag Women's Movement. *Space to Speak: Study on Female Domestic Workers in Sri Lanka*. Kandy: Red Flag Women's Movement, 2007.

RESPECT. *Accessibility of Services for Migrant Domestic Workers Survivors of Domestic Violence: Theory and Reality*. London: Kalayaan!, 2001.

Rodgers, Gerry, Eddy Lee, Lee Swepston, and Jasmien Van Daele. *The International Labour Organization and the Quest for Social Justice, 1919–2009*. Ithaca, NY: Cornell University Press; and Geneva: ILO, 2009.

Rottenberg, Catherine. *The Rise of Neoliberal Feminism*. New York: Oxford University Press, 2018.

Salmon, Carol. "Violence Stalks Migrant Women." *Domestics' Cross-Cultural News*, April 2, 1996.

"Sarah Balagbagan's Life Spared." *Nannies' Voice* 8, no. 11 (November 1995): 4.

Schwenken, Helen. "RESPECT for All: The Political Self-Organization of Female Migrant Domestic Workers in the European Union." *Refuge* 21, no. 3 (2003): 45–52.

"Sexual Harassment in the Workplace." *Domestics' Cross-Cultural News*, July 2000, 3–4.

Swepston, Lee. *The Foundations of Modern International Law on Indigenous and Tribal Peoples*, vol. 2: *Human Rights and the Technical Articles*. Brill: Leiden, 2018.

United Nations. *Report of the World Conference of the International Women's Year, Mexico City.* New York: United Nations, 1975.

United Nations. *Report of the World Conference of the United Nations Decade for Women: Equality, Development and Peace.* New York: United Nations, 1980.

United Nations. *Report of the World Conference to Review and Appraise the Achievements of the United Nations Decade for Women: Equality, Development and Peace.* New York: United Nations, 1985.

Tossing Men Out of Bars:
Consent in Today's Working Class

Anne Balay

In July 2020, Alexandria Ocasio-Cortez responded to Ted Yoho's flagrant harassment of her and his pitiful explanation by noting that she wasn't offended—that for her this was "just another day. His comments were not deeply hurtful or piercing to me because I have worked a working-class job."[1]

Maybe she means that in this type of work setting, this language is not rare, and that because of her class training, subway riding, and New York attitude, she just shrugged it off. But I'd like to suggest another reading.

AOC decided to respond publicly not because of the incident, but because of the excuse he gave in Congress the next day. She explains that because of her context as a worker, a subway commuter, a New Yorker, and a woman, she knew how to respond to such assaults by isolating herself from hurt. The comments, she says, did not "pierce" her. But it's within this same classed, raced, gendered, and regional context that she pivots to confronting him. When she adds, "I have tossed men out of bars that have used language like Mr. Yoho's," she is class-dragging him: using his formal title to contrast with his sleazy behavior.

Playing on class norms, she is treating an elite man the way she would treat a blue-collar customer. This allows her to accomplish an important recognition: *all* men engage in this behavior. Working-class women know how to respond effectively.

AOC ends by thanking Yoho for demonstrating that "you can be a powerful man and accost women . . . with impunity." Unconscious bias is notoriously hard to see—that's how it's defined and perpetuated. What Yoho does is make it visible, and that's what AOC wants us to notice. We *think* that working-class men harass—that construction workers wolf whistle—and we expect it from them. Actually, men of all ranks, types, and classes harass; we just don't notice this behavior when it comes from powerful, well-connected men. AOC's response not only draws attention to this

1. For this and all subsequent AOC quotations, see "Rep. Alexandria Ocasio-Cortez (AOC) House Floor Speech Transcript."

Labor: Studies in Working-Class History, Volume 19, Issue 1
DOI 10.1215/15476715-9475772   © 2022 by Labor and Working-Class History Association

convenient mistake but also demonstrates that it's working-class women who have the tools to respond appropriately and effectively. And that's where I focus my attention because too often the power of working-class women goes unrecognized. I want to cheer when AOC throws Yoho out of the bar (here the House of Representatives), and I want to model feminist responses to harassment on her working-class knowledge and high-femme skill set.

All women are targeted by sexual violence directed at them by all (kinds of) men. Working-class women like AOC have the tools to respond appropriately—to either shrug it off or to shut it down, depending on the context and the vulnerability of the target.

I have spent the past ten years doing oral histories of blue-collar queer workers, and the topics of harassment and consent come up often. One recent incident sheds light on how class shapes the way these are experienced.

First, the background. Several groups of women truckers have emerged online, with various emphases and missions. First came Women in Trucking (WIT), which deliberately avoids getting involved in industry debates about harassment, rape, and safety. The group's goal is to elevate the image of women truckers. They rely on corporate sponsorship for funds and publicity, which means that (a) they like a "positive" message and (b) they do not challenge the corporations.

Enter Desiree Wood, who had a child in her teens. From there her life bumped along in a typical working-class pattern. Eventually, shit happened and she found herself homeless and nearing middle age. Desperate, she chose trucking because she likes adventure, and though there's not a cowardly bone in her body, she wanted a safe place to sleep. She signed with a company called Covenant, which uses a team training model to maximize corporate profit. This put Desiree (as it had many women and men before her) in a truck with someone who demanded sex. When Desiree refused and reported him, Covenant brushed it off, didn't fire him, shifted her between trainer/codrivers until they realized she wasn't going to keep quiet in order to keep her job, and then fired her. Through these months, Desiree contacted WIT asking for help and got nowhere. They treated her the same as her would-be rapist and the company that protected him. They didn't really believe her and felt that an adequate remedy was to remove her, rather than address the widespread assumption that "the sleeper test" was just the price of a woman breaking into a male-dominated industry.

Desiree disagreed. She went to the media and stuck with it until Dan Rather picked up the story and featured her on PBS's documentary series *Frontline*. Although she moved to a different trucking company, she still wasn't done. Desiree found work as a trucker, but she also found a lifestyle she loved; driving a truck is a highly skilled, adrenaline-packed job, and its value is unmissable. People who do it well, especially those who have struggled previously, are proud and willing to fight. Desiree wanted other women to have this opportunity without paying the price she was asked to, so she formed a competing group, REAL Women in Trucking. This

Figure 1. Kira Wertz (call sign Foe Hammer) is a transgender woman and company driver based in Oklahoma City, here shown on an off-ramp just north of Ardmore, Oklahoma. She has been safely operating Class A trucks since 2014, and carries hazmat, tanker, and multiple trailer endorsements. Photo: Kira Wertz.

group does on-the-ground advocacy, puts pressure on policy makers, and provides a social hub for women who drive truck.

A bunch of us (I'm in this group, which welcomes former truckers as well as current drivers) decided to attend the Great American Truck Show in Dallas last year, renting an enormous house with a pool. Trucking keeps its workers isolated, and events like this are opportunities to talk and be visible. One of our goals at this event was to get signatures on a petition asking to meet with the Federal Motor Carrier Safety Association (FMCSA) to discuss patterns of rape and harassment in training fleets and to strategize how to address them nationwide. Women in Trucking had been consulted about this and had proposed that women only be trained by other women. REAL Women in Trucking objected to this "remedy" because (1) there are very few women who train, so a new trucker might have to wait months without income, probably far from home, before a female trainer could take her out on the road to begin earning an income, and (2) not all truckers are straight and not all truckers are cis and not all harassers are men and . . . Instead, we need a clear message to companies and truckers explaining consent, and we need a policy of removing offenders from the list of truckers who can train any new truck drivers.

Finally—my story. My friend Jess Graham and I were wandering the floor of the truck show asking everyone to sign our petition, and giving background if they asked. But we were on a mission: Jess wanted to approach the WIT booth and get them to sign. When she started driving truck a few years before, she had reached out to them and not felt welcome. She's a big woman with an even bigger mouth, and she got a vibe from them that she just wasn't their kind of woman.

Jess assured us she could "do" middle-class passing. She had makeup and a top and scarf and could talk the talk. She wanted to do this drag to get an audience with the enemy.

No one in that booth was going to engage anyone from Desiree's circle, or me (since I discuss their corporate entanglements in my book), but Jess was pretty new and wearing femininity as masquerade. As she approached the women at the counter, I hovered at the next booth, my back to them, listening. Jess explained what she wanted and what our goals were and asked for a response. And that trucker said that in her experience, most of the women out there want to have sex with their trainers—they have entered the profession to find men who will support them, and they deliberately "flaunt their femininity" to get laid.

The class message in this exchange is crucial. Just like in the statement AOC made, it could be read as a confirmation of stereotyped assumptions about class, sexuality, and bodily autonomy in which a working-class woman (the trucker standing at the WIT booth) performs attitudes about the loose morals and poor judgment of her peers in response to a middle-class presenting person. And certainly, that's part of the story. I've met countless people—men, women, and others—who believe that friendliness invites bad behavior and that businesslike focus deters it, and since this is their experience, they conclude that people who have run into trouble were just not acting right. So her comment and others do assert that being a woman in a male space is equivalent to inviting rape.

Yet there are other layers to her response. She isn't (necessarily) saying these words because it's what she believes as a blue-collar worker. Prime Inc. is telling them to defend its enormous corporate profits. The freight industry is controlled by a handful of monoliths that own megacarriers (trucking fleets like Swift, JB Hunt, or Prime), and these people are Fortune 500 robber barons, not working stiffs with time cards who wear Carhartts (the ubiquitous brand of thermal workwear). Clearly the woman at the WIT booth has not mounted a feminist critique of this corporatespeak, but it didn't start with her, or with anyone in the working class.

Furthermore, lots of people at truck stops do want sex. They're out on the road for weeks or months at a time during which they have no life outside the truck,

Figure 2. Jess Graham with her truck Black Widow at a rest stop in Louisiana. Photo: Jessica Graham.

which is their home. Many live there permanently. Anyone who's spent any time in truck stops knows that lots of cruising goes on there.

Now clearly rape and cruising are not the same. But when people talk about workplaces and consent, they usually understand work, home, and the social sphere as separate, and they often portray workers (and especially women) without bodies or desires in the workplace. I hear echoes of a mythic female purity when they talk, and that mythic sexless figure is white, middle-class, and straight. Actual truckers out in the world, of all genders, are often raunchy and proud of it. Others keep to themselves and find all that embarrassing and low-class.

Consent is complicated. It doesn't mean the same thing across class lines and in different contexts. To understand what it means to particular people in particular places means letting go of it as a static, objective standard. We need to listen rather than instruct. And that means listen to the women at the Woman in Trucking booth as well as to my friend Jess. Which is both a very queer way of conceiving objectivity and truth, and a radical one.

We don't even need to ask truckers how they understand and enforce consent because they have already made their views known—in spades. A group of truckers wrote the petition I mentioned and got it signed by wads of truckers and their allies, and when the FMCSA held an informal "listening session" about an unrelated rule change, they presented it to the powers that be. Several truckers approached the microphone during the Q&A, explained who they were and what the petition was, and asked for a chance to discuss rape and harassment in training fleets with the federal regulators. Given the amount of witnesses and media present, FMCSA's talking head at the convention almost had to consent, and a bunch of my friends met with him in Washington, DC, a few weeks later. Probably nothing will come of it, but my point is that that's not because working-class women have trouble coming to or articulating their viewpoint.

While in DC, on an expensive trip they funded via GoFundMe, the truckers made the best of it by scheduling meetings with senators or representatives from each woman's home state and Elizabeth Warren—with anyone who agreed to listen. And they got connected to other activists to get their message out. They explained that the people who own corporations that maximize profits by training new truckers want their employees to be scared and vulnerable. Organized and educated workers might resist appalling pay and working conditions, up to and including rape, while isolated and blamed workers are likely to think that their future employment depends on their being quiet.

But the class lines are crucial here. I often hear that blue-collar and working-class women expect to be harassed or worse at work, and the assumption is that they're somehow responsible for this pattern, even accept or enable it. But it's the policy positions of owners and fat cats that perpetuate these patterns, using classist assumptions about sexual expectations as camouflage. Harassment at work is scripted and enabled by the middle and owning classes.

Listening and grassroots activism as resistance to this pattern are crucial components of the MeToo movement. Tarana Burke structures the movement around believing the stories of survivors, building communities of them, and asking what would help them heal. While the mainstream media might focus on punishing the perpetrators, Burke finds that irrelevant or worse, since it inevitably leads to carceral responses that are by definition both racist and ineffective. And it doesn't help the people who come forward—it's misdirection.

What Burke did was create a climate in which people realized that they had a story and provide a context in which they could tell it. Some experiences need that frame, and class is crucial to understanding why.

Gradually, imperceptibly, the US working class has been disappeared. Though the people are still there, the sense of cohesion—the collective identity and access to a meaningful narrative—has dissolved. A crucial mechanism of neoliberalism, this shift isn't new. But the power of telling one's story as an antidote to it is what I want to notice. Burke created a language and a context in which people could do that. Sure, it was hijacked by the media and white celebrities, but the movement's power remained that of articulating how telling a story shapes how we understand our experience and the world.

Certainly as an oral historian I have found that to be true. When I reach out to a worker and ask them to sit down and tell me their story, the first response is that they don't have one. Only when I create a context by sharing my experience, other people's stories, and my interest in them as a person do they start talking. Often they surprise themselves with what emerges. They understand what has been taken from them and what they can now retain.

Union organizing provides many such opportunities. I now work for the Service Employees International Union (SEIU) Local 1, and I organize adjunct professors at St. Louis Community College, St. Charles Community College, St. Louis University, and Washington University. Though Missouri is not a right-to-work state, public sector bargaining units (such as community colleges) follow right-to-work rules, and our governor ensures us a weak position from which to bargain. And adjuncts anywhere are hard to organize, since they often don't see themselves as workers. Therefore, my job is an uphill battle. And now, with COVID, I can't have face-to-face meetings, and there is sweeping job loss, and people are sick and scared.

All of which is to say that the union will not get these workers much, in terms of contract improvements or money. However, the adjuncts I organize have taught me repeatedly that what the union does give them is a story. And my job here, as always, is to shut up and listen. Only recently have Americans come to see unions as chiefly concerned with the job security and pay of their workers. My adjuncts can't access these things, but they can access an earlier, more revolutionary union goal: to change the structure of work. By sharing stories with each other and the wider public, they challenge what it means to labor, what a job should offer its workers, and how paid work fits within civil society and our various social worlds.

In late August 2020, I found out one Monday that our unit's supervisor, a union vice president, had been summarily fired. In shock, I spread the word to the workers I organize who knew her, and immediately the grad students at WashU were angry and began to strategize how to respond and resist. The adjuncts at the community colleges were upset, felt betrayed, and proceeded with their work. The difference says something about class, consent, and organizing.

WashU consists of middle-class students, and a smattering of people from poorer backgrounds who are pursuing an education designed to elevate them to the middle class. What it means to be middle-class or "elite," in this context and in most of my thinking, is to experience stability and status. I use *working-class*, by contrast, as shorthand for people and jobs that are about necessity rather than choice and that offer little advancement and minimal sense of nobility or purpose. Members of the middle class are not used to authority acting on them in an arbitrary and capricious manner. Typically, their feelings, wishes, and preferences are taken into account, which explains why the grad workers at WashU refused to continue full participation in an organization that did not seek their consent, let alone their input.

The adjuncts and janitors we organize are working class either by inheritance or by higher ed's punitive hierarchy. By definition, they are accustomed to being screwed over by authority—that defines their condition.

But one goal of organizing a union is to provide workers with the ability to give or withhold consent. For once in my life, rather than mock privileged grad student workers, I want to imitate them. They are the real union here. They actually believe that we get strength from standing together and that we can only control our own future if we fight back when other workers' futures are compromised.

I can turn to the strength through storytelling skills my members have been teaching me to bring that power to the community college adjuncts, similar to what Desiree did with her own story and the petitions. I can build a community by listening to other people's experiences, and it's community that makes consent possible. And the motivation and strategy for this type of organizing emerge from working-class history and activism.

I am clearly too enmeshed in this work to have a scholarly perspective—I love these adjuncts and want their world to be better. But I also don't think that being enmeshed is a bad thing. Early in the process of writing about LGBT steelworkers, I met Jan Gentry. She told me stories about her life in mill and mine that shaped my book and my outlook on life. Though she had never been out at work explicitly, the process of looking back on her life in steel and talking about it to me made her want that to change. She wanted other gay steelworkers to have more protections, and therefore more safety and room to expand into whatever space they chose. She and I became friends, and she led a movement to get the United Steelworkers (USW) to change their international contract, and all the contracts they will bargain forevermore.

We went to Vegas together to attend the convention where this motion was debated and passed. We drove together in my un-air-conditioned car to North Fort Myers, Florida, to stay at a lesbian trailer park and describe this process to the (mostly retired) residents. We became friends. But she was not there when I was talking about my next book to a small audience at a bar outside Philly and learned that strippers in the area were organizing and had chosen the USW as their union because of the protections for queer and trans workers that Jan and I had fought for. Jan wasn't there because she had died of mill-related cancer. Like AOC, she had been harassed plenty and knew how to handle it (the stories are in my first book, where her name is "Gail"). Those are the fighting skills she brought to ensuring that other gay steelworkers, and then strippers, could fight for the protection of all workers. ◪

ANNE BALAY is an organizer for the Service Employees International Union (SEIU) in St. Louis, Missouri. She has also worked as a car mechanic, a professor, and a truck driver. Her books are *Semi Queer: Inside the Lives of Gay, Trans, and Black Truck Drivers* (2018) and *Steel Closets: Voices of Gay, Lesbian, and Transgender Steelworkers* (2014).

References

"Rep. Alexandria Ocasio-Cortez (AOC) House Floor Speech Transcript on Yoho Remarks July 23." *Rev*, July 23, 2020. www.rev.com/blog/transcripts/rep-alexandria-ocasio-cortez -floor-speech-about-yoho-remarks-july-23.

Class: A Useful Category of Analysis in the History of Sexual Harassment

Christopher Phelps

In her 1888 report as director of women's work for the Knights of Labor, Leonora Barry declared,

> I would be derelict in my duty did I not refer to cases which come to my knowledge frequently, in which men use the power which their position as employes, superintendents, or foremen give them to debauch girls in their employ whose employment is dependent on their good-will. It seems to me that our Order should use its influence everywhere to have laws passed for the protection of women against this wrong. It should be made a criminal offense for a man holding any position which gives him power over women to make in any way improper advances to them.[1]

An Irish immigrant widowed at an early age, Barry became a hosiery millworker to support her three children. Having joined the Knights and then traversed the country as their organizer, Barry was well acquainted with the "thousands of underpaid women and girls in our large cities," as she put it in the prior year's report. She called upon every Knights district assembly to establish a body of "three intelligent women" to investigate "any abuse existing which a female Local would be delicate in mentioning to the General Executive Board."[2]

When Barry made these statements, neither workplace sexual exploitation nor resistance to it were new. Consider a story concerning what Adrienne D. Davis calls the "sexual economy" of slavery, a racialized class relation in which owners "compelled sexual and reproductive labor."[3] Interviewed by the Federal Writers' Project in 1937, the elderly Fannie Berry, enslaved before the Civil War in Petersburg, Virginia, recalled a "big strappin'" slave named Sukie who decisively fended off her master:

Many thanks to Eileen Boris, Johanna Brenner, Patrick Dixon, Kaisha Esty, Leon Fink, Carol Hollier, and Mara Keire for astute criticism of prior drafts. Susan Levine and Lara Vapnek identified Leonora Barry in the photograph.

1. Barry, "Report of the General Instructor," 4. "Employe" is an archaic spelling of *employee*.
2. Quoted in Vapnek, *Breadwinners*, 46.
3. Davis, "'Don't Let Nobody Bother Yo' Principle,'" 17, 32.

Labor: Studies in Working-Class History, Volume 19, Issue 1
DOI 10.1215/15476715-9475786   © 2022 by Labor and Working-Class History Association

She used to cook for Miss Sarah Ann, but ole Marsa was always tryin' to make Sukie his gal. One day Sukie was in the kitchen makin' soap. Had three gra' big pots o' lye jus' comin' to a bile in de fireplace when ole Marsa come in. . . . Den he tell Sukie to take off her dress. Den he grabbed her an' pull it down off'n her shoulders. . . . He grab hold of her an' try an' pull her down on the flo'. Den dat black gal got mad. She took an' punch ole Marsa an' made him break loose an' den she gave him a shove an' push his hindparts down in de hot pot o' soap. Soap was near to bilin', an' it burnt him near to death. He got up holdin' his hindparts and ran from de kitchen, not darin' to yell, 'cause he didn't want Miss Sarah Ann to know 'bout it. . . . Marsa never bother slave girls no more.[4]

Sukie's action was remarkably effective, made possible by her armed self-defense with a pot of boiling hot soap and her shrewd leveraging of her master's fear of exposure. If sexual abuse by masters, employers, overseers, and owners is rife in American history, so too is its fierce rejection and deft evasion by servants, enslaved people, factory hands, and office workers.

Leonora Barry's pronouncements to the Knights of Labor in 1887 and 1888 belonged to that tradition, but they represented something new as well, a passing beyond individual resistance to a vision of labor's potential for collective, class-wide action. That idea materialized at the Knights of Labor's 1886 convention, where sixteen of 660 delegates were women. Meeting as a committee, the women—shoeworkers, textile mill operatives, dressmakers, a machine hand, an ironer, and a housewife— recommended that the Knights establish a women's work department with a general investigator empowered to inquire, among other things, into "the abuses to which our sex is subjected by unscrupulous employers."[5] Barry was present, and the group recommended she fill the new post. When subsequently, as the Knights' only female national officer, she urged the Order to provide formal mechanisms enabling women workers to address sexual abuse and to promote legislation to outlaw it, Barry advanced the earliest known program for the American labor movement to act against sexual harassment.[6]

4. Perdue, Barden, and Phillips, *Weevils in the Wheat*, 48–49.

5. Quoted in Flexner, *Century of Struggle*, 196.

6. A competing claim requires weighing, namely that labor's first initiative on the question came from the millworkers of Lowell, Massachusetts. Linda Gordon, in a brief passage in a brilliant talk first published in *Radical America* in 1981, stated that in the 1820s Lowell working women objected to vulgar language and indecent propositions (Gordon, "Politics of Sexual Harassment," 8). The passage had no citation, and decades later Gordon cannot specify the source (email to author, October 22, 2018). In the #MeToo moment, a millennial cohort of socialist-feminists, rightly admiring Gordon's essay, extended its claim. One stated that the Lowell strikes of the 1830s were motivated by "sexual harassment and assault by supervisors, which left them humiliated, enraged, and often pregnant" (Leonard, "How to Stop the Predators"), while another wrote that sexual harassment was "one of the key issues" in "the Lowell textile mill union campaigns" (Press, "Sexual Harassment").

The irony is that the Lowell millworkers would have taken such suggestions as an affront. When the mills were established in the 1820s, as former factory girl Harriet Robinson observed, the millworker of England and France had the disreputable image of being "subjected to influences that could not fail to destroy her purity and self-respect" (Robinson, *Loom and Spindle*, 61). To attract young, single girls from

Figure 1. Women delegates, Knights of Labor convention, Richmond, Virginia, October 1886. Leonora Barry stands at center, the only one wearing a hat, perhaps to symbolize her status as first among equals given the convention's appointment of her as national director of women's work. Elizabeth Rodgers, organizer of the Knights' largest district assembly in Chicago and the Irish-born wife of an iron molder, holds her twelfth child, two-week-old baby Lizzie, designated "Delegate No. 800" by the Knights and presented with a silver spoon and cup. Mary Anderson sits at left, Laura Graddick stands second from right; the others are unidentified. Prints and Photographs Division, Library of Congress, Washington, DC.

New England farms as cheap factory labor, Lowell mill owners intentionally countered that image by fostering an atmosphere of wholesome moral uplift. They sponsored literary and cultural activities, mandated church attendance, and required workers to live in strictly governed company boardinghouses. This encouraged a tractable, disciplined workforce, while the mill girls, for their part, appreciated the ethos of chastity as a way of safeguarding their reputations.

Thomas Dublin attributes the 1834 strike to wage reductions and the 1836 strike to boardinghouse room and board price increases, with no mention of sexual harassment. The strikers positioned themselves, rather, as free, independent New England citizens oppressed by a monied aristocracy (Dublin, *Women at Work*, 86–131).

It is worth considering the possibility that Gordon meant the 1840s, not the 1820s, and *Radical America* introduced a typo that cascaded into the subsequent poetical exaggerations. By the 1840s, allusions to sexual improprieties in the mills abounded as capitalist competition eroded the old Lowell paternalism and a

Contextually, this agenda was a product of the rare inclusivity of the Knights, who organized tens of thousands of women, African Americans, and immigrants. It also reflected the felt class power of wage-earning industrial labor amidst the Great Upheaval of 1886 and its aftermath. A transatlantic confluence can be detected in which broad industrial labor upsurges involving both men and women workers created a dawning working-class women's awareness of the potential for collective labor action to address workplace sexual abuse. In Britain's "new unionism" of the 1880s, for example, as less-skilled, lower-paid manual wage earners like dockers began to organize, women cotton factory operatives in Oldham, near Manchester, walked out in 1887 to protest sexual assaults by a male head carder in the earliest English textile industry strike over sexual harassment.[7]

In 1888, however, Barry recommended abolishing the Knights' woman's department in the belief that wage workers should not be distinguished by sex but organized together with men. This aspirational gender-blindness, combined with Victorian sexual reticence, indifference among laboring men, and the Knights' general decline, halted the progress of Barry's agenda. The initiative passed to a short-lived Working Women's Society (WWS) that brought together wealthy and working-class women in 1888–90 to protest "cruel and tyrannical treatment on the part of employers and their managers," including "abusive or insulting language."[8] The WWS sec-

---

permanent proletariat comprised largely of Irish immigrants replaced the temporary workforce of Yankee daughters. "Debate over the moral standards of factory women was most intense in the 1840s," writes David Zonderman (*Aspirations and Anxieties*, 136).

In 1840, Orestes Brownson wrote that few Lowell girls could return to their native place with "reputations unimpaired," to say that she worked in a factory being "almost enough to damn to infamy the most worthy and virtuous girl" (Brownson, *Laboring Classes*, 11). This brought indignation from Lowell girls (A Factory Girl, "Factory Girls," 17–19). When the Lowell Female Labor Reform Association, the first union, was formed in 1844, it focused on a ten-hour day and the speedup. Its militant organizer Sarah Bagley, writing in *Voice of Industry* in 1846, warned female workers away from "the steady gaze or stealthy touch of the *fiend* in human form," a likely allusion to sexual harassment, but simultaneously rejected smears on mill girls' reputations by declaring, "The standard of virtue in Lowell, is far above that of any city of its size in the Union" (Foner, *Factory Girls*, 167).

Even labor's champions at Lowell, then, considered virtuous individual conduct, not collective labor action, the remedy to sexual pressure. They objected to any suggestion that women workers had complied with coercive demands for fear that the cause of labor reform would be tarnished. This concession to conventional morality was understandable, but a trap. It ceded to overseers the power to discharge women by insinuating immorality. If Lowell illustrates anything, it is how bourgeois moral hegemony in the form of purity and reticence operated to inhibit women workers in the nineteenth century who wished to preserve an unsullied, unimpeachable character and did not wish to be designated "low class." Facing a world in which willingness of a woman to sell her labor power could be conflated with willingness to sell her body, working women sought to don a cloak of virtue that in the end impeded their ability either to organize or address sexual harassment.

Appreciation to Sylvia Cook, Thomas Dublin, Linda Gordon, Julie Husband, Judith Ranta, Ann Schofield, and David Zonderman for answering queries on this point; author alone responsible for the appraisal.

7. Lambertz, "Sexual Harassment in the Nineteenth Century English Cotton Industry," 31.

8. Quoted in Vapnek, *Breadwinners*, 74. On the WWS, see also McCreesh, *Women in the Campaign to Organize Garment Workers*, 58–60.

retary, Alice Woodbridge, had striking red hair and blue eyes that led others to compare her to models and made her a magnet for "insulting proposals from employers," disrupting her attempted office career.[9] The organization persuaded several state legislatures, including New York's, to appoint women factory inspectors on the grounds, as inspector Margaret Finn recalled, that women factory workers would "confide to women inspectors grievances relating to matters of propriety, that they would not tell to inspectors who are men." This reform, however, came just as the American Federation of Labor (AFL) presided over by Samuel Gompers took the lead in organized labor, guided by "pure and simple" trade unionism and uninterested in the organization of women workers. As Florence Kelley, a WWS leader, later recalled, the idea had "in no way" belonged "to the goals of the general workers' movement, although it found support among the unions."[10] Legislative backing proved fleeting, and women factory inspectors were not retained.

Despite their limited ultimate impact, these Gilded Age developments represented significant breakthroughs. Barry, in particular, went beyond demanding that the labor movement address sexual harassment to articulate a class analysis of it. The problem, she held, was not merely one of male license, for sexual exploitation was directly connected to class exploitation. The invasiveness of certain men was enabled by the power conferred to them in capitalist society over women whose employment was "dependent on their good-will." As Lara Vapnek writes, Barry "cast working women's low wages and vulnerability to sexual harassment as part of a larger system of wage slavery, to be corrected through workers' organization."[11]

Perspectives of Barry's sort have few echoes in contemporary academic analysis of sexual harassment. That may owe something to the structure of the neoliberal university, with its many institutes and centers of gender and sexuality, occasional centers of race and sexuality, and complete absence of centers of class and sexuality. As Eileen Boris suggests, "intersectionality" in practice refers almost entirely to gender and race, while class, despite ritual inclusion in intersectional trilogies, goes missing.[12] This is all the more true when class is understood not as a static function of education or income but as a dynamic, antagonistic relationship between capital and labor structured by the extraction of surplus value. Few theorists, writes Brooke Meredith Beloso in an extraordinary essay, have sufficiently explored "the class constitution of gender and sexuality" or "the gendered and sexual constitution of class."[13]

Located at precisely those intersections, this essay considers four historical phases—the Gilded Age, the Progressive Era, the Great Depression and the Second World War, and the present era since the 1970s—to maintain the value of class as an

9. Nathan, *Story of an Epoch-Making Movement*, 15–16.

10. Finn and Kelley quoted in Sklar, *Florence Kelley*, 142.

11. Vapnek, *Breadwinners*, 64–65. For more on Barry, see Flexner, *Century of Struggle*, 196–200; Levine, "Labor's True Woman," 331–37; McCreesh, *Women in the Campaign to Organize Garment Workers*, 1, 31–37.

12. Boris, "Class Returns," 74.

13. Beloso, "Sex, Work, and the Feminist Erasure of Class," 60.

analytic category in understanding sexual harassment and resistance to it in the history of American capitalism. Drawing synthetically upon a broad range of histories, it contests perspectives that erase or subordinate class while seeking to situate class, in turn, within a full-spectrum intersectionality. Bringing class back in reveals sexual harassment to be one form of the enactment of class, not merely gender. It indicates that sexual harassment deserves to be appreciated as a little-acknowledged but key variable in how a class in itself, the working class, becomes a class for itself, a self-aware, cohesive social force, even as it can also function as a disintegrative, divisive factor that short-circuits solidarity and class consciousness. While sexual harassment can in no way be reduced to class, class shapes sexual harassment and sexual harassment shapes class. This framing throws present history into sharp relief by making clear that from the 1880s through the 1940s resistance to sexual harassment was firmly grounded in working-class self-activity, while in the present era since the 1970s that tradition definitely persists but has simultaneously been decentered, the issue too often being refracted such that gender detaches artificially from class.

Factory Girls and Foremen: Sexual Class Struggles of the Progressive Era

The proletarian fiction that emerged in the socialist movement of the first decades of the twentieth century cast sexual harassment as employer exploitation. In *Diary of a Shirtwaist Striker* (1910), Theresa Malkiel referred to "a child of sixteen seduced by her employer."[14] In 1912, Margaret Sanger, a nurse and socialist not yet converted to birth control as her central focus, wrote a short story about a young nurse whose employer tries to rape her.[15] The vulnerability of a family in the face of a corporation's totalizing power was underscored by Upton Sinclair in *The Jungle* (1906), whose Lithuanian immigrant protagonist Jurgis Rudkus discovers that his wife Ona succumbed to her foreman at the Chicago meatpacking company where they and other relatives of theirs worked:

> "I did not want—to do it," she said; "I tried—I tried not to do it. I only did it—to save us. It was our only chance. . . . He told me—he would have me turned off. He told me he would—we would all of us lose our places. We could never get anything to do—here—again. He—he meant it—he would have ruined us. . . . He knew all about us, he knew we would starve."[16]

Mass-produced dime novels, which enjoyed a wider working-class audience than radical fiction and social criticism, also discussed sexual harassment explicitly, as chronicled by Nan Enstad.[17] Social criticism and commentary also took on the issue, as when Emma Goldman wrote in "The Traffic in Women" (1910) that since "nowhere is woman treated according to the merit of her work, but rather as a sex," it was

14. Malkiel, *Diary of a Shirtwaist Striker*, 128.
15. Sanger, "Unrecorded Battle" (in this issue).
16. Sinclair, *Jungle*, 181.
17. Enstad, *Ladies of Labor, Girls of Adventure*, 48–83, 140–45.

"almost inevitable that she should pay for her right to exist, to keep a position in whatever line, with sex favors."[18] These multifaceted trends in print culture both indicated and contributed to a shift in morality in the early twentieth century that afforded far greater public candor about sexuality than the Victorian Era did, accompanied by searches for sexual order, including regulatory action against red-light districts.[19]

This new public sexual discourse explains why the first American labor strikes with obvious themes of sexual harassment transpired in the Progressive Era, coinciding with increased numbers of women in the industrial workforce, an accelerating woman suffrage movement, mass immigration, and, as with the 1880s, a militant working-class upsurge. The garment industry was the epicenter, notably among Jewish women who experienced extensive sexual harassment in sweatshops and factories.[20] So legendary was this harassment that five decades later E. L. Doctorow would evoke it in his epic novel *Ragtime*, depicting a sweatshop worker who "became accustomed to the hands of her employer" until "one day with two weeks' rent due she let him have his way on a cutting table."[21] Daniel Bender has usefully observed that sweatshop harassment served multiple functions in that it "soothed relations between male workers and bosses and cemented hierarchies of skill," reinforcing male exclusivity in better-paid skilled trades.[22] Attentiveness to women workers' agency, however, reveals that their fire was overwhelmingly aimed at the employing class: contractors, foremen, owners, and bosses. That was for good reason, because those embodiments of capital, far more than skilled craftsmen, controlled not only livelihoods but many subtle gradations of workload and pay.[23]

In the context of the socialist-tinged industrial unionism of the early twentieth century, women organizers and workers objected to male "insults" (a term that usually referred to verbal offenses but also could encompass physical ones). This had the significant effect of shifting responsibility away from the traditional blaming of women as enticers and onto the offenders. As early as 1907, white goods workers struck in protest against the "insults of a male employee whom the company refused to discharge."[24] In the "Uprising of the Twenty Thousand" in the shirtwaist trade in 1909–10, Clara Lemlich complained to the *Evening Journal* that bosses "swear at us and sometimes they do worse—they call us names that are not pretty to hear," while Rose Pastor Stokes told *Collier's* of "foremen in certain factories who insult and abuse girls beyond endurance."[25] In the massive Chicago garment strike the following year,

18. Goldman, *Traffic in Women*, 20.

19. D'Emilio and Freedman, *Intimate Matters*, 202–35.

20. Baum, Hyman, and Michel, *Jewish Woman in America*, 132–36; Weinberg, *World of Our Mothers*, 198–99; Glenn, *Daughters of the Shtetl*, 147–48, 175; Tyler, *Look for the Union Label*, 54; Bender, "'Too Much of Distasteful Masculinity.'"

21. Doctorow, *Ragtime*, 20.

22. Bender, "'Too Much of Distasteful Masculinity,'" 109n6.

23. Contemporaneous awareness of the latter point is expressed in O'Reilly, "Story of Kalamazoo," 228.

24. Quoted in Dye, *As Equals and as Sisters*, 67.

25. Quoted in Enstad, *Ladies of Labor, Girls of Adventure*, 140–41.

an officer of the Women's Trade Union League (WTUL), an alliance of middle-class and working-class women, cited "the petty tyranny of the individual boss" bent on "an increase in profits," objected to the "abusive and insulting language" used by "those in authority in the shops," and vowed "no woman should be subjected by fear of loss of her job to unwarranted insults."[26] In 1913, a Jewish white goods striker in New York announced that "with the union behind us" the bosses "wouldn't dare use the same language to us."[27]

Such remarks were incidental to core demands of wages, hours, and union recognition, but workplace sexual violation acquired greater centrality in walkouts by women button makers of Muscatine, Iowa, in 1911, Cleveland garment workers in 1911, and corset workers of Kalamazoo, Michigan, in 1912.[28] That harassment abounded in such midwestern towns pointed to the universality of the experience. As Pauline Newman, an International Ladies' Garment Workers Union (ILGWU) organizer, wrote her friend Rose Schneiderman,

> You know as well as I do that there is not a factory today where the same immoral conditions does not exist! You remember your factories where you have worked and so do I, and both of us know that the cloak factories and all other shops in the city of New York or Chicago, every one of the men will talk to the girls, take advantage of them if the girls will let them, the forman and superintendents will flirt with the girls, and it is nothing new for those who know that this exists today everywhere.[29]

The ILGWU's women organizers debated the wisdom of making this pervasive condition a public issue. Josephine Casey and Leonora O'Reilly saw exposing sexual harassment as valid, but Newman viewed it as inevitable with working-class fatalism and saw it as a distraction from economic issues likely to misfire given default norms blaming women for sexual transgressions; instead, she advocated, young women should be educated to fend it off.[30] Indeed, calling attention to sexual exploitation did not always play to strikers' advantage. Neither the Muscatine nor the Cleveland nor the Kalamazoo strike was won. Nevertheless, the strategy could generate favorable publicity, as when the *Daily Times* of Erie, Pennsylvania, stated during the Cleveland strike, "No foreman of any shop should be permitted to hold a club over any girl and refuse to pay for work faithfully performed or compel her to sacrifice her woman-hood in order to secure an advance in wages."[31] In this way, the new labor discourse

26. Coman, "Sweated Industry," 14.

27. Quoted in Glenn, *Daughters of the Shtetl*, 175.

28. Rousmaniere, "Muscatine Button Workers' Strike"; Barnum, "How Industrial Peace Has Been Brought About," 780–81; Mason, "Feeling the Pinch"; O'Reilly, "Story of Kalamazoo"; Foner, *Women and the American Labor Movement*, 357–58; Orleck, "'There Is Not a Factory Today'" (in this issue).

29. Newman to Schneiderman, July 11, 1912, quoted in Dye, *As Equals and as Sisters*, 22–23; spelling and syntax as in original.

30. Kessler-Harris, "Organizing the Unorganizable," 16; Segrave, *Sexual Harassment of Women*, 52–54; Orleck, *Common Sense*, 72–74.

31. Quoted in *Ladies' Garment Worker*, "Warning to Merchants," 8.

about bosses' outrages, crafted primarily by women union organizers defending predominantly female workforces, laid bare the sexual class struggle and positioned it in wider class struggles.

Sometimes such struggles were waged by working men. The 1909 steel strike of sixteen mostly "Slavic" nationalities at McKees Rock, Pennsylvania, objected to foremen engaging in what the *Pittsburgh Leader* called "the swapping of human souls, the souls of women, for the lives of their babes"; the strike ended in victory with the corporation's "pledge that any foreman or agent found guilty of demanding sexual favors from workers' wives or daughters as a condition of continued employment would be immediately discharged," as Philip Foner records.[32] In the Colorado coalfields, company gunmen routinely threatened miners' wives in the camps as the miners worked underground. One former miner wrote President Woodrow Wilson telling of a camp marshal "trying with a revolver in his hands . . . when man was in mine, [to coerce] a wife to unjust purposes, and the mining foreman and Superintendent was clearing him the way to flee before he could be arrested."[33] Such conditions festered until the Colorado Fuel and Iron strike of 1913–14 erupted, culminating in the Ludlow Massacre.

From the 1880s to the 1920s, working-class women saw "insults" and "immorality" in the workplace as primarily a class matter. Middle-class reformers such as the Women's Christian Temperance Union sought to increase the age of consent, use seduction tort law, or pass protective legislation to prohibit night work, limit working hours, ban women from certain occupations, or otherwise constrict women's access to equal employment.[34] Individual working-class women employed some of these methods—filing seduction lawsuits, for example—but as a group strategy, working-class women favored unionism. That did little, to be sure, for Black women, who, outside of sharecropping, were concentrated in domestic service, where isolation and close quarters fostered ubiquitous harassment by employers, as one Georgia nursemaid testified in 1912:

> I remember very well the first and last place from which I was dismissed. I lost my place because I refused to let the madam's husband kiss me. He must have been accustomed to undue familiarity with his servants, or else he took it as a matter of course, because without any love-making at all, soon after I was installed as cook, he walked up to me, threw his arms around me, and was in the act of kissing me, when I demanded to know what he meant, and shoved him away. I was young then, and newly married, and didn't know then what has been a burden to my mind and heart ever since: that a colored women's virtue in this part of the country has no protection. . . . I believe nearly all white men take, and expect to take, undue liberties with their colored female servants—not only the fathers, but in many cases the sons

32. *Pittsburgh Leader* in Duchez, "Strikes in Pennsylvania," 197; Foner, *Women and the American Labor Movement*, 423.

33. Quoted in Long, "Women of the Colorado Fuel and Iron Strike," 67.

34. Larson, "'Even a Worm Will Turn at Last'"; McLean, "Confided to His Care or Protection."

also. Those servants who rebel against such familiarity must either leave or expect a mighty hard time, if they stay.[35]

Such vulnerability left little recourse but to capitulate or give notice—or, as Darlene Clark Hine observes, migrate northward.[36] Factory labor, by contrast, entailed proletarian aggregation, enabling working women—very heavily immigrant—to begin to imagine superseding individual susceptibility. As Gertrude Barnum of the ILGWU wrote during the clash at Kalamazoo, where native-born white workers predominated, "The Union alone can keep up the good work of protecting the helpless young country girls who are lured from their farm homes by inviting advertisements and are then left at the mercy of the greed of men—greed for money and greed for the flower of our young womanhood."[37]

Elided in such public pronouncements were other realities, as when Newman observed privately that John Dyche, the ILGWU's conservative Gompersite secretary-treasurer, appointed women organizers on grounds that "they too are not bad looking, and one is rather liberal with her body"; she further revealed to her friend Rose Schneiderman that she herself had "many times to struggle against him and be annoyed by his love, so-called."[38] Such uncomfortable truths notwithstanding, Progressive Era working women had boldly asserted that insults were a social problem in need of social solutions and had hewn steadily to the hope that union power would protect working women against the unchecked tyranny of the foreman. That aspiration was not hollow. Unionism could and did block employer harassment. A 1915 broom strike, recalled the Swedish immigrant unionist and Chicago WTUL member Mary Anderson, resulted in a sexually brutal foreman being fired.[39] In a New York case, a white goods employer who routinely pinched his workers' behinds was confronted by his unionized employees; when he justified the behavior by claiming he considered them his children, they retorted, "We would rather be orphans"—and he stopped.[40]

Sit Down and Hands Off:
Underappreciated Sexual Class Struggles of the CIO Era

Far less visible or remembered is the role of sexual harassment in the consolidation of class consciousness in American labor's great breakthrough during the Great Depression and Second World War. The independent women's movement all but evaporated after passage of the Nineteenth Amendment, and the onset of hard times in the 1930s fostered gender and sexual conservatism, explaining why in the Depression the issue was subterranean instead of openly declared, as it had been in the Progressive Era.

35. A Negro Nurse, "More Slavery at the South," 197–98.
36. Hine, "Rape and the Inner Lives of Black Women," 914.
37. *Ladies' Garment Worker*, "Trial of Women," 7.
38. Quoted in Kessler-Harris, "Organizing the Unorganizable," 15; and Orleck, *Common Sense*, 70.
39. Anderson, *Woman at Work*, 56.
40. Lang, "62," 178–79; Schneiderman, *All for One*, 86.

Sexual injustice was nonetheless one key to the auto organizing drive at the heart of the great industrial upsurges of 1934–37 that culminated in both the United Auto Workers (UAW) and Congress of Industrial Organizations (CIO). Labor historians consistently emphasize that the sit-down strikes were about the arbitrary power of the foreman and irregularity of work, not only wages, but most have yet to fully absorb the findings of certain scholars, such as Stephen Meyer and Ruth Meyerowitz, that one of the most invidious forms of that arbitrary authority was sexual behavior damaging to both female and male workers.

Women in sex-segregated departments such as upholstery or small-parts assembly, as one *Auto Workers News* item noted in the 1920s, "have to allow the assistant foreman considerable liberty in order to keep their jobs, as I saw him run his hand through a girl's hair as he passed her machine."[41] Such entitlement became harder to circumvent in the 1930s. As union militant Genora Johnson Dollinger recalled, conditions were so bad before the 1936–37 sit-down strike in Flint, Michigan, that in one department of the AC Sparkplug division of General Motors (GM) "the girls had all been forced to go to the county hospital and be treated for venereal disease traced to one foreman" because young women "earned just enough to provide food for the family and they couldn't lose their jobs because nobody else in the family had a job."[42] Bud Simons, a Flint sit-downer, confirmed that among women in the GM cut-and-sew department "it was generally known if you wanted to hold your job and if there was a foreman wanted a date with you, the proper thing to do was to date him."[43] When Meyerowitz conducted oral histories of Depression-era women workers at a Detroit GM plant, "virtually all the women autoworkers interviewed commented on the problem of sexual harassment and the prevalence of exchanging sexual favors for jobs."[44]

Supervisors also coerced male autoworkers into delivering up their wives and daughters, a humiliation that generated immense resentments. John W. Anderson recalled that it was "common talk around the shop" that a man who wanted to keep his job "often had to respond with his wife or his daughter to the wishes of the foreman," who would "visit the home or he would take them out."[45] Male workers placed in this position experienced both defensive protectiveness of family *and* anger and humiliation at the violation of their traditional patriarchal property in women, resentment at the affront to women's dignity *and* vitiation of the pride, strength, and independence of working-class "manliness."[46] As Gramsci observed, working-class consciousness is always "contradictory consciousness" as workers unite to create a new

41. Quoted in Meyer, "Workplace Predators," 81.
42. *Striking Flint*, 5–6.
43. Quoted in Meyer, "Workplace Predators," 82.
44. Meyerowitz, "Organizing the UAW," 256n7.
45. Lynd and Lynd, *Rank and File*, 44–45.
46. See, broadly, Meyer, *Manhood on the Line*.

world but think in received categories.[47] In this gendered and sexual constitution of class, violated working-class women and humiliated men experienced the obliteration of the sanctity of family, venerated in American culture but consistently honored only for the business and professional classes.

Sexual harassment similarly motivated another CIO union, the left-led United Cannery, Agricultural, Packing, and Allied Workers of America (UCAPAWA). On the West Coast, part of its appeal for Mexicana and Chicana cannery women was its challenge to conditions that regularly meant "a good pinch on the butt."[48] In the southern tobacco industry, Black women spearheaded the creation of UCAPAWA Local 22 during the Second World War, which became central to postwar freedom struggles in Winston-Salem, North Carolina. Local 22 was born out of a 1943 sit-down strike at RJ Reynolds Tobacco Company (RJR) among Black women who comprised the overwhelming majority of stemmers, a dangerous, health-threatening job. The Jim Crow order dominated by white men presumed Black women's sexual availability, just as slavery had, making sexual exploitation part of a continuum of psychological intimidation reinforcing class, race, and gender. In the RJR plant, white foremen awarded better wages and preferential treatment in exchange for sex. Robert Black, a union organizer, remembered that foremen would "just walk up and pat women on their fannies and they'd better not say anything," adding, "if her husband was working right next to her, that husband better not say anything." Ruby Jones, a worker, recollected, "When you go to the restroom, you was timed. If you didn't come out at that time . . . the foreman would come in the dressing room, where the women were. . . . Come in there, and you had your clothes off. Come in the toilet!"[49]

Sexual favoritism and sexual tyranny were searingly existential, holding the potential to convert all wage labor into sex work—whether momentarily, episodically, or as an implicit, constant threat. Sexual harassment compounded the innate alienation of labor under capitalism with the alienation of a worker's sexuality. Far from being individual or arbitrary, it was a critical means by which a white male managerial corps enacted shopfloor rule. As Robin D. G. Kelley notes, Black women tobacco workers devised many personal strategies for evading verbal and physical abuse, some honed in prior work as domestics. As they discussed it among themselves, this "experience of, and opposition to, sexual exploitation probably reinforced bonds of solidarity," he observes, obliging historians to "see resistance to sexual harassment as a primary struggle to transform everyday conditions at the workplace."[50]

In a vivid demonstration of Beloso's "gendered and sexual constitution of class," the militant, class-conscious labor movement at the point of production in the 1930s and 1940s must at least in part be understood as a rebellion against patterns

---

47. Gramsci, *Prison Notebooks*, 333.

48. Ruiz, *Cannery Women*, 73–74.

49. Quoted in Griffin and Korstad, "Class as Race and Gender," 431; and Kelley, "'We Are Not What We Seem,'" 97.

50. Kelley, "'We Are Not What We Seem,'" 98.

of supervisory sexual abuse. Amid capitalist crisis, with few options available, some workers were terrified into compliance with the sexual demands of foremen, but the resultant humiliation, shame, and resentment fed discontent with the job and visceral antagonism toward management. This provides one clue as to why the working class coalesced in the 1930s despite widespread Depression-era joblessness. Sexual exploitation made workers understand acutely that as individuals they usually held insufficient leverage, making common labor action compelling. When Frank Marquart asked a young woman striker at Midland Steel why she joined the union, thinking she would cite wages, she replied, "When you belong to a union the foreman can't screw you. Last month my foreman asked me to go out with him. I told him 'to hell with you, Charlie, I know what you want.' He got mad, but he didn't try to spite me. He knew damn well the union would be on his neck if he did."[51]

The hopes invested in industrial unionism did see results—sometimes dramatic—in the CIO era. "Sexual harassment and sexual abuse diminished," writes Meyerowitz, relaying her UAW subjects' memories, "as unionization weakened the power of the foremen to demand favors in exchange for employment."[52] Sadie Rosenberg of United Electrical, Radio and Machine Workers of America (UE) Local 427 in Bayonne, New Jersey, who witnessed women compelled to sleep with foremen and endure groping on the assembly line, stated, "I don't think it was ever completely eliminated, but certainly the situation improved during the period of the union's strength increasing."[53] This was a function not simply of new formal mechanisms such as grievance procedures and seniority systems but also of a heightened consciousness of class power. With the Second World War's conversion to war production and full employment, wildcat strikes multiplied just as the numbers of women workers tripled. Women workers responded to "wolf whistles" by whistling back, and spoke out against harassment in "indignation meetings" in large plants.[54] Mary Pollard, an aircraft worker, remembered how a group of women in her shop dealt with an offending supervisor responsible for training new women workers: "They bodily took him up—well, the office was on the poop-deck, which is a half level overlooking the department—and insisted he be fired on the spot. And he was."[55] The élan of class militancy that lasted from the sit-downs of 1936–37 to the epochal postwar strike wave of 1945–46 thus included women workers' direct action to counter sexual harassment.

In the postwar era, however, at the high point of union density in American history, the problem of sexual harassment did not come to an end. Far from it: unions, overwhelmingly male-led and increasingly bureaucratic and conservative in the Cold War, tended to trivialize or ignore sexual complaints, a trend accelerated by the post-

51. Marquart, *Auto Worker's Journal*, 72.
52. Meyerowitz, "Organizing the UAW," 251.
53. Quoted in Milkman, *Gender at Work*, 40.
54. Lipsitz, *Rainbow at Midnight*, 53–54.
55. Quoted in Meyer, "Workplace Predators," 84.

war reassertion of American gender traditionalism. This shows another important side of the gendered and sexual constitution of class, the inherited culture's conditioning of male workers and union officers. Ostensibly class institutions, unions often discouraged women workers' equal participation. As shopfloor militancy receded, some UAW shop stewards proved to be harassers, while certain locals refused to grieve the issue.[56] In 1955, the African American Chrysler worker James Major, in an episode reconstructed by Kevin Boyle, kissed his white female co-worker Leona Hunt in a playful moment as the production line shut down for Christmastime. He was fired, she was sexually harassed by white male workers, and the union declined to aid either of them. Women autoworkers considered foremen "the most likely sexual threats," Boyle notes, but unions were unreliable counterweights.[57] In the postwar garment trades, likewise, Xiaolin Bao found in her oral histories that when Puerto Rican and African American women "brought complaints of this nature to the union, they were either told that they should feel 'flattered' by the interest of their employers or resolve the matter quietly through monetary settlement."[58] Did the failed promise of unions to consistently address sexual harassment produce a disenchantment contributing, in some measure, to industrial unionism's long subsequent decline? Historians have yet to even ask the question.

Harassment and Class in the New Gilded Age

For decades, producer Harvey Weinstein—"producer" being Hollywood for capitalist, or what Marx called "capital personified," with "the soul of capital"—used so-called business meetings to coerce sex from his assistants and dozens of young women who hoped to act in one of his films.[59] Bidding them to his hotel suite, he would open his bathrobe, badger them relentlessly, and take pleasure in their fear. "I could feel that the more I was freaking out, the more he was excited," actress Emma de Caunes told Ronan Farrow. "It was like a hunter with a wild animal. The fear turns him on."[60] Weinstein the sadist was a hitmaker, delivering Oscars and box-office profits for his backers. Savvy for all his vulgarity, he endowed a professorship in Gloria Steinem's name and forged an alliance with Hillary Clinton, for whom he raised millions of dollars. His legal representatives included David Boies, the Democratic lawyer in *Bush v. Gore*; the feminist Lisa Bloom; and, as testament to his networking, another attorney recommended by Rudolph Giuliani. Whenever Weinstein could not intimidate and browbeat victims into submission, he retaliated through his network of gossip columnists and private detectives—including Black Cube, made up of former Mossad operatives, hired for $100,000 a month—to undermine anyone who would testify against him or report the truth. His company board, aware of the swirling alle-

56. For appalling examples, see Gabin, *Feminism in the Labor Movement*, 175; Meyer, "Workplace Predators," 86.

57. Boyle, "Kiss," 512.

58. Bao, *Holding Up More Than Half the Sky*, 40.

59. Marx, *Capital*, 233.

60. Farrow, *Catch and Kill*, 250.

gations, formulated a harassment policy to protect itself and looked away. His attorneys drafted settlements providing cash payouts to victims, who had to turn over all evidence and keep silent. The journalistic convention is to call Weinstein a "power broker," but a stronger nomenclature is warranted. With connections reaching from the Clintons to Giuliani, with the best lawyers, private eyes, and non-disclosure agreements that money could buy, Weinstein epitomized nothing less than class power.[61]

Yet as the #MeToo movement broke open in 2017, class was marginal to typical portrayals of the issue. The tendency to filter such issues through an almost exclusively gendered prism traces to the 1970s, when feminists first coined the very term "sexual harassment." Even then, however, alternative perspectives vied for consideration. The Alliance Against Sexual Coercion (AASC), a Boston women's collective, characterized "male power and class power" as the "two sources of power" operating in sexual harassment, which fostered "the economic insecurity of working women" and helped ensure "male dominance under capitalism."[62] Why did such consciousness dissipate? It is not that class society disappeared, for the 1970s are precisely when capitalism, like Weinstein, disrobed and showed its naked self in a sadistic neoliberal turn, ushering in a new Gilded Age of never-before-seen inequalities in income and wealth.

Much of the answer lies in the particular forms of feminism that gained ascendance as labor experienced its long decline. As economic imperatives drew ever-greater numbers of women into the American workforce in the 1960s and 1970s, they encountered a workplace suffused with a sexual revolution centered on male gratification, typified by *Playboy*. Betty Friedan revived feminism with *The Feminine Mystique* (1963), but in conceding to Cold War culture by not disclosing her youthful days in radical unionism and focusing instead on white suburban women, she revived not only feminism but its white middle-class center of gravity dating back to the suffrage movement.[63] Soon afterward, Title VII of the 1964 Civil Rights Act prohibited employment discrimination on the basis of sex, women's lobbying being key to gender's inclusion in the measure despite the persistent myth that it was a legislative fluke.[64] By the late 1960s, a youthful, more radical women's liberation movement sought both women's sexual autonomy and liberation from sexual objectification.[65] This profusion of liberal and radical feminisms coincided with an expansive liberal state and a host of other radicalisms, while rank-and-file rebellions, advancing public-sector and service-sector unionism, and manufacturing's erosion began to reshape and diminish organized labor in the 1960s and 1970s.[66]

Amid these transformations, working-class women were central to making sexual harassment an issue. When National Airlines required stewardesses to wear

61. This paragraph draws on books by the *New York Times* and *New Yorker* journalists who broke the Weinstein story: Kantor and Twohey, *She Said*; and Farrow, *Catch and Kill*.

62. AASC, "Organizing against Sexual Harassment," 18, 22–23.

63. Horowitz, *Betty Friedan*.

64. Osterman, "Origins of a Myth"; Thomas, *Because of Sex*, 81–105.

65. Echols, *Daring to Be Bad*.

66. Brick and Phelps, *Radicals in America*, 88–217.

"Fly Me" buttons in 1971, followed by Continental's 1972 advertising campaign featuring stewardesses who "really move our tail for you," flight attendants formed Stewardesses for Women's Rights, filed lawsuits, denounced "sexploitation," and pushed union leaders on women's concerns, resulting in a culture shift in the airline industry.[67] Blue-collar women entering male-dominated hard-hat trades such as construction and mining experienced immense sexual and racial harassment not only from foremen but fellow workers and union officers seeking to drive them out—and many pushed back. A member of Local 717 of the International Union of Electrical Workers (IUE) in Youngstown, Ohio, filed a complaint in 1967 with the Equal Employment Opportunity Commission (EEOC), whose investigator reported that union officials "continually harassed" her; one shop steward told her the "men were waiting" and "would take care of me."[68] This complaint was advanced, given that the EEOC would not issue formal guidelines on sexual harassment until 1980 under Eleanor Holmes Norton. Other workers took direct action. One Latina worker who entered construction in New York City told Susan Eisenberg that in the 1970s she ripped up the wall-to-wall porn covering her worksite's shanty walls; by the 1990s, she noted with satisfaction, "there's no pornography on the jobs" because "it's unacceptable anymore."[69]

Working-class women were the plaintiffs in the first six Title VII cases seeking to categorize sexual harassment as sex discrimination between 1971 and 1975. All involved "a male supervisor firing or forcing out a female subordinate employee after she rejected his sexual advances," writes Carrie N. Baker. Three of the six were African-American, including the first, in 1976, to secure a favorable judgment, a young Black federal public information specialist named Diane Williams whose married Black supervisor retaliated against her for refusing him sex.[70] Those cases were followed by *Meritor Savings Bank, FSB v. Vinson*, filed in 1978 by Mechelle Vinson, a bank employee whose supervisor forced her to have intercourse many times. Vinson quit rather than being discharged, but the Supreme Court in 1986 unanimously found the bank liable for sex discrimination because management had created "a hostile or offensive environment."[71] Because most litigants in these cases were African American, some histories isolate race as the decisive variable.[72] Black women's long history of resistance to their stereotypical sexualization definitely has bearing—as does their greater propensity to recognize "civil rights" as human rights. Since all but one of the Black women's cases entailed Black supervisors, however, what actually unified these early plaintiffs, regardless of race, was their gendered subordination in employer-employee relationships. What the Combahee River Collective in 1977 called the "specific class position of black women who are generally marginal in the labor

67. Cobble, *Other Women's Movement*, 209–11; Cobble, "'A Spontaneous Loss of Enthusiasm,'" 337–42.

68. Quoted in Deslippe, *"Rights, Not Roses,"* 169.

69. Quoted in Eisenberg, *We'll Call You*, 193.

70. Baker, *Women's Movement against Sexual Harassment*, 15–16, 21–25.

71. Thomas, *Because of Sex*, 102.

72. Hirshman, *Reckoning*, 17–19.

force" is important.[73] Gender, race, *and* class were crucial in early legal challenges by working women to sexual harassment.

Feminists of the 1970s made brilliant new insights into sexual harassment. They recast it as more about power and misogyny than sex, identified it as practiced by clients and co-workers as well as bosses, and connected it to occupational sex-segregation, lower pay for women, women's status as a reserve labor force, and male violence and aggression. The term "sexual harassment" itself arose out of collective discussion among young feminists in 1975 who founded Working Women United (WWU).[74] WWU involved women in Ithaca, New York, who had worked as cashiers, saleswomen, waitresses, nurses, letter carriers, and clerical workers.[75] Yet its most prominent leader, Lin Farley, did much to diminish the significance of class. "Patriarchal relations, not capitalism, are at the root of working women's problems," she wrote on the first page of *Sexual Shakedown: The Sexual Harassment of Women on the Job* (1978), the first major book on the topic.[76] New insights thus commingled with a turn—sometimes called "radical feminism," although other feminists questioned its radicalism—that replaced the old oversimplification that class is primary with a new oversimplification that sex oppression is primary. Gender *was* class.

That outlook informed Catherine MacKinnon, whose book *Sexual Harassment of Working Women* (1979) proved highly influential in American law, and who repurposed Marxist categories to imagine women as the proletariat and men capitalists.[77] Law is now so central to sexual harassment that histories of sexual harassment often begin with it in the 1970s. One account literally starts and ends with MacKinnon, daughter of a Republican corporate lawyer and federal judge who first took up the issue as a Yale law student.[78] Such narratives overlook earlier working-class contributors such as Leonora Barry, who called for outlawing workplace sexual abuse in 1888. They tend, furthermore, to elevate law as an instrument of social transformation above all other battlegrounds, not least workplace struggles. In this, radical feminism dovetailed in ways not always recognized with liberal feminism and liberal legal theory, in whose lexicons "class" often means groups warranting similar status under the law. In 1975, Karen DeCrow, lawyer and National Organization for Women president, called sexual harassment "not a personal problem, but rather a class problem, which we as females share."[79]

To a competing strand of feminism, typified by the AASC, emphasis on patriarchy alone was "simplistic," class was premised on relations of production, and

73. Combahee River Collective, "Black Feminist Statement," 366.

74. For persuasive analysis that the phrase arose out of brainstorming and cannot be attributed to any single person, see Baker, *Women's Movement against Sexual Harassment*, 31, 208–9n36.

75. Nemy, "Women Begin to Speak Out"; Baker, *Women's Movement against Sexual Harassment*, 27–40.

76. Farley, *Sexual Shakedown*, iv.

77. MacKinnon, *Sexual Harassment of Working Women*. Excellent critiques of MacKinnon's gender theory are Beloso, "Sex, Work, and the Feminist Erasure of Class"; and Sutherland, "Marx and MacKinnon."

78. Hirshman, *Reckoning*, dedication page, 11–22, 255.

79. Quoted in Baker, *Women's Movement against Sexual Harassment*, 32.

"patriarchy and capitalism reinforce *each other* in the phenomenon of workplace harassment."[80] The AASC, which grew out of the rape crisis center movement, saw women workers' lack of "autonomy or control over working conditions," along with racism, as part of the superexploitation required by the system, making it an open question "whether or not it is possible to eliminate these conditions without abolishing capitalism itself."[81] Yet the AASC's analysis was supple, as when member Mary Bularzik wrote, "Sexual harassment is a phenomenon that crosses class lines, though it does have a class dimension. It cannot be reduced to bosses exploiting workers, because the problem of harassment by co-workers is so extensive. In addition, harassment by supervisors and co-workers does not necessarily support the needs of a rationalized, profit-oriented system, and may even work at cross-purposes to it." This nuanced approach further viewed harassment as a "danger to workers' solidarity" and held out hope for more democratic, egalitarian workplaces.[82] "Sexual harassment," the AASC wrote, "occurs within the work setting because of strict hierarchies which result from and reinforce capitalist economic organization."[83]

Such materialist outlooks and the working-class feminist praxis to which they gave theoretical expression proved difficult to sustain through the 1980s and 1990s as the New Right gained sway, liberalism and the left retreated, and labor came in for sustained, ultimately devastating assault by corporate America. Linda Gordon warned in 1981 that "legalism" could transform the issue of sexual harassment into "a bureaucratized, mechanistic set of procedures for disallowing certain very narrowly defined behavior."[84] In the neoliberal era, that is precisely what transpired. Considerable ink has been spilled over the strange 1980s alliance of MacKinnon and her collaborator Andrea Dworkin with the New Right on pornography, far less regarding the co-option of MacKinnon's legal ideas on sexual harassment. *Meritor* drew upon her theories in a decision written by William Rehnquist that was both a concession to the women's movement and a containment of firms' liability if written harassment policies and employee reporting mechanisms were in place. Sexual harassment entered the realm of HR, which inevitably had a mission to protect the company first and foremost. By the time Anita Hill testified against Clarence Thomas before the Senate in 1991 in televised hearings that did more than anything else to catapult sexual harassment into the public eye, commentators discussed the issue almost exclusively in terms of gender and race. "No one in a position to be widely heard articulated support for Anita Hill grounded in class or status solidarity," observed Nancy Fraser, who called class "the great unarticulated American secret."[85]

Working-class women nevertheless remained central. When the Iron Range miner Lois Jenson experienced a hostile work environment and her United Steel-

---

80. Klein, "Book Review," 34–35.
81. Hooven and McDonald, "Role of Capitalism," 32–33.
82. Bularzik, "Sexual Harassment at the Workplace," 37, 40.
83. AASC, "Organizing against Sexual Harassment," 33.
84. Gordon, "Politics of Sexual Harassment," 10.
85. Fraser, "Sex, Lies, and the Public Sphere," 607, 609.

workers (USW) local failed to defend her, she initiated the first class-action sexual-harassment lawsuit, *Jenson v. Eveleth Taconite Co.* (1997), as depicted in the best-seller *Class Action* (2002) and the movie *North Country* (2005).[86] Just before #MeToo erupted, the Ya Basta! Coalition of the Service Employees International Union (SEIU) United Workers West won contractual improvements for women janitors' safety in California, and UNITE HERE's "Hands Off Pants Off" campaign achieved ordinances in Seattle and Chicago requiring panic buttons for housekeepers in hotel rooms.[87] Yet #MeToo exposed harassing officials in the AFL-CIO and the SEIU-led Fight for $15 campaign, showing that unions remain a painfully imperfect vehicle of redress.[88] Conversely, the Time's Up Legal Defense Fund underwrote lawsuits, including by McDonald's workers, but devoted no resources to unionizing the heavily female service sector, where workers today, like those in the Muscatines and Flints of yesteryear, know unions would offset the power of franchisees, shift supervisors, and CEOs.

Worker-centered strategies could and did gain traction in the #MeToo era, as when workers at McDonald's and Google staged one-day walkouts—bringing down, at Google, compulsory arbitration procedures that protected serial harassers and disadvantaged victims.[89] But visions of workers' control, of a democratic workplace, are not prominent in recent public campaigns against sexual harassment even though scholarship continues to identify it as a valuable part of the solution.[90] Unions, one potential instrument of workplace transformation, can best cultivate respect and solidarity, say advocates, by negotiating specific contract language against sexual harassment, empowering women and people of color in leadership, investigating member-on-member harassment, offering self-defense training, and devising informal resolution mechanisms that, paradoxically, work better than corporate "zero tolerance" policies that sound good but deter women from coming forward for fear they will destroy a co-worker's life. Both feminists and unionists ought to build labor-oriented political coalitions to raise the tipped minimum wage, achieve free childcare and Medicare for all, resuscitate the right to organize and strike, and otherwise mitigate the precarity that fosters "I need this job" vulnerability.[91]

Class and political economy, in short, remain highly salient in sexual harassment. Many male corporate executives responded to #MeToo with exclusionary sexism—ceasing to meet one-on-one with women, for example.[92] The sensational

86. Bingham and Gansler, *Class Action.*

87. Yeung, *In a Day's Work*, 186, 194; Lyons, "'Hands Off Pants On.'"

88. Eidelson, "U.S. Labor Leaders Confront Sexual Harassment in Top Ranks."

8.9 Abrams, "McDonald's Workers across the U.S. Stage #MeToo Protests"; Wakabayashi et al., "Google Walkout"; McGregor, "Google and Facebook Ended Forced Arbitration."

90. Williams, "Sexual Harassment and Sadomasochism."

91. Avendaño, "Sexual Harassment in the Workplace"; Crain and Matheny, "Sexual Harassment and Solidarity"; Hodges, "Strategies for Combating Sexual Harassment"; McAlevey, "What #MeToo Can Teach the Labor Movement."

92. Tan and Porzecanski, "Wall Street Rule"; Bennhold, "Another Side of #MeToo"; Bower, "#MeToo Backlash."

#MeToo takedowns of the rich and famous in publicity-sensitive sectors such as media barely affected the low-wage women farmworkers, food service employees, building cleaners, and domestic helpers, chiefly people of color, for whom sexual assault is a pervasive hazard.[93] #MeToo erupted in an era when the working class lacks coherence and organization, but if history is any guide, heightened awareness of sexual harassment may presage coalescences yet to come.

Such is the ambition of a revived social-justice feminism of millennials and sixties veterans in the era of Occupy Wall Street, the Movement for Black Lives, and Alexandria Ocasio-Cortez. These feminists resist punitive carceral measures in favor of collective power on the job and in social movements and unions.[94] They hold solidarity with men not only possible but necessary. They recognize that harassment may take same-sex forms—sometimes with queer intentions but most often homophobic, and directed against trans, gay, lesbian, genderqueer, and heterosexual workers alike—revealing the limitations of the legalistic "sex discrimination" framework.[95] Refusing to drive out the desirable along with the derogatory, they celebrate women's sexual freedom and reject a puritanical, moralistic tone on sex as well as blanket prohibitions on all co-worker sexual relationships motivated by corporate worries over liability, just as the AASC once declined "desexualization of the workplace."[96] They caution against trial by social media and indiscriminate slogans like "Believe Women" in favor of verifiable evidence, due process for accusers and accused, and proportionality in punishment, conditions necessary to make victims come forward and draw men away from controlling, entitled masculinities.[97] Tarana Burke, originator of the "Me Too" expression, likewise emphasizes the value of sharing stories of healing rather than trauma.[98] Given the weight of social structure and history, true intersectional syntheses have been rare and fleeting in the quest to end work-related sexual coercion, but perhaps recognition is finally dawning that dignity and power for women, people of color, and workers are best achieved together. ◲

CHRISTOPHER PHELPS teaches American history in the Department of American and Canadian Studies at the University of Nottingham.

93. For stunning reportage, see Yeung, *In a Day's Work*.

94. Press, "#MeToo Must Avoid 'Carceral Feminism'"; Leonard, "How to Stop the Predators."

95. Numerous examples may be found in Balay, *Steel Closets*, and Balay, *Semi Queer*.

96. AASC, "Organizing against Sexual Harassment," 21. For excellent reflections on how campaigns against sexual exploitation may easily shade into puritanism, see Halperin and Hoppe, *War on Sex*.

97. Out of a literature too vast to cite, consider writings in the past five years by Masha Gessen, Laura Kipnis, Daphne Merkin, Zephyr Teachout, Susan Watkins, and JoAnn Wypijewski.

98. Harris, "She Founded Me Too."

References

Abrams, Rachel. "McDonald's Workers across the U.S. Stage #MeToo Protests." *New York Times*, September 18, 2018. www.nytimes.com/2018/09/18/business/mcdonalds-strike-metoo.html.

AASC (Alliance Against Sexual Coercion). "Organizing against Sexual Harassment." *Radical America* 15, no. 4 (1981): 17–34.

Anderson, Mary. *Woman at Work*. Minneapolis: University of Minnesota Press, 1951.

Avendaño, Ana. "Sexual Harassment in the Workplace: Where Were the Unions?" *Labor Studies Journal* 43, no. 4 (2018): 245–62.

Baker, Carrie N. *The Women's Movement against Sexual Harassment*. Cambridge: Cambridge University Press, 2008.

Balay, Anne. *Semi Queer: Inside the World of Gay, Trans, and Black Truck Drivers*. Chapel Hill: University of North Carolina Press, 2018.

Balay, Anne. *Steel Closets: Voices of Gay, Lesbian, and Transgender Steelworkers*. Chapel Hill: University of North Carolina Press, 2014.

Bao, Xiaolan. *Holding Up More Than Half the Sky: Chinese Women Garment Workers in New York City, 1948–92*. Urbana: University of Illinois Press, 2001.

Barnum, Gertrude. "How Industrial Peace Has Been Brought About in the Clothing Trade." *Independent* 73, no. 3331 (1912): 777–81.

Barry, L. M. "Report of the General Instructor and Director of Woman's Work." In *Proceedings of the General Assembly of the Knights of Labor of America, Twelfth Regular Session, Held at Indianapolis, Indiana, November 13 to 27, 1888*, 1–5. Philadelphia: Journal of United Labor, 1889.

Baum, Charlotte, Paula Hyman, and Sonya Michel. *The Jewish Woman in America*. New York: Plume, 1977.

Beloso, Brooke Meredith. "Sex, Work, and the Feminist Erasure of Class." *Signs: Journal of Women in Culture and Society* 38, no. 1 (2012): 47–70.

Bender, Daniel E. "'Too Much of Distasteful Masculinity': Historicizing Sexual Harassment in the Garment Sweatshop and Factory." *Journal of Women's History* 15, no. 4 (2004): 91–116.

Bennhold, Katrin. "Another Side of #MeToo: Male Managers Fearful of Mentoring Women." *New York Times*, January 27, 2019. https://ww.nytimes.com/2019/01/27/world/europe/metoo-backlash-gender-equality-davos-men.html.

Bingham, Clara, and Laura Leedy Gansler. *Class Action: The Story of Lois Jenson and the Landmark Case That Changed Sexual Harassment Law*. New York: Doubleday, 2002.

Boris, Eileen. "Class Returns." *Journal of Women's History* 25, no. 4 (2013): 74–87.

Bower, Tim. "The #MeToo Backlash." *Harvard Business Review*, September–October 2019. https://hbr.org/2019/09/the-metoo-backlash.

Boyle, Kevin. "The Kiss: Racial and Gender Conflict in a 1950s Automobile Factory." *Journal of American History* 84, no. 2 (1997): 496–523.

Brick, Howard, and Christopher Phelps. *Radicals in America: The U.S. Left since the Second World War*. Cambridge: Cambridge University Press, 2015.

Brownson, O. A. *The Laboring Classes*. New York: Elton's, 1840.

Bularzik, Mary. "Sexual Harassment at the Workplace: Historical Notes." *Radical America* 12, no. 4 (1978): 25–43.

Cobble, Dorothy Sue. *The Other Women's Movement: Workplace Justice and Social Rights in Modern America*. Princeton, NJ: Princeton University Press, 2004.

Cobble, Dorothy Sue. "'A Spontaneous Loss of Enthusiasm': Workplace Feminism and the Transformation of Women's Service Jobs in the 1970s." In *Rebel Rank and File: Labor Militancy and Revolt from Below during the Long 1970s*, edited by Aaron Brenner, Robert Brenner, and Cal Wilson, 335–54. London: Verso, 2010.

Coman, Katherine. "A Sweated Industry." *Life and Labor* 1, no. 1 (1911): 13–15.

Combahee River Collective. "A Black Feminist Statement." In *Capitalist Patriarchy and the Case for Socialist Feminism*, edited by Zillah R. Eisenstein, 362–72. New York: Monthly Review Press, 1979.

Crain, Miriam, and Ken Matheny. "Sexual Harassment and Solidarity." *George Washington Law Review* 87, no. 1 (2019): 56–123.

Davis, Adrienne D. "'Don't Let Nobody Bother Yo' Principle': The Sexual Economy of American Slavery." In *Black Sexual Economies: Race and Sex in a Culture of Capital*, edited by Davis and the BSE Collective, 15–38. Urbana: University of Illinois Press, 2019.

D'Emilio, John, and Estelle Freedman. *Intimate Matters: A History of Sexuality in America*. New York: Harper and Row, 1988.

Deslippe, Dennis A. *"Rights, Not Roses": Unions and the Rise of Working-Class Feminism, 1945–80*. Urbana: University of Illinois Press, 2000.

Doctorow, E. L. *Ragtime*. New York: Bantam, 1981.

Dublin, Thomas. *Women at Work: The Transformation of Work and Community in Lowell, Massachusetts, 1826–1860*. New York: Columbia University Press, 1979.

Duchez, Louis. "The Strikes in Pennsylvania." *International Socialist Review* 10, no. 3 (1909): 193–203.

Dye, Nancy Schrom. *As Equals and as Sisters: Feminism, Unionism, and the Women's Trade Union League of New York*. Columbia: University of Missouri Press, 1980.

Echols, Alice. *Daring to Be Bad: Radical Feminism in America, 1967–1975*. Minneapolis: University of Minnesota Press, 1989.

Eidelson, Josh. "U.S. Labor Leaders Confront Sexual Harassment in Top Ranks." *Bloomberg Businessweek*, November 7, 2017. www.bloomberg.com/news/articles/2017-11-07/u-s-labor-leaders-confront-sexual-harassment-in-their-top-ranks.

Eisenberg, Susan. *We'll Call You if We Need You: Experiences of Women Working Construction*. Ithaca, NY: ILR Press, 1998.

Enstad, Nan. *Ladies of Labor, Girls of Adventure: Working Women, Popular Culture, and Labor Politics at the Turn of the Century*. New York: Columbia University Press, 1999.

A Factory Girl. "Factory Girls." *Lowell Offering*, December 25, 1840.

Farley, Lin. *Sexual Shakedown: The Sexual Harassment of Women on the Job*. New York: McGraw-Hill, 1978.

Farrow, Ronan. *Catch and Kill: Lies, Spies, and a Conspiracy to Protect Predators*. New York: Little, Brown, 2019.

Flexner, Eleanor. *Century of Struggle: The Woman's Rights Movement in the United States*. New York: Atheneum, 1970.

Foner, Philip S., ed. *The Factory Girls*. Urbana: University of Illinois Press, 1977.

Foner, Philip S. *Women and the American Labor Movement: From Colonial Times to the Eve of World War I*. New York: Free Press, 1979.

Fraser, Nancy. "Sex, Lies, and the Public Sphere: Some Reflections on the Confirmation of Clarence Thomas." *Critical Inquiry* 18, no. 3 (1992): 595–612.

Gabin, Nancy F. *Feminism in the Labor Movement: Women and the United Auto Workers, 1935–1975*. Ithaca, NY: Cornell University Press, 1990.

Glenn, Susan A. *Daughters of the Shtetl: Life and Labor in the Immigrant Generation*. Ithaca, NY: Cornell University Press, 1990.

Goldman, Emma. *The Traffic in Women and Other Essays in Feminism*. New York: Times Change Press, 1970.

Gordon, Linda. "The Politics of Sexual Harassment." *Radical America* 15, no. 4 (1981): 7–40.

Gramsci, Antonio. *Selections from the Prison Notebooks*. New York: International Publishers, 1971.

Griffin, Larry J., and Robert R. Korstad. "Class as Race and Gender: Making and Breaking a Labor Union in the Jim Crow South." *Social Science History* 19, no. 4 (1995): 425–54.

Halperin, David M., and Trevor Hoppe, eds. *The War on Sex*. Durham, NC: Duke University Press, 2017.

Harris, Aisha. "She Founded Me Too. Now She Wants to Move Past the Trauma." *New York Times*, October 15, 2018. www.nytimes.com/2018/10/15/arts/tarana-burke-metoo-anniversary.html.

Hine, Darlene Clark. "Rape and the Inner Lives of Black Women in the Middle West." *Signs* 14, no. 4 (1989): 912–20.

Hirshman, Linda. *Reckoning: The Epic Battle against Sexual Abuse and Harassment*. Boston: Houghton Mifflin Harcourt, 2019.

Hodges, Ann C. "Strategies for Combating Sexual Harassment: The Role of Labor Unions." *Texas Journal of Women and the Law* 15, no. 2 (2006): 183–228.

Hooven, Martha, and Nancy McDonald. "The Role of Capitalism: Understanding Sexual Harassment." *Aegis* (May–June 1979): 31–33.

Horowitz, Daniel. *Betty Friedan and the Making of "The Feminine Mystique."* Amherst: University of Massachusetts Press, 1998.

Kantor, Jodi, and Megan Twohey. *She Said: Breaking the Sexual Harassment Story That Helped Ignite a Movement*. New York: Penguin, 2019.

Kelley, Robin D. G. "'We Are Not What We Seem': Rethinking Black Working-Class Opposition in the Jim Crow South." *Journal of American History* 80, no. 1 (1993): 75–112.

Kessler-Harris, Alice. "Organizing the Unorganizable: Three Jewish Women and Their Union." *Labor History* 17, no. 1 (1976): 5–23.

Klein, Freada. "Book Review: *Sexual Shakedown*." *Aegis* (May–June 1979): 33–35.

Ladies' Garment Worker. "Trial of Women Labor Leaders for Violating Injunction." 3, no. 6 (1912): 4–7.

Ladies' Garment Worker. "Warning to Merchants Issued by the Committee." 3, no. 1 (1912): 8.

Lambertz, Jan. "Sexual Harassment in the Nineteenth Century English Cotton Industry." *History Workshop*, no. 19 (1985): 29–61.

Lang, Harry. *"62," Biography of a Union*. New York: Undergarment and Negligee Workers' Union, Local 62, ILGWU, 1940.

Larson, Jane E. "'Even a Worm Will Turn at Last': Rape Reform in Late Nineteenth-Century America." *Yale Journal of Law and the Humanities* 9, no. 1 (1997): 1–71.

Leonard, Sarah. "How to Stop the Predators Who Aren't Famous." *New York Times*, November 16, 2017. https://nytimes.com/2017/11/16/opinion/stopping-predators-sexual-harassment.html.

Levine, Susan. "Labor's True Woman: Domesticity and Equal Rights in the Knights of Labor." *Journal of American History* 70, no. 2 (1983): 323–39.

Lipsitz, George. *Rainbow at Midnight: Labor and Culture in the 1940s*. Urbana: University of Illinois Press, 1994.

Long, Priscilla. "The Women of the Colorado Fuel and Iron Strike, 1913–14." In *Women, Work and Protest: A Century of U.S. Women's Labor History*, edited by Ruth Milkman, 62–85. London: Routledge, 1987.

Lynd, Alice, and Staughton Lynd, eds. *Rank and File: Personal Histories by Working-Class Organizers*. New York: Monthly Review Press, 1988.

Lyons, Sarah. "'Hands Off Pants On': The Collective and Radical Art of Shedding Self-Doubt." *Labor Studies Journal* 43, no. 4 (2018): 263–68.

MacKinnon, Catherine A. *Sexual Harassment of Working Women*. New Haven, CT: Yale University Press, 1979.

Malkiel, Theresa A. *The Diary of a Shirtwaist Striker*. Ithaca, NY: ILR Press, 1990.

Marquart, Frank. *An Auto Workers' Journal: The UAW from Crusade to One-Party Union*. University Park: Pennsylvania State University Press, 1975.

Marx, Karl. *Capital*. Vol. 1. Moscow: Progress Publishers, 1965.

Mason, Karen M. "Feeling the Pinch: The Kalamazoo Corsetmakers' Strike of 1912." In *"To Toil the Livelong Day": America's Women at Work, 1780–1980*, edited by Carol Groneman and Mary Beth Norton, 141–60. Ithaca, NY: Cornell University Press, 1987.

McAlevey, Jane. "What #MeToo Can Teach the Labor Movement." *In These Times*, December 27, 2017. https://inthesetimes.com/article/me-too-workers-women-unions-sexual-harassment-labor-movement-lessons.

McCreesh, Carolyn Daniel. *Women in the Campaign to Organize Garment Workers: 1880–1917*. New York: Garland, 1985.

McGregor, Jena. "Google and Facebook Ended Forced Arbitration for Sexual Harassment. Why More Companies Could Follow." *Washington Post*, November 12, 2018. www.washingtonpost.com/business/2018/11/12/google-facebook-ended-forced-arbitration-sex-harassment-claims-why-more-companies-could-follow/.

McLean, Sara. "Confided to His Care or Protection: The Late-Century Crime of Workplace Sexual Harassment." *Columbia Journal of Gender and Law* 9 (1999): 47–90.

Meyer, Stephen. *Manhood on the Line: Working-Class Masculinities in the American Heartland*. Urbana: University of Illinois Press, 2016.

Meyer, Steve. "Workplace Predators: Sexuality and Harassment on the U.S. Automotive Shop Floor, 1930–1960." *Labor: Studies in Working-Class History of the Americas* 1, no. 1 (2004): 77–93.

Meyerowitz, Ruth. "Organizing the United Automobile Workers: Women Workers at the Ternstedt General Motors Parts Plant." In *Women, Work and Protest: A Century of U.S. Women's Labor History*, edited by Ruth Milkman, 235–58. London: Routledge, 1987.

Milkman, Ruth. *Gender at Work: The Dynamics of Job Segregation by Sex during World War II*. Urbana: University of Illinois Press, 1987.

Nathan, Maude. *The Story of an Epoch-Making Movement*. Garden City, NY: Doubleday, Page, and Company, 1926.

A Negro Nurse. "More Slavery at the South." *Independent* 72, no. 3295 (1912): 196–200.

Nemy, Enid. "Women Begin to Speak Out against Sexual Harassment at Work." *New York Times*, August 19, 1975, 38.

O'Reilly, Leonora. "The Story of Kalamazoo." *Life and Labor* 2, no. 8 (1912): 228–30.

Orleck, Annelise. *Common Sense and a Little Fire: Women and Working-Class Politics in the United States, 1900–1965*. Chapel Hill: University of North Carolina Press, 1995.

Osterman, Rachel. "Origins of a Myth: Why Courts, Scholars, and the Public Think Title VII's Ban on Sex Discrimination Was an Accident." *Yale Journal of Law and Feminism* 20, no. 2 (2009): 409–40.

Perdue, Charles, Thomas E. Barden, and Robert K. Phillips, eds. *Weevils in the Wheat: Interviews with Virginia Ex Slaves*. Charlottesville: University Press of Virginia, 1976.

Press, Alex. "#MeToo Must Avoid 'Carceral Feminism.'" *Vox*, February 1, 2018. www.vox.com/the-big-idea/2018/2/1/16952744.

Press, Alex N. "Sexual Harassment Is Everyone's Problem." *Jacobin*, December 7, 2017. www.jacobinmag.com/2017/12/harvey-weinstein-sexual-harassment-feminism-unions.

Robinson, Harriet H. *Loom and Spindle: Life among the Early Mill Girls*. Boston: Thomas Y. Crowell, n.d. [1898].

Rousmaniere, Kate. "The Muscatine Button Workers' Strike of 1911–12." *Annals of Iowa* 46, no. 4 (1982): 243–62.

Ruiz, Vicki. *Cannery Women, Cannery Lives: Mexican Women, Unionization, and the California Food Processing Industry, 1930–1950*. Albuquerque: University of New Mexico, 1987.

Schneiderman, Rose. *All for One*. New York: Paul S. Eriksson, 1967.

Segrave, Kerry. *The Sexual Harassment of Women in the Workplace, 1600 to 1993*. Jefferson, NC: McFarland and Company, 1994.

Sinclair, Upton. *The Jungle*. Boston: Bedford/St. Martin's, 2005.

Sklar, Kathryn Kish. *Florence Kelley and the Nation's Work*. New Haven, CT: Yale University Press, 1995.

Striking Flint: Genora (Johnson) Dollinger Remembers the 1936–37 General Motors Sit-Down Strike. Chicago: L. J. Page, 1996.

Sutherland, Kate. "Marx and MacKinnon: The Promise and Perils of Marxism for Feminist Legal Theory." *Science and Society* 69, no. 1 (2005): 113–32.

Tan, Gillian, and Katia Porzecanski. "Wall Street Rule for the #MeToo Era: Avoid Women at All Cost." *Bloomberg*, December 3, 2018. www. bloomberg.com/news/articles/2018-12-03/a-wall-street-rule-for-the-metoo-era-avoid-women-at-all-cost.

Thomas, Gillian. *Because of Sex: One Law, Ten Cases, and Fifty Years That Changed American Women's Lives at Work*. New York: St. Martin's, 2016.

Tyler, Gus. *Look for the Union Label: A History of the International Ladies' Garment Workers Union*. Armonk, NY: M. E. Sharpe, 1995.

Vapnek, Lara. *Breadwinners: Working Women and Economic Independence, 1865–1920*. Urbana: University of Illinois Press, 2009.

Wakabayashi, Daisuke, Erin Griffith, Amie Tsang, and Kate Conger. "Google Walkout: Employees State Protest over Handling of Sexual Harassment." *New York Times*, November 1, 2018. www.nytimes.com/2018/11/01/technology/google-walkout-sexual-harassment.html.

Weinberg, Sydney Stahl. *The World of Our Mothers*. Chapel Hill: University of North Carolina Press, 1988.

Williams, Christine L. "Sexual Harassment and Sadomasochism." *Hypatia* 17, no. 2 (2002): 99–117.

Yeung, Bernice. *In a Day's Work: The Fight to End Sexual Violence against America's Most Vulnerable Workers*. New York: New Press, 2018.

Zonderman, David A. *Aspirations and Anxieties: New England Workers and the Mechanized Factory System, 1815–1850*. New York: Oxford University Press, 1992.

Margaret Sanger, "The Unrecorded Battle" (1912)

Preface by Christopher Phelps

Published here for the first time, "The Unrecorded Battle" is a short story written in 1912 by Margaret Sanger, later the most famous American advocate of women's access to birth control. A dramatization of a doctor's sexual harassment of a nurse, the story drew on elements of Sanger's life. In 1912, Sanger was a nurse in New York City. She was thirty-two or thirty-three years old, having been born Margaret Higgins on September 14, 1879, in the middle of her working-class Irish immigrant parents' eleven children. Upon her father's death, Higgins trained as a nurse between 1899 and 1902 at White Plains Hospital in Westchester County, at which time she lived in a boardinghouse, much like the story's protagonist. A few months' residence at the Manhattan Eye and Ear Hospital followed, but her nursing career was sidetracked when she married the Jewish architect and artist William Sanger and gave birth to three children. In 1910, the family returned to New York City, where Margaret Sanger again took up work as a nurse while the couple joined the Socialist Party, then at its electoral peak. In their flat they hosted evenings attended by Industrial Workers of the World (IWW) leaders Big Bill Haywood and Elizabeth Gurley Flynn, radical intellectual John Reed, and anarchist Emma Goldman.[1]

Tacking between the worlds of working-class radicalism and nursing, Sanger developed her view that women's sexual liberation is integral to the struggle for social justice. Her nursing career took her into Lower East Side tenements, where she delivered babies. As she met impoverished families who could ill afford more children but did not know how to prevent pregnancy, and as she saw the devastation produced by gonorrhea and syphilis, she came to see a pressing need for candid sex education. That led her to write astonishingly frank columns for the socialist newspaper the *New York Call* in 1911 and 1912 in which she used such words as "vagina" and brought down the censorship of Anthony Comstock. Ardently involved in the revolutionary working-class movement, Sanger spent the first half of 1912 assisting the Lawrence,

---

1. Details on Sanger in this preface drawn from Chesler, *Woman of Valor*; Gordon, *Woman's Body, Woman's Right*; and Sanger, *Autobiography*.

Labor: Studies in Working-Class History, Volume 19, Issue 1
DOI 10.1215/15476715-9475817   © 2022 by Christopher Phelps and Margaret Sanger

Figure 1. Margaret Sanger in uniform as a nurse trainee in her early twenties in White Plains, New York, circa 1899–1902. Margaret Sanger Papers, Special Collections, Smith College.

Massachusetts, IWW textile strike as a key organizer in the evacuation of strikers' children to temporary adoptive families in New York City.

"The Unrecorded Battle" captures a moment when nursing was akin to domestic service, menial labor carried out chiefly by young women in a phase before marriage. Nurses took cases with private patients or individual doctors on an as-needed basis at the whim of private placement agencies. One nurse depicted in the story, the socialist suffragist Miss Willets, is perhaps the story's best ideological proxy for Sanger herself, since she imagines resolving nursing's precarity through a single public booking agency. In the absence of such systematic solutions, Peggy the protagonist is deliriously happy at the highly paid position promised by a doctor who turns out to be a scoundrel and tries to sexually assault her. Her plight captures vividly how class and economic circumstances can invite acquiescence in sexual exploitation and require every element of one's being to resist. It also gives expression to a predicament so many women experienced that the Women's Trade Union League in 1904 called for "a law to prevent the hiring of workers under false pretenses."[2]

The name Peggy, is, of course, a variation on Margaret, but whether Sanger ever experienced sexual harassment on the job is unknown. It may have bearing that her younger sister Ethel Byrne was also a nurse in New York City. In the end, Sanger came to view nursing as a palliative and instead embarked on birth control advocacy by launching her periodical *The Woman Rebel* and publishing the pamphlet *Family Limitation* in 1914. Two years later she opened her first birth control clinic, which was rapidly closed by the police. When socialism, feminism, and the labor movement all collapsed in the course of the First World War and 1919, Sanger was unmoored from the movements that initially gave her project its meaning and purpose. She shifted to a medical model of contraception under doctors' authority, leading her to downplay her radical past, depend on wealthy philanthropists, de-emphasize working-class liberation in favor of a rhetoric of population control, and ally with eugenicists in ways that have left her legacy compromised and tarnished.[3]

"The Unrecorded Battle" carries hints of these themes by attributing Peggy's resistance to her American Revolutionary bloodline and by positioning medical professionalism as the counterweight to her assaulter's ruling-class network. Those very points, however, might be equally said to reflect more innocuous strains of labor republicanism and nurses' struggles for dignity within medicine's sex-segregated and hierarchical occupational structure. While "The Unrecorded Battle" is defined by a melodramatic clash of heroine and villain of a type commonplace in Progressive Era popular culture, it avoids the anti-Semitism of some "white slavery" exposés. While it resorts to tropes of country innocence and urban degeneracy, it broaches the subjects of sexual harassment and attempted rape at a time when even divorce was still considered a mildly scandalous topic, and it is strikingly advanced in its insight into how

---

2. Quoted in McCreesh, *Women in the Campaign to Organize Garment Workers*, 90.

3. Stewart, "Planned Parenthood in N.Y. Disavows Margaret Sanger"; Pollitt, "Canceling Margaret Sanger."

sexual harassment can function to drive women from the workforce. "The Unrecorded Battle" defends women's sexual autonomy and fiercely rejects working-class women's sexual exploitation to the point of warning that perpetrators might someday draw armed retribution. For all its period markers, the story has contemporary resonance, given that a systematic review of worldwide studies finds that most nurses today encounter sexual harassment at work.[4]

Sanger's manuscript contained innumerable errors of punctuation, spelling, and grammar, here corrected, with a light editorial hand, for readability. The original is found in Margaret Sanger Papers, box 203, reel 131, Manuscript Division, Library of Congress. Publication graciously permitted by Alexander Sanger.

Margaret Sanger, "The Unrecorded Battle"

"A case, a case, my kingdom for a case" were the words that rang through the room where several nurses were gathered one afternoon in June.

The words were uttered by a small, fair, healthy specimen of the female sex, who, tilting her nose a trifle more if possible than was naturally inclined, threw the stockings she was darning from her, gathered her knees within her folded hands, and continued, "No joking girls, it's three weeks today since I've had a case, and tomorrow not only my rent here is due, but——." She was interrupted by the telephone. "Yes, yes, certainly I'll take it. I'll go right down. Goodbye." She turned from the phone, and the light in her eyes, the expression of happiness on her face, made one who saw it say what a pretty girl she is.

"Lucky dog!" said the girls in a chorus. "Where is it?" asked one. "What is it?" said another.

"No time for questions, girls, I must don my best togs and see if I can't cinch that job. Get out of here, all of you, and come back later on. I must dress."

A half hour later, she was neatly attired, boarding a downtown car. In her hand was a card upon which was written the address of the physician who wanted an office nurse.

She arrived at the address given. "Ah, yes," she thought. "I expected a brownstone front. Now, Peggy Taylor, smile your prettiest." A colored butler took her card and told her to be seated, but before she had time to glance at her surroundings, the doctor stood before her in operating gown. "Ah, Miss Taylor, yes, I'm glad to see you. Yes, I want an assistant nurse, one who is capable and understands her business. I require a certificate of health, a reference from two reliable physicians, and your hospital diploma. I wish it understood that I pay well for your services, Miss Taylor, twenty-five dollars a week and board, five dollars for every operation done outside, and two and a half for all done in the house. We average ten operations a day." At this information she beamed happiness. Her heart beat so loudly she straightened in her chair to get control of herself. He saw the look and was satisfied. Yes, he thought to himself, she will do nicely. "Is there anything you do not understand, Miss Taylor?

4. Lu et al., "Worldwide Prevalence of Sexual Harassment towards Nurses."

Very well, then, if you wish to accept the position bring the required references at 10 a.m. tomorrow and consider yourself engaged." He arose, shook hands in a most businesslike way, ushered her to the door, closed it after her, watched her as she boarded an uptown car, smiled as only he could smile, and went back to his work.

Peggy had no knowledge of when she got back to her room. She had known what it is to be happy, but never before had she been so favored by the gods that she called herself "lucky," until now. "Me," she said aloud. "Me, Peg Taylor, to fall into such luck. What a dress I'll give to Kit for her graduation. I'll write at once to mother and tell her about it." She wrote the following:

> Dear dearest mother mine,
>
> Stop that garden work. Get a man to do it for you, and I'll pay him, or get one to peddle the milk and let father do the garden work. Delay your trip to New Haven until my next letter, when I shall send you money enough to buy a new dress for yourself and one for Kit. I want her graduation dress to be a real dress, Muddy dear, a point d'esprit over silk with baby ribbon would be right, I should think. Oh, I'm so happy. Don't you worry about that horrid old mortgage and note which fall due soon, for I'm coining money. Will write you about it later on, love to all the kiddies, and be happy,
>
> Your devoted Peggy

She finished writing this and with pen upraised sat pondering for a moment, then brought forth another sheet of paper and wrote:

> Dear old Dick,
>
> Yours rec'd. If I had answered it yesterday as I was inclined to do, you should have had "yes" for an answer instead of the one I am going to give today.
>
> Dick, for three weeks I have not earned one cent. All the nurses were desperate. I have had only a few cases so far this spring and short ones too. I was foolish to come to New York when I did. Summer is always bad, so I am told. Yesterday I felt I could keep up no longer and was strongly tempted to shake it all off and go back to the farm and—be yours. But the thought of the mortgage due shortly, of mother bending over the strawberry bed trying to sell enough to make ends meet, the thought of a thousand things needed for those little ones, and I their only hope—I thought of these, Dick, and I could not give up; but today I am well-rewarded, for yours truly is to be assistant to a M.D. and you, dear Dick, must be content to wait, oh, a little longer and then I'll be forever your
>
> Peg

She caressingly sealed this letter, took her hat and gloves, and departed to get the required references.

"Let me see, there is Dr. Clark, yes, I'll go to him. I nursed his wife and sick baby, and he will be glad to hear of the turn of fortune I've had." She had not long to wait before she was telling this great specialist of the wonderful opportunity she had before her and of the part he was to play in her realization of it.

This man of experience looked at her fondly, as he would a child. He hesitated to dampen the spirits of this happy girl, and yet he was suspicious of the location, and urged her to delay going there until he could find out for her a little more concerning this generous physician who was not registered among the legitimates.

She laughed at his concern and called him "stupid," assured him she was capable of judging conditions better than he was as she had seen the person in question, and if he would just jot down a few words that would serve as a reference, she would be off and not trouble him again—until she wanted something else. At which they both laughed, and she was soon on her way to the general practitioner where she obtained the required health certificate and reference. Back again to her little room to say goodbye to this "dinky box" and dream the dreams which should have come true to so faithful, generous, and loyal a girl. She had not long to dream, however, for she was soon aroused from her reveries by a loud knocking at the door, and girls' voices saying, "Hello, Taylor, let us in. Say, did you get the job? Bully for you. Tell us all about it." She told them simply. "Ye gods!" said one of the girls, a Miss Ryan, "was ever such luck. I'll give you all fair warning, girls, if I don't get a case in twenty-four hours, I'll marry—a street cleaner." "Indeed," said Miss Willets, an auburn-haired girl with a twinkle in her eye who was a staunch suffragist. "You'd have done that long ago had you the slightest opportunity."

"Well," said Miss Ryan, "so would you, Willie, if you were on twenty-four hour duty with a typhoid for six weeks without one cent, and then after you had pulled this skeleton out of the jaws of—well, it might be presumptuous of me to say just where—but the nerve of those people to refuse to pay me twenty-five dollars a week, to question the right of a woman to demand such a price."

"Oh, yes, of course," interrupted Miss Willets. "They dispute your right, they question your price, but would they dare to question a doctor? Would they refuse a man the salary he asks? No," she continued, rising from the bed on which she was sitting, "they would not dare to, but we women—we are so alone and foolishly divided, that not until we demand our rights politically will we be respected in any vocation."

"Hooray, hooray," cheered the voices. "Go on, Willie." "Keep it up." She was willing to, but was silenced by the tall figure of the matron of the registry, who had knocked several times, and receiving no response—walked in. She smiled as she heard the closing words of the enthusiastic orator. Upon seeing Miss Daly who was next on the list she informed her she had been called by Dr. Russell for an obstetrical case, to report at once. A groan from the crowd. "Beat it, Daly," and "twins for yours." She was off. The matron told Miss Ryan to get her bag ready, for it was her turn next. "Ready, why Mrs. Robinson, I've been ready for weeks." They all laughed, and the matron, a kindly woman of middle age, left them to their follies.

Miss Willets had not forgotten her subject. "No, Ryan, there is no use in kicking about abuses here and there. The first thing all working women must do is organize. Do you hear, girls? To organize. That's the first step out of darkness for women. Why, look at us, we nurses do practically all the work in many cases, and what do we get out of it? We pay, first, five dollars to belong to a registry, then out of every case we pay the registry ten percent on all our earnings, and room and telephone. Figure it up how much we get out of it. We do the work, that's the point, and what right have these parasitical registries to take ten percent, or any percent? Why not work together, have one central registry where all nurses register and any doctor wanting a nurse can call for one there? How much more economical. Think of the three hundred or more registries with their three hundred telephones, clerks, and other encumbrances, and a doctor not knowing where to get a nurse, and hundreds of nurses hanging in the air, lots of them on the verge of starvation, waiting for a call. Isn't it foolish? Why, even Taylor, the innocent from Connecticut, can see it, can't you, hon?"

"If you mean me, Miss Willets," said Miss Taylor, "I can see that point all right, but I cannot understand why you are so hard on the matrons of the registries. They must do something in order to live. Why not that?"

"Yes," said the suffragette sarcastically, "they must live, that's true, but don't you, personally, find it rather expensive charity? Could not such an intelligent woman as Mrs. Robinson, for instance, be doing something worthwhile? I dare say if you talk to her, she is longing to do something, some service to humanity, instead of this monotonous existence."

"Say, Willie," said Miss Ryan, who had been closing her eyes in boredom. "If ever you get a patient with insomnia, reel off that rot you just gave us and either he will be cured, or he will be compelled to change his residence—to Bellevue. For heaven's sake, cut it out and let us hear about Taylor's case."

"Is he handsome, Peggy?" asked Miss Willets.

"Well, yes and no."

"That's a bad sign to begin with, can't you say which?"

Peggy thought a minute and then said, "No, I can't just tell. He has a peculiar face, but I'm not going to dissect his looks until I know him better. All I know is it's a good job, girls, and I need the money."

"That's true," said Miss Willets, "but are you sure everything is straight down there? You are such a kid in some things, Peggy, and yet—and yet," she said thoughtfully, "I sometimes think it is your innocence which somehow protects you."

"Perfect nonsense," said Miss Taylor. "I'm sure he is a gentleman. He's very courteous. Even if he isn't, nurses must stand the cross and disagreeable, as well as the polite, people."

So they chatted and discussed the problems that trouble the thinking people of all nations, until bedtime, when wishing each other good night and Peggy good luck. They left her. She threw herself upon her knees and poured out her heartfelt thanks to the Great Unknown for this happiness, this great and beautiful happiness, of being able to do for others, and especially those we love. So she slept the sleep that only youth and a good conscience can sleep.

The next morning promptly at ten she found herself again at the brownstone front, but instead of the dark butler, the doctor himself opened the door. He was immaculately dressed, his hair almost shone, mustache curled, which together with the pink carnation in his coat lapel made her say "dandy" to herself. He bowed long and low over her hand, not quite the business air of the day before.

"Allow me to assist you," he said as he took her suitcase, and, leading the way through the house, summoned Mrs. Thomas, the housekeeper, and George the butler, introducing them, saying, "This is your future mistress Miss Taylor. Hereafter she is to be consulted concerning affairs of the house, and I wish it understood that her wishes are mine."

She followed him up the soft luxurious stairs through this house of elegance to a large, spacious, elegantly furnished room the sight of which made her heart beat for joy. He pushed open the door, allowed her to enter, put the bag inside the door, and quickly stepped inside and closed the door. She held her breath a moment, not daring to think. Then he spoke. "This is your room, Miss Taylor, do you like this color?" He watched her closely. "These flowers I had sent in for you today. These books are yours. In fact, little one, the desires of your life shall be filled in my house. You are mistress of this entire place." Stepping to her side he said softly, "This is your little bed, sweetheart," and stepping to a screen on the other side of the bed pulled it back. "And this is mine," he said, pointing to another bed which the screen had so cunningly hidden.

During all this conversation she had stood as one petrified, but at these last words she gave one bloodcurdling scream and rushed for the door. He was there before her, caught her by the throat, and roughly pushed her against the closed door. "You little devil," he hissed. "What are you here for? Ha ha, then here you've come and here you'll stay, miss. Scream, kick to your heart's delight, for no one shall heed you," he thundered.

At these terrible words, the blood left her face, her knees trembled, for she at last realized into what a demon's den she had come. She had seen men in joy, sorrow, agony, and death, but this was her first experience at seeing a living devil smile. But at that smile the fighting blood of her New England ancestors arose in her. She knew a time had come to fight, and fight to the death—rather than that.

Quicker than it takes to tell these thoughts flashed through her mind. She raised her head, looked him square between the eyes, and said, "Doctor, I have one thing to say. You are mistaken in me. I am not that kind of woman. I came here innocently. I wish to go away. Look into my face, look closely, and should you see in that look other than purity, then God help me."

At these words he came closer, anger and passion fighting for possession. "You lie," he said. "You lie, you hussy. You have come here to spy. You have come here pretending innocence, to pry into my work, but your game won't work with me. Listen," he said hoarsely, "look you into my eyes."

"Oh, God, that horrible face."

"Learn what power is. It is greater than the purity which you claim is in yours. One word from me and into this house you'd remain until I gave the word to release you. A word from me and to the workhouse you would go—as a prostitute. Yes, I have that much power, and far more. Think, little fool, could I run an establishment of this kind without power? Could I perform from ten to twenty operations a day without power? Could I?" he screamed. "No, no, with all your pretended innocence you must know that. And further, anything you might say of me would be laughed at. No newspaper in New York City dare, I repeat it, dare, to print what I have told you. Why? Power. Power from on high in the world of capital, influence, and prestige, all whom I have favored and in turn favor me."

During this time he had released her, much to her relief, and stood a little distance from her in order to use his hands, for he gesticulated much, but as he told her of the favors he had done his face softened and he came toward her with outstretched arms. Here was no longer the frightened bird. Here was a woman holding anger and pride in check, standing resolutely against the door, head held high, lips tightly closed ready for fight. She had aged five years since she came into that room.

Here was something new, something worth winning, he thought. His whole being shook with passion as he said, "Forgive me, can't you? You're here, you have all to gain by staying here, why make a mess of this?"

He kept coming closer as he spoke. She felt in another second it would be too late. "Stop!" she cried, as she raised her arm and pointed at him. Her eyes blazed. Her face was pale and drawn. "Stop, I say, not one step nearer. You have had your say, now I'll have mine. I'm not afraid of you. Your tyranny and boasted power are nothing new to me. Of one thing I am certain," she said calmly. "I leave this room as pure as I have entered it, or I leave it not at all. Your lies about your influence with scoundrels in this city does not frighten me, for I too am protected by men who are men. On high, I have back of me the vast army of medical men in the United States, two of whom know I came here today. Knowing this I defy you to touch me." Her turn had come now, and all fear was gone.

At these words and the reliant look of this slip of a girl the coward cringed. He knew she spoke the truth. He realized she was not the ordinary girl, and not to be bullied. He knew he must give her up. But not until his cruelty had some relief. He folded his arms, put his head cunningly on one side, and said, "You are not trying to make me believe you are pure, are you?" She looked him fully in the eyes and answered, "I am." He changed his position slightly by shifting the other foot forward, bent forward, and continued, "Do you mean to tell me you are a virgin?" She gasped at this cruelty but looked at him and said, "I do." "Swear it," he thundered, his right arm raised high, his whole being aroused to anger. "I swear," she said, her head erect, and eyes dancing fire.

She saw she had won. He stepped to the door, unlocked it, and shouted, "Go!" She went. Then the air was rent with peal after peal of the most diabolical laughter. For a second her blood seemed to freeze in her veins. She put her hands to her ears to shut out that terrible laugh, but the sight of her suitcase tumbling down the stairs brought her to her senses. Soon she was safe outside that den of torture. On, on, she plodded she knew not where, she cared not where. She was safe, safe, safe. That was enough for the present.

She had won the battle for her soul. Ah, God, was ever such a battle fought! Sometime in the afternoon, we see her at the Grand Central Station, buying a ticket for her hometown. Later we see her walking along the dusty road nearing the farm.

At a distance we can see a figure bending over a green patch, with sunbonnet pushed far back on her head, and we feel it is her mother. Peggy sees her and a lump comes into her throat as she thinks of the disappointments in store for them all.

She is soon enfolded in the strong arms of that dear mother, and as they sit together under the elm tree, she relates her agonizing experience to that loyal heart.

A glance at the New England mother will at once tell us better than words where the daughter got her courage and spirit in time of danger. Proud, brave, and tireless, she took her daughter's face in her hands and said, "Peggy, you are a wonderful girl. I'm prouder of you today than I *ever* was of your great-grandfather who fought and died so valiantly at the battle of Bunker Hill. This unrecorded battle!" She shook her head. "And you, my Peggy, the victor!"

They sat thus for some time. "I'll not go back, mother. I'm so tired of it all, and Dick has waited so patiently. Yes, I've quite decided to stay."

After the house was quiet that night, the father and mother walked up and down the kitchen floor, up and down, hour after hour, arm in arm. For miles around this honest and sturdy farmer was called Uncle Sam, so vividly did he remind us of our "Uncle Sam."

On, on, he walked, up and down far into the dawn, head bent, eyes fixed on the floor, fists clenched, thinking, thinking.

At last he stopped, went to a shelf, took down a rifle he kept there, blew off the dust, wiped it carefully with his sleeve, looked at it fondly, even tenderly, aimed at something on his wall, and wiped it again. "For goodness sake, what are you going to do with that gun, Tom Taylor?" said the little mother, for once greatly agitated.

He gave the gun another wipe with his sleeve and said, "I'm going to New York, wife, to take that man's blood." ◪

References

Chesler, Ellen. *Woman of Valor: Margaret Sanger and the Birth Control Movement in America.* New York: Simon and Schuster, 1992.

Gordon, Linda. *Woman's Body, Woman's Right: Birth Control in America.* New York: Penguin Books, 1977.

Lu, Li, et al. "Worldwide Prevalence of Sexual Harassment towards Nurses." *Journal of Advanced Nursing* 76, no. 4 (2020): 980–90.

McCreesh, Carolyn D. *Women in the Campaign to Organize Garment Workers: 1880–1917.* New York: Garland, 1985.

Pollitt, Kathy. "Canceling Margaret Sanger." *The Nation,* September 7/14, 2020. www.thenation.com/article/society/canceling-margaret-sanger.

Sanger, Margaret. *An Autobiography.* New York: Norton, 1938.

Stewart, Nikita. "Planned Parenthood in N.Y. Disavows Margaret Sanger over Eugenics." *New York Times,* July 21, 2020. www.nytimes.com/2020/07/21/nyregion/planned-parenthood-margaret-sanger-eugenics.html.

Printed and bound by CPI Group (UK) Ltd, Croydon, CR0 4YY

13/04/2025

14656486-0002